Starting and Running
a Nonprofit

Steven M. Bragg

AccountingTools®

ISBN 978-1-64221-341-6

Table of Contents

About the Author

Steven Bragg, CPA, has been the chief financial officer or controller of four companies, as well as a consulting manager at Ernst & Young. He received a master's degree in finance from Bentley College, an MBA from Babson College, and a Bachelor's degree in Economics from the University of Maine. He has been a two-time president of the Colorado Mountain Club, and is an avid alpine skier, mountain biker, and certified master diver. Mr. Bragg resides in Centennial, Colorado. He has written more than 300 books and courses, including *New Controller Guidebook*, *GAAP Guidebook*, and *Payroll Management*.

Steven maintains the accountingtools.com web site, which contains continuing professional education courses, the Accounting Best Practices podcast, and thousands of articles on accounting subjects.

Chapter 1
Understanding Nonprofits

What is a Nonprofit?

Nonprofit organizations, often referred to as "nonprofits" or "not-for-profit entities," are institutions that exist primarily to serve a mission rather than to generate profit for private individuals or shareholders. Unlike businesses that distribute earnings to owners or investors, nonprofits reinvest surplus revenues back into their programs, services, and operations. They are typically organized under federal and state laws as tax-exempt entities, often under provisions like section 501(c) of the Internal Revenue Code in the United States. This legal status allows them to operate without paying federal income taxes, provided that their activities are consistent with their charitable, educational, religious, or other qualifying purposes.

The defining feature of nonprofits is their mission-driven nature. Their primary goal is to create public or community value, whether by advancing education, alleviating poverty, improving health, protecting the environment, or promoting the arts. This orientation fundamentally distinguishes them from both for-profit businesses and government agencies. Businesses focus on maximizing shareholder wealth, while government entities function under political mandates; nonprofits operate in the space between, often filling gaps in services where markets fail or governments are constrained. Their accountability is to their stakeholders (donors, beneficiaries, communities, and regulators) rather than to investors seeking financial returns.

Nonprofits play several essential roles in society. First, they provide vital services to vulnerable or underserved populations. Charitable organizations, for example, may operate food banks, shelters, or health clinics that serve individuals who cannot otherwise afford such services. In this way, nonprofits act as safety nets, helping to reduce inequality and promote social welfare. Because their missions prioritize community needs, they often take on responsibilities that neither the private sector nor the government is fully positioned to address.

Second, nonprofits serve as vehicles for civic engagement. They provide opportunities for individuals to volunteer their time, contribute resources, and advocate for causes they believe in. This participatory function strengthens democratic societies by fostering community involvement and giving voice to diverse groups. Civic associations, advocacy groups, and cultural organizations encourage individuals to participate in public life beyond the realm of politics, cultivating social capital and reinforcing bonds of trust and reciprocity within communities.

Third, nonprofits contribute significantly to the economy. They employ millions of people worldwide and generate substantial economic activity. In the United States alone, the nonprofit sector accounts for a notable share of the workforce, with hospitals, universities, and charitable organizations among the largest employers in many regions. Their economic footprint extends beyond employment, influencing local and national development through purchasing goods, providing training, and fostering innovation in service delivery.

Nonprofits also play a critical role in shaping policy and public discourse. Advocacy organizations, think tanks, and professional associations use research, lobbying, and public education to influence legislation and social norms. Environmental groups, for instance, have shaped public understanding of climate change and influenced regulatory frameworks, while civil rights organizations have advanced justice and equality. By providing independent perspectives, nonprofits can act as checks on government and corporate power, ensuring that diverse voices are represented in decision-making processes.

Another distinctive role of nonprofits is their flexibility and innovation. Because they are mission-oriented and less constrained by market profitability or political cycles, nonprofits can experiment with new approaches to social problems. Philanthropic funding and grants often support pilot projects and innovative models that, if successful, may later be adopted by governments or businesses. For example, nonprofits have pioneered community health models, microfinance, and sustainable development practices that have since been mainstreamed into broader policy and commercial frameworks.

Despite their many strengths, nonprofits also face challenges. They must balance the need for financial sustainability with the imperative to serve their missions. Dependence on donations and grants can make them vulnerable to shifts in funding priorities, economic downturns, or donor expectations. Moreover, because they operate in the public trust, nonprofits are held to high standards of accountability and transparency. Issues such as governance, ethical fundraising, and performance measurement are central to their credibility and effectiveness.

In sum, nonprofits are mission-driven organizations that exist to create public benefit rather than private gain. They provide essential services, foster civic engagement, contribute to economic vitality, influence policy, and often serve as laboratories for social innovation. By filling gaps left by the market and government, nonprofits embody the principle of collective responsibility, helping societies pursue shared values such as equity, justice, and human dignity. Their role is indispensable in ensuring that social needs are met, voices are heard, and communities thrive.

Differences from Other Organizational Types

Nonprofits, for-profits, and government agencies represent three distinct organizational forms that operate with different purposes, structures, and accountabilities. Each of these entities contributes to society in meaningful ways, but they do so with differing missions, governance models, funding sources, and measures of success. Understanding their differences sheds light on how they complement and at times overlap with each other in addressing economic, social, and political needs.

At the heart of the distinction lies the purpose of the entity. For-profit businesses exist primarily to generate financial returns for their owners or shareholders. Their legitimacy stems from their ability to deliver products or services that consumers value enough to purchase, thereby creating profits that sustain and expand the enterprise. Nonprofits, in contrast, exist to fulfill a mission that produces public or community value, rather than personal financial gain. Their goals might include feeding the hungry, advancing education, supporting the arts, or protecting the environment. Unlike for-profits, nonprofits are prohibited from distributing surplus revenue to private individuals; instead, they must reinvest all surpluses into programs, staff, and organizational capacity that advance their mission. Government agencies, by comparison, are mission-driven in a different sense: they exist to carry out the mandates of elected officials and the laws enacted by legislatures. Their purpose is inherently political and administrative, focused on providing public goods, regulating behavior, and ensuring the collective welfare through the exercise of authority backed by law.

The differences in funding further illustrate these divergent purposes. For-profit businesses rely on revenue from the sale of goods or services, supplemented in some cases by investment capital from shareholders or lenders. Profitability is essential, not only for survival but also for growth and investor confidence. Nonprofits typically draw on a mix of funding sources, including donations from individuals, grants from foundations, contracts with governments, and revenue from fee-based services. Their sustainability depends on cultivating trust among donors and demonstrating that resources are being used effectively to achieve impact. Government agencies, in contrast, rely on taxation and appropriations from legislatures. Their budgets are determined through political processes, and their resources are allocated according to policy priorities rather than market demand or voluntary contributions. This creates both stability, since governments have the power to tax, and vulnerability, since funding is tied to political negotiations and shifts in leadership.

Accountability is another critical point of differentiation. For-profits are accountable primarily to their owners and shareholders, who demand returns on their investment. Markets also serve as a form of accountability, since a business that fails to satisfy its customers will struggle to survive. Nonprofits are accountable to a wider array of stakeholders. Donors expect financial stewardship and evidence of impact, beneficiaries expect meaningful services, and regulators require adherence to laws governing tax-exempt status. Because nonprofits operate in the public trust, they are also subject to scrutiny from watchdog groups, media, and the communities they serve. Government agencies, meanwhile, are accountable to elected officials and, ultimately, to citizens. Their performance is judged not by profitability or fundraising success but by their ability to implement laws fairly, provide public goods, and manage resources responsibly. This accountability is exercised through elections, oversight hearings, audits, and the rule of law.

Differences also emerge in governance structures. For-profit businesses are typically managed by executives under the oversight of a board of directors that represents shareholder interests. Decision-making authority is concentrated in the pursuit of financial performance, though companies increasingly incorporate social responsibility into their strategies. Nonprofits are usually governed by volunteer boards of directors or trustees, who are charged with safeguarding the mission and ensuring that resources are used for the public good. These boards do not represent shareholders but act as stewards of the organization's values and compliance with regulations. Government agencies are governed through bureaucratic hierarchies, with authority delegated from elected officials to appointed administrators and civil servants. The chain of command is designed to ensure adherence to policy directives, though it can also create rigidity that limits innovation and responsiveness.

Measures of success further highlight the distinctions. For-profit organizations are judged by profitability, growth, and market share. Financial metrics dominate, though customer satisfaction and brand reputation are increasingly recognized as critical to long-term success. Nonprofits, however, measure success by the degree to which they achieve their mission. This can include quantitative outcomes, such as the number of meals served or students educated, as well as qualitative impacts like improved community well-being. Because outcomes are often difficult to measure, nonprofits must balance storytelling with data-driven evaluations to convey their effectiveness. Government agencies, on the other hand, measure success by their ability to implement programs as mandated, deliver services efficiently, and maintain public trust. Their performance metrics may include compliance rates, service delivery times, or reductions in social problems, though political considerations often shape perceptions of their effectiveness.

Another important difference lies in flexibility and innovation. For-profits, driven by competition, are often more agile in responding to market trends and consumer preferences. Innovation is rewarded when it leads to higher profits or market advantage. Nonprofits, while mission-driven rather than profit-driven, can also be highly innovative, especially in developing new approaches to entrenched social problems. However, their reliance on restricted funding and donor priorities can sometimes limit their degree of experimentation. Government agencies are typically the least flexible, given their bureaucratic nature, political oversight, and risk aversion. Yet governments hold unique authority to scale solutions nationwide or regulate markets in ways that neither nonprofits nor businesses can achieve on their own.

Employment practices also reflect these differences. For-profit businesses often offer competitive salaries, benefits, and incentives to attract talent, aligning employee performance with profitability goals. Nonprofits, by contrast, may offer lower compensation but attract individuals motivated by mission and values. Many nonprofit staff view their work as a form of public service, deriving satisfaction from contributing to societal change. Government agencies provide stable employment with standardized pay scales, strong benefits, and job security, though they may struggle to reward high performance or attract entrepreneurial talent compared to other sectors.

Despite these distinctions, the three sectors interact and overlap in significant ways. Nonprofits often partner with government agencies to deliver services under contract, blending public funding with community-based implementation. Businesses increasingly engage in corporate social responsibility or create hybrid models, such as social enterprises, that combine profit-making with mission-driven goals. Governments regulate both nonprofits and for-profits, while also relying on them for expertise and execution. This interdependence reflects the complexity of modern societies, where no single sector can meet all needs effectively.

In conclusion, nonprofits, for-profits, and government agencies differ fundamentally in their purposes, funding, accountability, governance, and measures of success.

For-profits pursue financial gain through markets, nonprofits pursue mission impact through community trust and reinvestment, and government agencies pursue public mandates through taxation and authority. Their contrasts reveal the strengths and limitations of each: businesses excel in efficiency and innovation, nonprofits in mission and community connection, and governments in authority and scale. Together, they form a complementary ecosystem, each playing roles that the others cannot, and collectively shaping the economic, social, and political fabric of society.

Common Misconceptions About Nonprofits

Nonprofit organizations hold a unique place in society, bridging gaps between markets and governments by pursuing missions that promote the public good. Yet, despite their visibility and impact, they are often misunderstood. A variety of misconceptions surround their funding, operations, and effectiveness, which can undermine trust, distort expectations, or limit their ability to achieve their goals. Exploring these misunderstandings reveals not only how nonprofits truly function but also why it is important for the public, donors, and policymakers to recognize their realities.

A frequent misconception is that nonprofits do not need to make money. Because the word "nonprofit" implies the absence of profit, many assume these organizations should operate with little regard for financial surplus. In reality, nonprofits must generate revenue in order to survive. While they cannot distribute profits to private individuals, they must still bring in more income than expenses to remain financially stable. Surpluses allow nonprofits to build reserves, invest in infrastructure, and weather periods of fluctuating funding. Expecting them to operate on the brink of insolvency not only misrepresents their purpose but also undermines their capacity to deliver on their missions.

Closely related is the belief that nonprofits should rely exclusively on volunteers rather than paid staff. While volunteers play a critical role in extending capacity, professional staff are essential for ensuring consistent, high-quality services. Running a hospital, managing an after-school program, or operating a housing shelter requires specialized expertise, training, and full-time commitment. To attract and retain talent, nonprofits must offer competitive salaries and benefits. The misconception that nonprofit employees should accept low or even symbolic pay disregards their professionalism and contributes to burnout and turnover. Just as society values skilled work in for-profit and government sectors, nonprofit expertise deserves recognition and fair compensation.

Another common misunderstanding is that nonprofits are inherently inefficient or less professional than for-profit businesses. This stereotype often stems from the perception that nonprofits are small, underfunded, or overly dependent on goodwill. While some organizations do struggle with limited resources, many nonprofits operate with a high level of professionalism, incorporating best practices in management, finance, and governance. Hospitals, universities, and major cultural institutions, for instance, are among the most complex organizations in society, requiring sophisticated planning and accountability systems. Moreover, nonprofits must maintain rigorous reporting and compliance standards to satisfy regulators and funders. Far from being casual or amateurish, nonprofit management demands a high degree of skill and adaptability.

A particularly damaging misconception is that low overhead costs are the best measure of a nonprofit's effectiveness. Donors and watchdog groups often focus narrowly on the percentage of funds spent on programs versus administration or fundraising, assuming that the lower the overhead, the more effective the organization. This view ignores the reality that effective nonprofits must invest in infrastructure, technology, staff training, and evaluation to succeed. Overhead is not waste; it is the cost of building organizational capacity to deliver impact sustainably. Pressuring nonprofits to keep administrative costs unrealistically low forces them into a "starvation cycle," where they underinvest in their own growth and thereby undermine their long-term effectiveness. The true measure of a nonprofit's impact lies in its outcomes and mission fulfillment, not artificially minimized overhead.

Nonprofits are also often assumed to be small, local charities operating on shoestring budgets. While many do fit this description, the nonprofit sector is remarkably diverse. It includes large hospitals, universities, international aid organizations, cultural institutions, and research centers that operate with budgets in the millions or even billions of dollars. These institutions employ thousands of people, engage in global partnerships, and shape public policy. Equating nonprofits solely with neighborhood charities diminishes recognition of the sector's scope and economic significance. The reality is that nonprofits constitute a major share of employment and gross domestic product in many countries, influencing health, education, and cultural life at the national and global levels.

Another misconception is that nonprofits are automatically altruistic and beyond criticism. The assumption that mission-driven organizations always act ethically can obscure instances of mismanagement, mission drift, or even outright fraud. Nonprofits, like all organizations, are run by people and are therefore vulnerable to human error, poor judgment, or misconduct. Healthy skepticism is necessary to ensure accountability, but this does not negate the enormous good that the vast majority of nonprofits accomplish. Recognizing that nonprofits can face governance and ethical challenges helps foster better oversight and stronger performance.

It is also often believed that nonprofits operate independently of markets, relying purely on donations and grants. In truth, many nonprofits earn significant portions of their income through fee-for-service models, membership dues, or product sales. Museums may charge admission, universities collect tuition, and hospitals bill insurance providers. These earned revenue streams diversify funding and provide stability, complementing philanthropic support. The misconception that nonprofits depend entirely on donations fails to acknowledge their entrepreneurial strategies and the ways they blend philanthropy with business-like models to remain sustainable.

Another misunderstanding is that nonprofits are politically neutral or disengaged. While restrictions on lobbying and partisan activity exist, nonprofits are often deeply involved in shaping public policy, advocating for social change, and amplifying community voices. Environmental organizations influence climate policy, civil rights groups push for equity, and professional associations shape industry standards. Their ability to mobilize constituencies and advocate for systemic reforms is a central aspect of their societal role. To assume they are apolitical diminishes their contributions to democracy and civic life.

Finally, many people think that the impact of nonprofits is easy to measure or obvious from the scope of their activities. In fact, measuring social outcomes is complex. Feeding a hundred people or educating fifty students is tangible, but the long-term impacts—such as improved health, greater civic participation, or reduced inequality—are harder to quantify. Unlike for-profit companies, which can rely on profit margins as a clear indicator, nonprofits must grapple with multidimensional outcomes that require nuanced evaluation methods. The misconception that their impact can be easily captured through simple numbers underestimates the depth and breadth of their contributions.

In conclusion, nonprofits are often misunderstood in ways that distort expectations and hinder their effectiveness. Misconceptions that they should not earn surpluses, that staff should work for little pay, that overhead is wasteful, or that they are inherently altruistic fail to reflect reality. Nonprofits are professional organizations that require financial sustainability, skilled staff, infrastructure, and accountability to fulfill their missions. They are diverse in size and scope, blending philanthropy with earned income and engaging in advocacy as well as service delivery. Recognizing and dispelling these misconceptions is crucial for strengthening public trust, improving support, and enabling nonprofits to play their full role in advancing social welfare, justice, and community well-being.

Types of Nonprofits

Nonprofit organizations occupy a wide and varied space in society, encompassing institutions as diverse as food banks, hospitals, trade associations, and advocacy groups. While they share the defining characteristic of being mission-driven rather than profit-driven, nonprofits differ significantly in their purposes, structures, and activities. Some focus on alleviating immediate social needs, others concentrate on advancing professional standards, and still others seek to influence public policy. Understanding the different types of nonprofits helps clarify their distinct contributions to social, economic, and political life, while also highlighting the diversity and adaptability of the nonprofit sector.

Among the most widely recognized types of nonprofits are charitable organizations. These entities are formed with the purpose of providing services or relief to individuals and communities in need. Charitable nonprofits include food banks, homeless shelters, hospitals, educational foundations, and organizations that serve vulnerable populations such as children, the elderly, or people with disabilities. Their missions often align with what tax law defines as "charitable purposes," including the relief of poverty, the advancement of education, the promotion of health, and other activities that improve social welfare. Donations to charitable organizations are typically tax-deductible, making them attractive vehicles for philanthropy. The scale of these nonprofits can range from small community-based groups serving local neighborhoods to international organizations like the Red Cross, which mobilize resources across borders. While charitable nonprofits may sometimes be perceived as limited to short-term relief efforts, many engage in systemic change by investing in long-term solutions such as education, housing, and healthcare reform.

Religious organizations represent another major category of nonprofits. Churches, mosques, synagogues, and temples fall under this classification, as do faith-based organizations that operate schools, hospitals, and relief agencies. In the United States, religious organizations enjoy special tax treatment, often without the need to formally register for tax-exempt status. Their missions extend beyond worship, frequently encompassing community support, moral guidance, and social services. Many faith-based nonprofits are among the largest providers of humanitarian aid worldwide. Their significance lies not only in the spiritual life of communities but also in their capacity to mobilize resources, volunteers, and moral authority to address social issues.

Educational nonprofits also occupy a significant share of the sector. These include universities, private schools, research institutes, and scholarship foundations. While many educational institutions charge tuition and generate revenue, they operate under nonprofit status because their surplus funds are reinvested into their mission rather than distributed as profit. Universities and colleges, for example, use their resources to expand research, fund scholarships, build facilities, and enhance academic programs. Beyond traditional schools, educational nonprofits can include organizations that provide adult literacy programs, job training, or early childhood development services. Their impact is far-reaching, as education serves as a foundation for social mobility, economic development, and civic engagement.

Healthcare nonprofits are another important type. Hospitals, community clinics, mental health centers, and nursing homes often operate as nonprofit entities, particularly in the United States where nonprofit hospitals form a significant portion of the healthcare system. These organizations provide care regardless of a patient's ability to pay, and their revenues are reinvested into improving medical services, expanding access, and funding research. Nonprofit healthcare providers are expected to offer "community benefits," such as free clinics or preventive health programs, as part of their tax-exempt status. Their mission-driven focus distinguishes them from for-profit healthcare providers, which prioritize shareholder returns.

Beyond service-oriented organizations, trade associations represent a distinct category of nonprofits. Unlike charities, trade associations are designed to serve their members rather than the general public. They typically consist of businesses, professionals, or industries that unite to promote common interests, set standards, and advocate for favorable policies. Examples include the American Bar Association, chambers of commerce, and industry-specific organizations in fields such as manufacturing, technology, or construction. These associations provide professional development, networking opportunities, research, and lobbying efforts. Although they do not serve the public in the same way that charities do, they fulfill an important role by fostering professional standards, supporting economic development, and influencing public policy. Donations to trade associations are not tax-deductible as charitable contributions, reflecting their member-serving focus rather than public-serving mission.

Advocacy groups form another crucial category of nonprofits, distinguished by their role in shaping public opinion and influencing policy. These organizations focus on issues such as civil rights, environmental protection, healthcare reform, or consumer safety. Examples include the American Civil Liberties Union (ACLU), Human Rights Watch, and the Sierra Club. Advocacy nonprofits engage in research, public education, lobbying, and grassroots mobilization to advance their causes. While they must adhere to certain restrictions on political activity, particularly regarding partisan campaigns, they play a vital role in democratic societies by amplifying marginalized voices, holding institutions accountable, and driving systemic change. Their impact is often measured not in direct service delivery but in policy reforms, legal victories, and shifts in public attitudes.

Cultural and arts organizations also make up a distinctive segment of the nonprofit world. Museums, theaters, symphonies, and historical societies are often organized as nonprofits, reflecting their mission to preserve and promote culture rather than to generate profits. These organizations enrich society by fostering creativity, preserving heritage, and providing opportunities for public engagement with the arts. They rely heavily on philanthropic support, grants, and earned revenue from admissions or performances. Their sustainability often depends on balancing accessibility with financial viability, as cultural institutions are expected both to serve the public and to maintain professional standards of preservation and performance.

Foundations represent another type of nonprofit, though their structure is somewhat unique. Private foundations, such as the Ford Foundation, are funded by individuals, families, or corporations and primarily exist to distribute grants to other nonprofits. Public foundations, like community foundations, gather donations from a wide pool of donors to support local projects and initiatives. Foundations do not generally provide direct services but instead play a crucial role in financing and shaping the nonprofit landscape. They set priorities through their grantmaking, influence the direction of social change, and provide resources for innovation.

Mutual benefit organizations, though less publicly visible, also fall within the nonprofit sector. These include social clubs, fraternal organizations, and recreational associations that primarily exist to serve the interests of their members rather than the public. Country clubs, alumni associations, and professional fraternities often operate as nonprofits because their revenues are reinvested in member services rather than distributed as profits. While their missions may appear narrower than those of charitable or advocacy groups, they contribute to social cohesion, networking, and personal development.

The diversity of nonprofit types highlights the breadth of their contributions. Charitable organizations address immediate social needs, religious groups provide moral and material support, educational and healthcare nonprofits strengthen the foundations of human capital, and cultural institutions preserve and promote the arts. Trade associations and mutual benefit groups advance professional and member interests, while advocacy groups and foundations push for systemic change and resource distribution. What unites them is their nonprofit status, which ensures that resources are reinvested into mission rather than extracted as private profit.

In conclusion, nonprofits are far from homogeneous. They range from small neighborhood charities to massive international organizations, from service providers to advocacy coalitions, from cultural stewards to professional associations. Each type plays a unique role in addressing needs, shaping communities, and influencing policy. Recognizing this diversity is essential to appreciating the full scope of the nonprofit sector and its indispensable contributions to society. While their missions, structures, and funding sources may vary, nonprofits collectively embody the principle that organizations can exist not for private gain but for the advancement of shared values and the common good.

The Nonprofit Lifecycle

Nonprofit organizations, like for-profit businesses and government institutions, evolve through a natural lifecycle. While their missions differ from those of commercial enterprises, the growth trajectory of nonprofits – from inception to maturity – often follows predictable patterns marked by opportunities, challenges, and transformations. Understanding this lifecycle is crucial for nonprofit leaders, boards, donors, and stakeholders, as it provides a roadmap for strategic decision-making, sustainability, and mission fulfillment.

The nonprofit lifecycle can be described in several distinct stages: idea conception and startup, early growth, organizational development, maturity, and in some cases, decline or renewal. Each stage reflects the evolving priorities of the organization, the changing role of leadership, and the balance between mission and sustainability. What follows is a detailed discussion of each stage, highlighting the characteristics, challenges, and strategies that shape the journey from startup to maturity.

Conception and Startup

The lifecycle of a nonprofit begins with an idea: a vision to address an unmet need, to solve a pressing social problem, or to promote a cause. This idea may come from individuals with lived experience, community leaders, or professionals who see gaps in existing services. At this stage, the nonprofit exists primarily as an aspiration, requiring founders to articulate the mission clearly, identify potential beneficiaries, and begin laying the groundwork for legal and organizational structures.

During the startup stage, establishing legitimacy is a primary challenge. Founders must secure initial support from stakeholders (volunteers, donors, and community members) who believe in the mission. They must also navigate the legal process of incorporating the nonprofit, applying for tax-exempt status, and creating bylaws and governance structures. The board of directors is often formed during this stage, though early boards may consist of friends or colleagues of the founder, serving more as supporters than as strategic advisors.

Funding is a particularly difficult hurdle in the startup phase. With limited track records and visibility, new nonprofits often rely on small donations from friends and family, grassroots fundraising events, or modest grants. Resources are scarce, and staff are frequently volunteers or part-time workers. This scarcity can foster creativity but also imposes significant strain, as organizations must deliver meaningful results without the infrastructure of established nonprofits.

The key task in this stage is to prove the concept: to demonstrate that the nonprofit's mission addresses a genuine need and that its programs have the potential for impact. Piloting programs, gathering testimonials, and documenting early outcomes are vital to building credibility. Success is measured less by scale and more by validation – that the organization has a role to play in the community.

Early Growth

If the startup proves viable, the nonprofit enters the growth stage. Here, the focus shifts from survival to expansion. The organization begins to professionalize its operations, formalize governance, and diversify its funding sources. Growth often involves hiring the first paid staff, expanding the board with individuals who bring expertise and networks, and creating systems for program delivery and evaluation.

During this stage, nonprofits face the tension between opportunity and capacity. Increased visibility often brings more demand for services, but the organization may not yet have the infrastructure to scale effectively. Leaders must balance the desire to serve more people with the need to build strong internal systems. Overextending too quickly can jeopardize quality and sustainability, while moving too cautiously can result in missed opportunities and diminished relevance.

Fundraising begins to evolve beyond grassroots efforts. Grant applications, corporate partnerships, and major donor cultivation become more prominent. With new funding comes the expectation of accountability, requiring nonprofits to adopt more formal financial management practices and begin measuring outcomes more rigorously. Donors and funders want evidence that their contributions are making a difference, and nonprofits must adapt to these expectations.

Board development is also critical in this stage. Early boards that primarily served as cheerleaders must transition into more strategic roles, including financial oversight, fundraising support, and governance responsibilities. This evolution can create tension if founding board members are unprepared for the shift. Leaders must be intentional in recruiting board members who bring relevant expertise and connections while remaining committed to the mission.

The hallmark of the growth stage is the professionalization of the nonprofit. The organization is no longer a fledgling idea but a recognized entity with growing credibility, impact, and sustainability.

Organizational Development

As the nonprofit continues to grow, it enters a phase of organizational development marked by consolidation and system-building. The focus turns inward, with attention on strengthening infrastructure, refining strategy, and managing complexity. At this stage, the nonprofit has established programs, a track record of impact, and stable funding streams, though it still faces challenges of scale and sustainability.

Human resources become a central concern. With more staff and volunteers, nonprofits must implement personnel policies, job descriptions, performance evaluations, and professional development opportunities. Leadership transitions may also arise, as founders sometimes step aside or share responsibilities with new executives better suited to managing complexity. These transitions can be fraught, as founder-led organizations often struggle with identity and continuity when leadership changes.

Financial systems also become more sophisticated. Audited financial statements, internal controls, and budget forecasting are essential to maintaining credibility with funders and ensuring accountability. Nonprofits may begin to pursue multi-year grants or build endowments, seeking financial stability beyond year-to-year fundraising. Program evaluation evolves into a more systematic process, with organizations measuring not just outputs but outcomes and impact.

Governance matures as well. Boards at this stage function as true fiduciary bodies, balancing oversight with strategic vision. They become more diverse and intentional, incorporating members with legal, financial, and community expertise. Committees and advisory councils may be formed to distribute responsibilities and deepen engagement.

Externally, nonprofits at this stage often build networks and collaborations. Partnerships with other nonprofits, businesses, and government agencies enhance impact and visibility. Advocacy efforts may also expand, as organizations seek to influence policies and systems that affect their mission. The nonprofit begins to shift from simply delivering programs to positioning itself as a thought leader in its field.

The organizational development stage is characterized by the shift from growth to stability. The nonprofit becomes a professional, credible institution, capable of sustaining itself and delivering measurable impact.

Maturity

The maturity stage represents the peak of the nonprofit lifecycle. At this point, the organization has established a strong reputation, diversified funding, effective leadership, and robust infrastructure. It is widely recognized as a trusted provider of services or an influential advocate for change. Programs are well-developed, staff are skilled, and governance structures are strong.

In maturity, the nonprofit enjoys stability, but it also faces the risk of stagnation. With established systems and steady funding, there can be a temptation to maintain the status quo rather than pursue innovation. Donors and beneficiaries may perceive the organization as successful, but internally, leaders must guard against complacency. The challenge is to remain dynamic and responsive to changing needs while preserving the stability that maturity affords.

At this stage, nonprofits often expand their focus from direct service delivery to systems-level change. For example, a mature nonprofit that once focused on running a local food pantry may now engage in statewide advocacy for food security policies. A health clinic that once treated individual patients may now influence healthcare policy or research. By leveraging credibility, networks, and expertise, mature nonprofits can extend their impact beyond their immediate programs.

Financially, mature nonprofits typically enjoy multiple funding streams, including earned income, government contracts, major gifts, and endowment income. However, dependence on large institutional funders can create vulnerabilities, particularly if those funders shift priorities. Mature nonprofits must balance stability with flexibility, ensuring that financial security does not come at the expense of mission relevance.

Leadership in maturity often emphasizes succession planning. Strong organizations recognize the importance of preparing future leaders, both in executive roles and on the board. Investing in leadership development ensures continuity and guards against the risks of abrupt transitions.

Mature nonprofits also focus on evaluation and accountability. With established reputations comes heightened scrutiny from funders, regulators, and the public. Demonstrating impact, transparency, and ethical practices is essential to maintaining trust. Mature organizations often become benchmarks for others in their field, setting standards and sharing best practices.

The maturity stage is characterized by stability, credibility, and influence. Yet it also presents the paradox of success: the very structures that sustain the nonprofit can make it resistant to change. Remaining innovative and adaptable is critical to avoiding decline.

Decline or Renewal

Not all nonprofits remain in maturity indefinitely. Some face decline due to shifts in funding, leadership challenges, mission drift, or external changes. Decline may manifest in shrinking budgets, staff turnover, loss of credibility, or irrelevance as needs evolve. In severe cases, nonprofits may dissolve, merge with others, or significantly downsize.

However, decline is not inevitable. Many nonprofits enter a phase of renewal, using strategic planning, innovation, and leadership change to reinvigorate their mission. Renewal often requires honest assessment, willingness to let go of outdated programs, and the courage to pivot in new directions. Successful renewal can transform an organization, enabling it to adapt to new realities while retaining its core mission.

Renewal also underscores the cyclical nature of the nonprofit lifecycle. Just as businesses reinvent themselves in response to changing markets, nonprofits must continually adapt to shifting social needs, funding landscapes, and political environments. The ability to innovate, collaborate, and embrace change determines whether a mature nonprofit sustains its influence or fades into irrelevance.

Conclusion

The nonprofit lifecycle mirrors the developmental patterns of living systems: birth, growth, maturity, and, in some cases, decline or renewal. Each stage, from startup to maturity, presents unique opportunities and challenges that shape the identity, effectiveness, and sustainability of the organization. Startups must prove their concept and establish legitimacy. Growth brings professionalization and expansion but also the risks of overextension. Organizational development consolidates systems and strengthens infrastructure. Maturity affords stability and influence but demands vigilance against stagnation. Decline or renewal represents the crossroads, where organizations either fade or transform.

Understanding the nonprofit lifecycle is vital for leaders, boards, and funders. It provides a framework for anticipating challenges, making strategic choices, and investing in capacity at the right times. More importantly, it underscores the dynamic nature of nonprofits, which must continually adapt while remaining true to their missions. By recognizing where they are in the lifecycle and responding accordingly, nonprofits can maximize their impact, sustain their relevance, and fulfill their vital role in advancing the public good.

Summary

In this chapter, we established that nonprofit organizations occupy a specific niche between governments and for-profit enterprises. This niche is an essential pillar of society, since nonprofits support many fundamental needs that would otherwise not be addressed. To be successful, these organizations must be prudently run, with solid revenue streams, reasonably-paid employees, and close attention to expenses. When well-managed, a nonprofit can grow rapidly, providing a variety of necessary services. However, its board and management team must pay attention to its financial health and purpose within the community, or else there will be a risk of long-term decline.

Chapter 2
Structuring a Nonprofit

Introduction

When creating a nonprofit entity, there are several key issues to address right away, such as choosing the correct legal structure, creating articles of incorporation and by-laws, and securing tax-exempt status. We address these issues and much more in the following pages.

Choosing a Legal Structure

The decision to create a nonprofit organization is rooted in the desire to pursue a mission that benefits society rather than to generate profits for private individuals. Yet turning that mission into a functioning entity requires a series of practical steps, none more consequential than choosing the legal structure. The legal form a nonprofit adopts, whether as an unincorporated association, a trust, or a nonprofit corporation, shapes its governance, liability, tax status, fundraising capacity, and long-term sustainability. Each structure offers advantages and limitations, and the choice depends on the nonprofit's mission, size, funding model, and growth ambitions. Understanding these options is essential for founders seeking to align legal form with organizational purpose.

An unincorporated association is often the simplest and most informal legal structure for a nonprofit. It arises whenever two or more individuals come together to pursue a common purpose without formally incorporating under state law. This model is particularly appealing in the earliest stages of a nonprofit's life, when a small group wishes to begin work quickly without navigating the complexities of incorporation. For example, neighbors organizing to run a local food drive or community members forming a cultural group may initially operate as an unincorporated association. The benefits of this approach are clear: it requires no formal filing, is inexpensive to establish, and allows groups to function with minimal administrative burden.

However, the informality of unincorporated associations creates significant risks and limitations. Because the association has no separate legal identity, its members may be personally liable for debts, contracts, or legal claims. If someone is injured at an event organized by the association, members could be held personally responsible. This exposure can deter volunteers and limit the scope of activities. Furthermore, unincorporated associations often face difficulties accessing funding. Many grantmakers, government agencies, and donors prefer or even require nonprofits to have incorporated status, as it demonstrates accountability and provides clearer governance. Without incorporation, an organization may struggle to build credibility, expand its operations, or secure tax-exempt recognition from the IRS. While an unincorporated association may suffice for short-term or small-scale projects, it is generally not suited to organizations seeking long-term sustainability or significant public funding.

A trust represents another option for organizing a nonprofit. In this structure, a donor (the settlor) transfers assets to trustees, who are legally obligated to manage those assets for charitable purposes. Charitable trusts are particularly common in philanthropy, where wealthy individuals establish trusts to support causes such as education, healthcare, or the arts. A trust offers several advantages: it ensures that assets are legally protected and dedicated to the mission, it provides a high degree of permanence, and it can offer significant tax benefits to donors. Because trustees are legally bound by fiduciary duties, trusts are viewed as reliable vehicles for ensuring that resources are managed prudently and in alignment with the donor's intent.

Nevertheless, the trust structure has limitations that make it less suitable for operating nonprofits. Trusts are rigid in nature, as the terms established by the settlor are difficult to amend. This rigidity can hinder an organization's ability to adapt to changing circumstances, social needs, or opportunities for innovation. Moreover, trusts are primarily designed as vehicles for managing assets rather than running programs. While they can fund charitable activities, they lack the flexibility and governance structures that operating nonprofits typically require. Trustees, rather than a board of directors, hold decision-making authority, and they are bound to act within the constraints of the trust deed. As a result, trusts are more often used as foundations or grantmaking entities than as direct service providers. For organizations that seek to operate programs, hire staff, and engage in advocacy, the trust model may prove restrictive.

The nonprofit corporation is the most common and versatile legal structure for nonprofits, particularly those seeking tax-exempt status under section 501(c)(3) of the IRS Code in the United States. By incorporating under state law, the organization becomes a separate legal entity distinct from its founders and members. This separation provides critical protection, as directors, officers, and members are generally shielded from personal liability for the organization's debts or legal claims. Incorporation also enhances credibility with funders, government agencies, and the public, signaling that the organization has a formal governance structure and is accountable under the law.

A nonprofit corporation is governed by a board of directors, which has fiduciary responsibility for ensuring that the organization pursues its mission and complies with legal and ethical standards. The board hires and oversees executive leadership, approves budgets, and sets strategic direction. This governance structure balances accountability with flexibility, allowing organizations to adapt as they grow. Nonprofit corporations also enjoy perpetual existence, meaning they can continue beyond the involvement of their founders, ensuring mission continuity over time.

From a funding perspective, incorporation opens doors to a wide range of opportunities. Foundations, corporations, and government agencies are far more likely to fund incorporated nonprofits, as incorporation provides assurance of oversight, stability, and accountability. Furthermore, nonprofit corporations can apply for federal tax-exempt status, enabling donors to claim deductions for contributions and exempting the organization from federal income taxes. These advantages significantly expand the fundraising potential of a nonprofit corporation compared to unincorporated associations or even trusts.

Despite its advantages, incorporation also brings responsibilities and costs. Nonprofit corporations must comply with state filing requirements, maintain bylaws, hold regular board meetings, file annual reports, and adhere to IRS reporting requirements, including filing the Form 990. Failure to comply with these requirements can jeopardize tax-exempt status and public credibility. Additionally, the governance structure can sometimes lead to tensions, particularly in founder-led organizations where the transition to board oversight may feel like a loss of control. The formalities of incorporation, while beneficial for accountability, require commitment to organizational discipline and transparency.

Choosing among these structures depends on the vision and needs of the nonprofit. For small, informal, or short-term efforts, an unincorporated association may provide a practical starting point. It allows founders to act quickly and focus on immediate community needs, though it exposes members to personal liability and limits long-term growth. For asset-based philanthropy, a trust can provide a powerful vehicle for ensuring that resources are managed responsibly and dedicated to charitable purposes. Its stability and fiduciary framework make it well-suited for foundations or grantmaking entities, though its rigidity and limitations in program operations may hinder adaptability. For organizations seeking to operate programs, raise funds broadly, and establish a lasting institutional presence, incorporation is typically the most appropriate choice. It provides legal protection, access to funding, and credibility, but it also requires ongoing compliance and governance.

The decision is not always permanent, and organizations may evolve from one structure to another as their needs change. A group that begins as an unincorporated association may later incorporate to pursue larger grants or protect members from liability. A philanthropist who establishes a charitable trust may complement it with a nonprofit corporation to carry out direct services. The flexibility to adapt legal structures over time allows nonprofits to align their form with their mission and capacity.

In all cases, founders should seek legal and tax advice when choosing a structure. Laws governing nonprofits vary by jurisdiction, and the implications for liability, taxation, and governance are significant. Careful consideration of the organization's mission, scale, funding strategy, and long-term goals ensures that the chosen structure supports, rather than hinders, its effectiveness.

Ultimately, the choice of legal structure is about more than compliance. It reflects the organization's identity, credibility, and potential for impact. An unincorporated association may embody grassroots energy and community trust. A trust may represent the enduring legacy of a donor's philanthropy. A nonprofit corporation may stand as a dynamic institution capable of growing, adapting, and serving society across generations. Each structure offers a different path toward advancing the public good, and the right choice depends on how the organization envisions its mission unfolding over time.

By aligning legal structure with mission and strategy, nonprofits can build a strong foundation for growth, accountability, and impact. The decision requires balancing simplicity with protection, flexibility with stability, and autonomy with accountability. When carefully considered, the legal form becomes not merely a technical requirement but a strategic choice that empowers nonprofits to thrive and fulfill their promise of serving the common good.

The Articles of Incorporation

Certain formal steps are required to create a recognized legal entity. One of the most critical steps is the drafting and filing of articles of incorporation. These articles serve as the legal foundation of the nonprofit, establishing its existence under state law and setting the parameters for how it will operate. They are more than a procedural requirement; they embody the organization's identity, purpose, and accountability to the public. Understanding the function and content of articles of incorporation is essential for anyone involved in founding a nonprofit, as this document shapes the organization's structure, credibility, and long-term viability.

At their core, the articles of incorporation are the nonprofit's charter. They provide the state with basic information about the organization, including its name, purpose, and governance structure. Filing the articles with the appropriate state agency (usually the secretary of state) legally creates the nonprofit as a corporation distinct from its founders. This legal separation is vital, as it provides limited liability protection for directors, officers, and members. The articles, therefore, not only establish legitimacy but also safeguard the people working to advance the mission.

One of the most important elements of the articles is the statement of purpose. For a nonprofit, this statement must describe the charitable, educational, religious, or other qualifying purpose for which the organization exists. The language used here has significant implications, particularly for organizations that intend to seek federal tax-exempt status under section 501(c)(3) of the Internal Revenue Code. The IRS requires that the purpose clause clearly limit the nonprofit's activities to those that qualify for exemption. Vague or overly broad language can create problems during the application for tax-exempt recognition, while precise language ensures compliance and reduces the likelihood of challenges later on. For example, a nonprofit created to "advance education in underserved communities through after-school tutoring" conveys a specific charitable purpose, whereas a vague statement like "to improve communities" might raise questions.

The articles also specify the nonprofit's name. Choosing a name is not only a branding decision but also a legal one, as the name must comply with state rules and be distinguishable from existing entities. The name reflects the organization's mission and helps establish its identity in the public's mind, but its inclusion in the articles makes it legally binding. Some states require that the name include a designation such as "Inc.," "Incorporated," or "Corporation," while others may exempt nonprofits from this requirement. Ensuring that the chosen name aligns with both legal and branding considerations is an important step in incorporation.

Another critical component of the articles is the designation of a registered agent. The registered agent is an individual or entity authorized to receive legal documents on behalf of the nonprofit, such as service of process or official notices from the state. Listing a registered agent ensures that the nonprofit can be contacted in legal matters, maintaining accountability and compliance with state regulations. Without this role, the nonprofit could fail to receive important legal documents, leading to default judgments or loss of good standing.

The governance structure of the nonprofit is also addressed in the articles, typically through the identification of the initial board of directors. While the details of board operations are usually spelled out in the bylaws rather than the articles, many states require that the articles list the names and addresses of the founding directors. This information confirms that the nonprofit has the governance capacity to function as a corporation. Boards hold ultimate responsibility for oversight, so including this information in the articles underscores the seriousness of the commitment being made.

Another essential provision concerns the nonprofit's disposition of assets upon dissolution. For organizations seeking 501(c)(3) tax-exempt status, the IRS requires that the articles specify that any remaining assets, after debts are paid, must be distributed for exempt purposes rather than to private individuals. This clause ensures that the nonprofit's resources remain dedicated to the public good, even if the organization ceases to exist. For example, the articles might state that upon dissolution, assets will be distributed to another tax-exempt organization with similar purposes. Including this provision is not only a legal requirement but also a moral safeguard, preventing the diversion of charitable resources to private gain.

The articles may also include other provisions required by state law or considered prudent by the founders. These can include limitations on political activity, indemnification of directors and officers, or statements about membership structure if the nonprofit is to be a membership organization. Some nonprofits are governed by a self-perpetuating board, while others allow members to elect directors; the articles often clarify this distinction. By outlining such provisions, the articles provide a clear framework for how the nonprofit will be governed and how it will interact with stakeholders.

While the articles of incorporation establish the nonprofit's legal foundation, they are not intended to address every operational detail. Instead, they function in conjunction with bylaws, which provide more specific guidance on governance, meetings, decision-making, and internal policies. In effect, the articles provide the broad strokes (the legal identity and purpose) while the bylaws supply the detailed rules of operation. Together, these documents create a comprehensive governance framework.

The process of drafting and filing the articles varies by state, but most states provide templates or forms to guide founders. Filing fees are typically modest, though they vary by jurisdiction. Once the articles are filed and approved, the state issues a certificate of incorporation, officially recognizing the nonprofit as a legal corporation. From that point forward, the organization exists as a separate legal entity capable of entering contracts, owning property, and conducting business in pursuit of its mission.

The significance of the articles extends beyond the legal act of incorporation. They are often the first document that potential funders, regulators, and partners review when evaluating the nonprofit. As such, they represent the organization's public commitment to accountability, transparency, and mission alignment. Poorly drafted articles can hinder the nonprofit's ability to secure tax-exempt recognition, attract donors, or defend itself in legal matters. Carefully crafted articles, on the other hand, provide clarity, stability, and credibility.

In conclusion, the articles of incorporation are foundational to the life of a nonprofit. They establish the organization as a legal entity, provide liability protection, and enshrine its mission, governance, and accountability. By defining the purpose, naming the organization, appointing directors and a registered agent, and specifying the disposition of assets, the articles set the stage for both legal compliance and mission fulfillment. They are not simply bureaucratic paperwork but the charter that anchors the nonprofit's identity and ensures that its resources remain dedicated to the public good. For founders, giving careful attention to the drafting of the articles is one of the most important steps in creating a nonprofit capable of growth, credibility, and lasting impact.

Drafting Effective Bylaws

Bylaws are among the most important governing documents of a nonprofit organization. While the articles of incorporation establish the nonprofit's legal existence under state law, the bylaws provide the internal framework for how the organization operates. They set the rules for governance, clarify responsibilities, and ensure accountability among leaders, staff, and members. Drafting effective bylaws requires balancing flexibility with structure, simplicity with detail, and legal compliance with the organization's mission and culture. Well-crafted bylaws not only provide stability but also serve as a practical guide for decision-making, conflict resolution, and organizational growth.

The primary purpose of bylaws is to define governance. At their core, bylaws outline how the nonprofit will be directed and controlled by its board of directors. They specify the roles and responsibilities of the board, how directors are elected or appointed, the length of their terms, and the process for filling vacancies. By clarifying these procedures, bylaws ensure that the board can function consistently and fairly, even as individual directors come and go. Effective bylaws also establish the fiduciary duties of board members (care, loyalty, and obedience to the mission), ensuring that governance remains aligned with both legal requirements and ethical standards.

Equally important is the treatment of meetings. Bylaws typically specify how often the board will meet, what constitutes a quorum, and how votes will be taken. These provisions prevent uncertainty and provide predictability, ensuring that decisions are made in a legitimate and transparent manner. Some nonprofits also include provisions for electronic meetings and remote participation, reflecting the growing reliance on technology in governance. Flexibility in these areas helps the organization adapt to changing circumstances without compromising accountability.

Another key area addressed by bylaws is officer roles. Most nonprofits appoint officers such as a president or chair, vice chair, secretary, and treasurer. The bylaws define the duties of these officers, how they are selected, and how long they serve. This clarity is essential for ensuring that leadership responsibilities are distributed effectively and that officers are accountable for their performance. For example, the treasurer is typically responsible for financial oversight, while the secretary ensures accurate records of meetings. Without clear definitions, roles can overlap or be neglected, undermining governance.

Membership is another issue that bylaws must address, depending on the structure of the nonprofit. Some nonprofits are membership-based, meaning that individuals or organizations join as members and may have rights to vote on directors, bylaws changes, or other key issues. Others operate solely with a self-perpetuating board and no formal membership. If a nonprofit has members, the bylaws must clearly define their rights, obligations, and procedures for admission and termination. Membership provisions can be complex, as they must balance inclusivity with accountability, ensuring that members contribute to the organization's mission without compromising governance.

Bylaws also play a vital role in managing conflicts and transitions. Provisions for removal of directors or officers, conflict-of-interest policies, and dispute resolution processes provide mechanisms for addressing challenges before they escalate. Including these elements demonstrates a commitment to ethical governance and reduces the risk of internal crises. For example, a conflict-of-interest clause might require board members to disclose personal or financial interests in any decision affecting the nonprofit. Such provisions not only protect the organization legally but also preserve public trust.

Flexibility is essential in drafting bylaws. While they must establish clear rules, bylaws should avoid being overly detailed or prescriptive. Too much detail can make it difficult to adapt to new circumstances, requiring frequent amendments that consume time and resources. For instance, specifying the exact date of board meetings may create unnecessary rigidity, whereas requiring a minimum number of meetings per year allows for flexibility. The goal is to provide a stable framework that ensures fairness and accountability while leaving room for adaptation.

Legal compliance is another critical consideration. Bylaws must conform to state nonprofit corporation laws, federal tax-exemption requirements, and any additional regulations applicable to the organization's activities. For example, the IRS expects tax-exempt nonprofits to include provisions ensuring that their resources are dedicated to charitable purposes and not to private benefit. State laws may also require certain quorum thresholds, director duties, or reporting procedures. Consulting legal counsel during the drafting process helps ensure that bylaws not only meet the nonprofit's internal needs but also comply with all external requirements.

Beyond compliance, effective bylaws reflect the nonprofit's mission and culture. They should embody the values of the organization and promote practices consistent with its goals. For instance, a nonprofit committed to grassroots participation might structure bylaws to encourage broad member involvement in governance. A foundation focused on grantmaking might emphasize board expertise and fiduciary oversight. By aligning bylaws with mission, nonprofits ensure that governance supports, rather than distracts from, their purpose.

Finally, bylaws should be seen as living documents. They must be reviewed periodically to ensure that they remain relevant and effective as the organization evolves. Growth, changes in funding, shifts in leadership, and new legal requirements can all necessitate updates. Including an amendment process within the bylaws ensures that changes can be made thoughtfully and transparently. Regular review also reinforces the board's commitment to strong governance and accountability.

In conclusion, bylaws are the backbone of nonprofit governance, providing the framework for leadership, decision-making, and accountability. Drafting effective bylaws involves careful consideration of board structure, meetings, officer roles, membership, conflict resolution, and compliance. They must balance clarity with flexibility, legal rigor with mission alignment, and stability with adaptability. Far from being mere formalities, bylaws are practical tools that guide nonprofits through growth, challenges, and change.

Securing Tax-Exempt Status

Once a nonprofit is incorporated and governance is in place, it can apply for tax-exempt recognition with the IRS. The primary form for most organizations seeking 501(c)(3) status is Form 1023, *Application for Recognition of Exemption Under Section 501(c)(3) of the Internal Revenue Code*. Smaller organizations with annual gross receipts of $50,000 or less and assets under $250,000 may be eligible to use the streamlined Form 1023-EZ, which is shorter and simpler.

Form 1023 requires extensive information about the organization, including the following:

- A narrative description of its activities, explaining how each activity furthers the stated exempt purposes.
- A copy of the articles of incorporation and bylaws.
- Names, addresses, and compensation of officers, directors, and key employees.
- Details about fundraising plans, grantmaking activities, and potential conflicts of interest.
- A financial history for existing organizations or projected budgets for new ones.

The narrative description is especially important. The IRS scrutinizes this section to ensure that the nonprofit's activities align with exempt purposes and do not involve substantial nonexempt activities, such as political campaigning. Clear, specific descriptions of programs, services, and beneficiaries strengthen the application and reduce the likelihood of delays or requests for additional information.

Once submitted, the application enters the IRS review process. Processing times vary: Form 1023-EZ applications are often approved within weeks, while full Form 1023 applications may take several months, particularly if the IRS requests additional information. The IRS evaluates whether the organization meets the requirements for tax exemption, focusing on its purpose, activities, governance, and financial arrangements.

To qualify for tax-exempt status, a nonprofit must satisfy several standards established by the IRS. These include the following:

- *Organizational test.* The nonprofit's articles of incorporation must limit its purposes to exempt activities and include the required dissolution clause.

- *Operational test.* The nonprofit must operate exclusively for exempt purposes, with only insubstantial nonexempt activities. This means that charitable activities must dominate, and unrelated business activities must not become the primary focus.
- *Private inurement prohibition.* The nonprofit's earnings cannot benefit private individuals or insiders, such as founders or board members. Compensation must be reasonable and tied to actual services.
- *Restrictions on lobbying and political activity.* While limited lobbying is permitted, substantial lobbying is not. Political campaign activity in support of or opposition to candidates is strictly prohibited for 501(c)(3) organizations.

Failure to meet these standards may result in the denial of tax-exempt status.

If the IRS approves the application, it issues a determination letter formally recognizing the organization's tax-exempt status. This letter is a critical document, as it provides proof to donors that their contributions are tax-deductible. It also serves as evidence for state regulators, foundations, and other stakeholders that the nonprofit meets federal standards for exemption. Organizations should keep the determination letter permanently, as it will be required in many future interactions with funders and regulatory bodies.

Securing tax-exempt status is only the beginning. Maintaining that status requires ongoing compliance with IRS rules. Most nonprofits must file annual information returns, such as Form 990, 990-EZ, or 990-N, depending on their size. These forms provide transparency by disclosing financial information, governance practices, and program accomplishments. Failure to file for three consecutive years results in automatic revocation of tax-exempt status.

In addition, nonprofits must avoid prohibited activities, such as excessive lobbying or political campaigning, and must ensure that compensation and transactions with insiders are reasonable. Engaging in unrelated business activities may trigger unrelated business income tax, and excessive reliance on such activities can jeopardize a nonprofit's exemption. Careful financial management, board oversight, and adherence to mission are essential for long-term compliance.

Obtaining IRS recognition as a tax-exempt organization under section 501(c)(3) or another relevant section is transformative. It enhances the organization's fundraising capacity, as donors are more likely to contribute when their gifts are tax-deductible. It provides credibility, signaling to the public and stakeholders that the nonprofit meets federal standards of accountability and mission alignment. It also offers financial benefits, exempting the nonprofit from federal income taxes and often enabling access to reduced postal rates, state sales tax exemptions, and eligibility for public and private grants.

State-Level Requirements and Registrations

When starting a nonprofit organization in the United States, most attention tends to focus on federal recognition of tax-exempt status with the IRS. However, just as important are the state-level requirements and registrations that govern how nonprofits are formed, operated, and monitored within each jurisdiction. Because nonprofits are created under state law, their existence and compliance begin at the state level, long before they apply for federal exemptions. These requirements vary from state to state but generally include incorporation, charitable solicitation registration, state tax exemptions, employment-related filings, and annual reporting obligations. Understanding and fulfilling these requirements ensures that nonprofits remain in good standing, avoid legal or financial penalties, and maintain the trust of donors, regulators, and the public.

The process begins with incorporation. To exist as a legal entity distinct from its founders, a nonprofit must file articles of incorporation with the appropriate state office, usually the secretary of state or a similar agency. Incorporation provides the organization with limited liability protections, ensuring that directors, officers, and members are not personally responsible for the nonprofit's debts or liabilities. The articles must typically include the organization's name, purpose, registered agent, initial board members, and provisions related to dissolution. States may impose their own requirements for what must be included, but for organizations intending to seek federal tax-exempt status under section 501(c)(3), it is critical to draft purpose and dissolution clauses that satisfy both state law and IRS standards. Without proper incorporation, a nonprofit lacks legal standing and cannot take advantage of many protections and benefits available to incorporated entities.

Following incorporation, many states require nonprofits to register with the attorney general or a designated charity oversight office if they intend to solicit donations from the public. Known as charitable solicitation registration, this step is designed to protect donors by ensuring that nonprofits raising funds are transparent and accountable. In some states, even organizations soliciting donations solely online must register, while others impose thresholds based on the amount of contributions received annually. Registration typically involves filing an application that includes the articles of incorporation, bylaws, IRS determination letter (once received), financial statements, and information about officers and directors. Nonprofits may also be required to renew this registration annually, updating their financial data and governance information. Failure to register before soliciting donations can lead to fines, penalties, or prohibition from fundraising activities in that state.

State-level requirements extend beyond registration for solicitation. Many states offer their own tax exemptions, parallel to federal exemptions, which relieve nonprofits from paying state income tax, sales tax, or property tax. Securing these exemptions generally requires separate applications filed with the state's department of revenue or taxation agency. For example, a nonprofit may need to submit a copy of its IRS determination letter to prove its federal tax-exempt status, along with state-specific forms demonstrating eligibility for exemptions. Sales tax exemptions are particularly important for nonprofits that purchase significant goods and services, as they reduce operating costs. Property tax exemptions can also be substantial, especially for nonprofits that own facilities such as schools, hospitals, or community centers. These exemptions are not automatic; nonprofits must actively apply for them and comply with reporting requirements to maintain their status.

Employment-related registrations also fall under state requirements once a nonprofit begins to hire staff. Like other employers, nonprofits must comply with state labor laws, register for unemployment insurance, and contribute to workers' compensation funds. This often requires filing with the state's labor department or employment security office. Even though nonprofits may be mission-driven, they are still subject to employment regulations concerning wages, workplace safety, and nondiscrimination. Some states impose additional compliance obligations on nonprofit employers, such as mandatory employee training programs or reporting on workforce demographics. Ignoring these requirements can expose nonprofits to fines and lawsuits, undermining their credibility and straining their resources.

Annual reporting is another common state-level obligation. Most states require nonprofits to file annual or biennial reports with the secretary of state to confirm their continued existence and provide updated information about officers, directors, and addresses. These reports are often relatively simple but are critical for maintaining good standing. If a nonprofit fails to file timely reports, it risks administrative dissolution, which would revoke its legal standing and prevent it from conducting business. In addition to corporate reports, nonprofits that are registered to solicit contributions must often file annual financial reports with the attorney general or charitable bureau. These reports provide transparency to donors and regulators by disclosing revenues, expenses, and program activities. States may require audited financial statements once an organization's revenue exceeds a certain threshold, ensuring independent oversight of larger nonprofits.

In addition to these general requirements, some states impose specialized rules depending on the nonprofit's activities. For example, nonprofits operating educational institutions may need approval from a state education department. Healthcare nonprofits, such as clinics or hospitals, may require licensure from state health authorities. Organizations running child care programs, housing initiatives, or social services often face additional layers of state regulation to ensure the safety, quality, and accountability of their programs. These sector-specific requirements reflect the high stakes of providing services to vulnerable populations and the state's interest in protecting the public.

Foreign qualification is another consideration for nonprofits that operate across state lines. If a nonprofit incorporated in one state intends to conduct business or solicit donations in another, it may need to register as a foreign corporation in that state. This process typically involves submitting the articles of incorporation, proof of good standing from the home state, and a fee payment. Foreign qualification ensures that the nonprofit is subject to local jurisdiction, enabling the state to enforce its regulations and protect local donors and beneficiaries. For nonprofits with national reach, this can mean maintaining registrations in multiple states, each with its own requirements and deadlines.

The cumulative effect of these state-level requirements is that nonprofit compliance is not a one-time event, but rather an ongoing process. Incorporation establishes the nonprofit, but annual reports, solicitation registrations, tax exemption renewals, and employment filings must be maintained year after year. Many organizations create compliance calendars or engage legal and accounting professionals to manage these responsibilities. Failure to comply can have serious consequences, including fines, revocation of fundraising privileges, loss of tax exemptions, or even dissolution of the corporation. More importantly, noncompliance can erode public trust, as donors and stakeholders expect nonprofits to uphold the highest standards of accountability.

It is also important to note that state-level requirements interact with federal compliance. For example, when applying for state income or sales tax exemptions, nonprofits often need to present their IRS determination letter. Similarly, state charitable solicitation offices may cross-reference nonprofit filings with the federal Form 990, the annual IRS information return. In this way, compliance at the state and federal levels is intertwined, and strong governance practices benefit both.

In conclusion, while federal tax-exempt recognition often garners the most attention, state-level requirements and registrations form the backbone of nonprofit legal compliance. From incorporation and charitable solicitation registration to tax exemptions, employment regulations, and annual reporting, states impose a comprehensive framework to ensure that nonprofits remain transparent, accountable, and mission-focused. These requirements safeguard donors, protect the public, and enhance the credibility of the sector. For nonprofit leaders, understanding and fulfilling state obligations is not simply a matter of legal compliance, but a commitment to good governance and public trust. By diligently maintaining state registrations and adhering to state laws, nonprofits position themselves for stability, sustainability, and long-term impact in the communities they serve.

Summary

Deciding on the type of legal structure for a nonprofit is a serious matter, but usually results in the formation of a corporation, for which articles of incorporation and by-laws must be written. The next step is filing with the state in which the nonprofit resides, which can involve a variety of filings, depending on the nature of the entity's operations. Following that, it is essential for a nonprofit to obtain tax-exempt status from the IRS, since this drives the organization's ability to raise money from donors. These three activities are essential to the future success of a nonprofit, so consider paying for expert legal advice to ensure that these filings are properly created.

Chapter 3
Developing a Strategic Plan

Introduction

A nonprofit will probably not succeed without proper up-front planning. This means developing a mission statement and using it as the basis for setting goals and developing a plan that drives how the organization spends it cash and provides services. In this chapter, we cover mission statements, goal setting, needs assessments, and other tasks that are essential for improving a nonprofit's long-term odds of success.

Crafting a Mission, Vision, and Values Statement

The identity of a nonprofit organization is defined not only by its legal structure, governance, and financial resources but also by the words it chooses to articulate its purpose and aspirations. Mission, vision, and values statements together provide the philosophical framework for a nonprofit's existence, serving as both a compass for its internal decision-making and a beacon for external stakeholders. They shape culture, guide strategy, inspire supporters, and hold the organization accountable to its promises. Crafting these statements is therefore one of the most important steps in establishing or refining a nonprofit. While they are often presented as simple sentences on a website or brochure, their development requires deep reflection, broad consultation, and a careful balance of clarity, aspiration, and authenticity.

The mission statement is the cornerstone of this framework. It defines why the nonprofit exists and what it seeks to accomplish in practical terms. A strong mission statement is concise but comprehensive, communicating the organization's purpose, the population it serves, and the approach it takes to achieve impact. Unlike slogans, which aim to market or inspire, mission statements must withstand the test of time and remain relevant across changing contexts. For example, a nonprofit dedicated to providing after-school programs in low-income communities might craft a mission such as "to empower children in underserved neighborhoods by offering safe, enriching, and affordable after-school learning opportunities." This statement identifies the beneficiaries (children in underserved neighborhoods), the purpose (empowerment through education), and the method (after-school programs). Crafting such a mission requires founders and leaders to ask difficult questions: What is the real problem we are addressing? Who specifically do we serve? What activities are central to our approach? If the answers are vague, the mission will be too broad, diluting focus and making accountability difficult. Conversely, if the mission is overly narrow, it may limit growth and adaptability. The process of drafting a mission statement often involves facilitated discussions among board members, staff, volunteers, and even community stakeholders, ensuring that the statement reflects shared understanding and collective commitment.

Where the mission anchors the nonprofit in the present, the vision statement propels it into the future. The vision describes what the world would look like if the nonprofit's mission were fully realized. It is aspirational and forward-looking, intended to inspire action and communicate the long-term impact the organization seeks to achieve. A vision statement is less about programs and more about outcomes. Returning to the example of the after-school nonprofit, its vision might be "a future where every child has equal access to education, opportunity, and a supportive community." The vision conveys the organization's broader hope, transcending the specifics of its current activities. Crafting such a statement requires imagination but also realism, as an unattainable or overly vague vision risks sounding hollow. A well-developed vision statement strikes a balance between ambition and plausibility, motivating both internal stakeholders and external supporters to work toward the envisioned future.

Values statements complement mission and vision by articulating the principles that guide how the nonprofit conducts its work. Values express the organization's ethical commitments and cultural norms, shaping behavior, decision-making, and relationships with stakeholders. They answer the question: "What do we stand for as we pursue our mission and vision?" Values might include commitments to integrity, inclusivity, collaboration, innovation, or accountability. For instance, the after-school nonprofit might emphasize values such as respect for diversity, dedication to equity, and belief in the potential of every child. While values statements can sometimes become generic, effective ones are rooted in the specific identity of the organization. They should not merely echo buzzwords but reflect genuine commitments that influence practice. For example, a nonprofit that claims inclusivity as a value must demonstrate this through diverse leadership, equitable hiring practices, and culturally responsive programming. Crafting values requires open dialogue and consensus-building, ensuring that the principles resonate across the organization and are not simply imposed from above.

The process of crafting mission, vision, and values statements is as important as the final product. A rushed or perfunctory exercise often produces statements that sound polished but fail to resonate with stakeholders or guide decisions. By contrast, a participatory process builds ownership, strengthens organizational culture, and clarifies strategic direction. Ideally, this process begins with research and reflection, including a review of the community needs the nonprofit seeks to address, an assessment of the organization's unique strengths, and a scan of similar organizations to avoid duplication. Stakeholder engagement is critical: board members, staff, volunteers, beneficiaries, and even funders can contribute perspectives that enrich the statements. Facilitated workshops, surveys, and interviews provide opportunities to gather diverse input, ensuring the statements are inclusive and authentic.

Clarity and simplicity are essential in the drafting process. While mission and vision statements often emerge from lengthy discussions, the final wording must be brief, memorable, and accessible to a broad audience. Overly technical or jargon-heavy language can alienate supporters and obscure the organization's purpose. A mission that cannot be easily explained by staff or board members fails in its most basic function. Testing draft statements with different audiences, including community members and donors, can help refine language and ensure resonance.

Another consideration in crafting these statements is alignment with strategy and operations. A nonprofit's mission should inform its strategic plan, program priorities, and allocation of resources. If an organization's programs drift significantly from its mission, it risks losing credibility with donors and confusing stakeholders. Similarly, the vision should provide direction for long-term goals, ensuring that day-to-day activities contribute to broader aspirations. Values, meanwhile, should be embedded in policies and practices, from hiring and training to decision-making and evaluation. In this way, mission, vision, and values are not abstract ideals but living documents that shape the nonprofit's daily work.

These statements also play an important role in communication and branding. Externally, they convey the nonprofit's identity to donors, funders, partners, and the public. A clear mission reassures donors that their contributions are directed toward a defined purpose. An inspiring vision attracts supporters who share the same long-term goals. Strong values build trust, demonstrating that the nonprofit operates with integrity and accountability. Internally, these statements motivate staff and volunteers, providing a sense of shared purpose and belonging. In times of conflict or uncertainty, returning to mission, vision, and values can provide guidance and reaffirm commitment.

However, crafting these statements is not a one-time task. As nonprofits grow, evolve, and adapt to changing environments, their mission, vision, and values may need to be revisited. An organization that began as a local food pantry may evolve into a regional advocacy group addressing systemic food insecurity. In such cases, the mission may need updating to reflect broader activities, while the vision may expand to encompass systemic change. Regular reviews (perhaps during strategic planning cycles) ensure that the statements remain relevant and aligned with current realities. Updating them does not mean abandoning the organization's roots, but rather affirming its continued commitment in light of new opportunities and challenges.

Ultimately, mission, vision, and values statements are powerful tools for aligning purpose, inspiring action, and guiding decision-making in nonprofits. They embody the identity of the organization and communicate its commitments to the world. When done well, they become more than words on paper; they become touchstones for culture, strategy, and impact. They help nonprofits stay true to their purpose while navigating change, building trust with communities and donors, and inspiring collective action toward a better future.

In conclusion, the crafting of mission, vision, and values statements is a foundational exercise for nonprofits, shaping their identity, guiding their work, and inspiring their stakeholders. The mission grounds the organization in the present, articulating what it does and for whom. The vision points toward the future, describing the world the organization strives to create. The values define the principles that guide its journey, shaping behavior and culture. Together, they provide a coherent and compelling framework that enables nonprofits to remain focused, accountable, and impactful. Far from being perfunctory statements, they are essential tools for building legitimacy, attracting support, and sustaining the organization's commitment to public good.

Setting Short-Term and Long-Term Goals

For nonprofits, clarity of purpose is the foundation of effectiveness. Mission, vision, and values articulate why an organization exists and what it aspires to achieve, but it is through goal setting that these guiding principles are transformed into concrete action. Goals provide structure to ambitions, define measurable benchmarks, and align staff, volunteers, and stakeholders around shared priorities. They also serve as accountability mechanisms, ensuring that a nonprofit's limited resources are directed toward outcomes that advance its mission. In practice, nonprofits must balance short-term and long-term goals, weaving together immediate operational needs with broader aspirations for systemic change. Understanding how to set, differentiate, and integrate these goals is essential to achieving both sustainability and impact.

Short-term goals are typically those that can be achieved within a year or less. They focus on immediate priorities, operational improvements, or the execution of specific projects. For nonprofits, these goals often revolve around fundraising campaigns, program implementation, staff development, or communications strategies. For instance, a nonprofit dedicated to reducing homelessness might set a short-term goal of securing funding to expand shelter capacity for the coming winter season. Another short-term goal could be launching a new website to improve donor engagement. The defining characteristic of short-term goals is their immediacy: they address pressing needs or opportunities and produce tangible results that can be measured within a relatively short timeframe.

Short-term goals are important because they generate momentum and demonstrate progress. Nonprofits frequently operate under financial constraints and in environments where donors and funders demand accountability. Achieving short-term objectives shows stakeholders that the organization is capable of delivering results, which in turn builds trust and support for larger initiatives. Internally, short-term goals provide staff and volunteers with achievable targets that boost morale and prevent burnout. They help create a sense of accomplishment and lay the groundwork for pursuing more ambitious, long-term objectives.

While short-term goals keep nonprofits focused on the present, long-term goals anchor them in the future. These goals often span three to ten years and reflect the organization's vision for systemic change or sustained impact. Long-term goals go beyond immediate projects to address the root causes of social issues, build institutional capacity, and secure organizational sustainability. For example, the same nonprofit addressing homelessness might establish a long-term goal of reducing the city's homeless population by 25 percent over the next five years by combining shelter expansion, job training, and policy advocacy. Another long-term goal might be to establish a permanent endowment that provides stable funding for future programs.

Long-term goals are inherently more complex and challenging than short-term ones. They require strategic planning, significant resource allocation, and adaptability in the face of changing circumstances. Because social problems are rarely solved quickly, nonprofits must embrace patience and persistence when working toward long-term goals. At the same time, long-term objectives provide inspiration and direction, reminding stakeholders of the broader purpose behind day-to-day operations.

They ensure that nonprofits remain committed to systemic impact rather than being consumed entirely by immediate demands.

The relationship between short-term and long-term goals is not one of opposition but of complementarity. Short-term goals provide stepping stones toward long-term aspirations. They break down ambitious visions into manageable pieces, making progress tangible and sustainable. For example, if a nonprofit's long-term goal is to increase college access for underrepresented students, then short-term goals might include recruiting fifty new mentors this year, securing a grant to fund scholarships, or partnering with three local high schools. Each short-term accomplishment contributes to the long-term outcome, creating a coherent pathway from vision to reality. Without short-term goals, long-term ambitions risk remaining abstract; without long-term goals, short-term objectives risk becoming disconnected or reactive.

Setting effective goals requires intentionality and a structured process. Nonprofits must first root their goals in the mission and vision statements, ensuring alignment with the organization's core purpose. Goals that stray too far from the mission create confusion and risk diluting resources. For instance, a nonprofit dedicated to environmental conservation should be cautious about pursuing short-term funding opportunities unrelated to its environmental mission, even if they promise immediate revenue. Anchoring goals in mission provides clarity and legitimacy.

Next, nonprofits should strive to make their goals specific, measurable, achievable, relevant, and time-bound – often summarized as SMART goals. *Specificity* ensures that goals are concrete rather than vague aspirations. *Measurability* allows the organization to track progress and demonstrate accountability. *Achievability* ensures that goals are realistic given current resources and constraints, though they should still stretch the organization's capacity. *Relevance* ties goals directly to the mission, while *time-bound* parameters establish urgency and focus. For example, a SMART short-term goal might be: "Secure $250,000 in new grants from three foundations by the end of the fiscal year to expand after-school programming." A SMART long-term goal might be: "Increase high school graduation rates among program participants by 20 percent within five years."

Another key element in goal setting is inclusivity. Nonprofit leaders must involve staff, board members, volunteers, and even beneficiaries in the process of defining goals. This inclusiveness ensures that goals reflect the realities of implementation and the perspectives of those most affected by the nonprofit's work. It also builds buy-in, creating a sense of ownership across the organization. When staff and volunteers see how their daily efforts contribute to larger goals, motivation and cohesion increase.

Nonprofits must also remain flexible in their goal setting, particularly when it comes to long-term objectives. External conditions (such as economic downturns, changes in government policy, or public health crises) can disrupt even the best-laid plans. The COVID-19 pandemic, for example, forced many nonprofits to shift short-term goals toward emergency relief while recalibrating long-term aspirations. Flexibility does not mean abandoning goals altogether but adapting timelines, strategies, and metrics to new realities. Building in regular review periods allows nonprofits to assess progress, identify obstacles, and make necessary adjustments.

Measuring progress is critical to both short-term and long-term goals. For short-term goals, success can often be measured by outputs, such as funds raised, people served, or programs launched. For long-term goals, outcomes and impacts are more important, requiring nonprofits to invest in evaluation methods that capture changes in behavior, systems, or conditions. Demonstrating impact not only satisfies funders but also strengthens the nonprofit's learning culture, enabling it to refine strategies and increase effectiveness over time.

Donor and funder expectations also play a significant role in goal setting. Many funders require nonprofits to articulate both short-term and long-term goals in grant proposals and to report progress through measurable indicators. While this can create pressure, it also pushes nonprofits to clarify their objectives and align their resources strategically. Successful nonprofits use these requirements as opportunities to refine their goals and communicate impact to external audiences. Transparency in progress, whether goals are met, exceeded, or still in progress, reinforces credibility and trust.

In addition, goal setting serves as a mechanism for accountability and governance. Boards of directors rely on clearly articulated goals to evaluate the performance of executive leadership and ensure that the organization remains mission-driven. Staff performance reviews can be linked to progress toward short-term objectives, while strategic plans chart progress toward long-term outcomes. In this way, goals permeate every level of the organization, creating alignment from the boardroom to the front-lines.

In conclusion, setting short-term and long-term goals is fundamental to the success of nonprofits. Short-term goals provide immediate focus, demonstrate progress, and build momentum, while long-term goals keep the organization aligned with its vision and committed to systemic change. Together, they create a balanced framework that integrates urgency with aspiration. Effective goal setting requires alignment with mission, clarity through SMART principles, inclusivity in process, flexibility in response to change, and rigor in measurement. For nonprofits operating in environments of scarce resources and high expectations, the discipline of goal setting transforms ideals into impact. It ensures that every dollar, every hour of volunteer time, and every programmatic effort contributes not only to short-term achievements but also to lasting change in the communities they serve.

Conducting a Needs Assessment

When a group of individuals comes together to form a new nonprofit, they are often motivated by passion, conviction, and a desire to make a difference. Yet passion alone is not sufficient for building an effective and sustainable organization. To ensure that a nonprofit addresses genuine gaps in services, avoids duplicating existing efforts, and aligns its mission with community priorities, it must begin with a thorough needs assessment. This process involves gathering and analyzing information about the population to be served, the problems they face, the resources already available, and the opportunities for intervention. Conducting a needs assessment not only validates the necessity of the nonprofit's mission but also provides a foundation for strategic planning, program design, and fundraising.

The first step in a needs assessment is defining its scope. A nonprofit must determine which issues, populations, and geographic areas it intends to study. Without a clear scope, the process can become unfocused and overwhelming, leading to information that is broad but not useful. For example, a group interested in starting a nonprofit to address youth unemployment must decide whether it will focus on a specific city, region, or demographic segment. Narrowing the scope ensures that the data collected is relevant and manageable, setting the stage for meaningful analysis.

Once the scope is defined, data collection begins. Effective needs assessments draw from both quantitative and qualitative sources. Quantitative data provides measurable evidence of the problem, such as statistics on poverty rates, school dropout levels, housing shortages, or health disparities. These numbers can often be obtained from government agencies, academic research, or publicly available reports. For instance, census data or labor statistics may reveal high unemployment rates in a particular neighborhood. While quantitative data establishes the scale of the problem, it rarely captures the lived experiences of those affected.

This is where qualitative data plays a critical role. Through interviews, focus groups, surveys, or community meetings, nonprofits can hear directly from the people they seek to serve. These methods uncover personal stories, perceptions, and insights that numbers alone cannot convey. A community experiencing food insecurity may reveal not only a shortage of affordable groceries but also barriers such as lack of transportation, cultural preferences, or distrust of assistance programs. By blending statistical evidence with community voices, nonprofits can develop a nuanced understanding of needs that is both empirically grounded and human-centered.

As data is collected, it is equally important to map existing resources and services. A common mistake of new nonprofits is assuming that unmet needs are synonymous with a lack of services. In many communities, services may exist but may be underutilized, inaccessible, or misaligned with actual needs. For example, job training programs may exist but may not accommodate parents with child care responsibilities. By cataloging the organizations, agencies, and programs already in place, nonprofits can identify gaps rather than duplicating efforts. This step also opens the door to potential partnerships, as collaboration with existing organizations can enhance effectiveness and avoid unnecessary competition for resources.

Analyzing the data collected requires careful attention to patterns, gaps, and priorities. Quantitative statistics can be compared against benchmarks, such as state or national averages, to highlight areas where the community is particularly disadvantaged. Qualitative data can be coded to identify recurring themes or concerns. The aim is to move beyond raw information to actionable insights. For instance, if survey results show that young people cite lack of transportation as a major barrier to employment, the nonprofit may conclude that addressing transit access is as important as offering job training.

Prioritization is an essential part of analysis. Communities face multiple challenges, and no single nonprofit can address all of them effectively. Needs assessments help organizations determine which problems are most urgent, which are most solvable, and which align most closely with their mission. This prioritization must balance objective data with community input, ensuring that the organization's agenda is not imposed from outside but reflects the lived priorities of those it aims to serve. A nonprofit that ignores community voices risks irrelevance or mistrust, no matter how compelling its data may appear.

Once priorities are identified, the needs assessment should articulate them in a clear and accessible format. This often takes the form of a written report summarizing findings, highlighting key data points, and outlining gaps in services. The report may include both statistical evidence and illustrative stories, bringing the issues to life for funders, partners, and community stakeholders. Transparency in reporting builds credibility, demonstrating that the nonprofit has done its homework and is grounded in real community needs rather than assumptions or anecdotes.

Conducting a needs assessment is not only a technical exercise but also a relationship-building process. Engaging stakeholders throughout the assessment fosters trust and buy-in. Community members who are invited to share their experiences feel valued and are more likely to support the nonprofit's work in the future. Other nonprofits and agencies that are consulted may become collaborators rather than competitors. Funders who see that an organization has conducted a rigorous needs assessment are more inclined to invest, confident that their resources will be directed toward genuine needs. In this way, the process itself lays the groundwork for partnerships, legitimacy, and sustainability.

The needs assessment also has direct implications for program design. By identifying specific barriers and priorities, nonprofits can tailor their programs to meet actual needs rather than assumed ones. For example, rather than launching a generic tutoring program for youth, a nonprofit might focus on after-school STEM activities if the assessment reveals a gap in science and technology opportunities. Similarly, a nonprofit aiming to address hunger might establish mobile food pantries if the assessment highlights transportation barriers. Programs grounded in needs assessments are more likely to achieve meaningful impact because they address the root causes of problems.

Beyond program design, the needs assessment supports strategic planning. It informs the nonprofit's mission statement, vision, and long-term goals, ensuring they are aligned with community realities. It provides the evidence base for setting measurable objectives and tracking progress. It also guides resource allocation, helping the organization decide where to invest limited funds and staff time. By linking strategic priorities to documented needs, nonprofits strengthen their accountability and enhance their ability to adapt to changing conditions.

The process of conducting a needs assessment is not without challenges. Data may be incomplete, outdated, or difficult to interpret. Community members may be hesitant to participate due to distrust or fatigue from repeated surveys. There may also be tension between what data suggests and what stakeholders perceive as most urgent. For example, statistics may indicate high rates of obesity, while community members prioritize access to affordable housing. Navigating these tensions requires sensitivity, transparency, and willingness to acknowledge limitations. A needs assessment should not present itself as the definitive account of a community's needs but as a thoughtful contribution to ongoing dialogue.

Finally, needs assessments are not one-time events. Communities change, new challenges emerge, and programs evolve. A nonprofit that relies indefinitely on an assessment conducted at its founding risks becoming outdated and irrelevant. Periodic reassessment ensures that the organization remains responsive and adaptive. For some nonprofits, this may mean formal assessments every three to five years; for others, it may involve ongoing feedback loops through surveys, advisory committees, or community meetings. By embedding needs assessment into organizational culture, nonprofits remain dynamic and closely attuned to those they serve.

In conclusion, conducting a needs assessment is a foundational step in creating a new nonprofit organization. It moves the organization from passion to purpose, grounding its mission in evidence and community voices. By defining scope, gathering quantitative and qualitative data, mapping resources, analyzing priorities, and engaging stakeholders, nonprofits identify where they can make the most meaningful contribution. The process strengthens credibility with funders and partners, informs program design, and guides strategic planning. While challenges exist, they can be overcome through transparency, inclusivity, and ongoing reassessment. Ultimately, a needs assessment is not just a prerequisite for forming a nonprofit – it is a commitment to accountability, responsiveness, and impact, ensuring that the organization truly serves the communities it seeks to uplift.

SWOT Analysis for Nonprofits

Nonprofit organizations operate in complex environments that are shaped by community needs, donor expectations, government regulations, and competition for resources. To remain effective and sustainable, nonprofits must regularly assess their internal capacities and external circumstances. One widely used tool for this purpose is the SWOT analysis, which examines an organization's strengths, weaknesses, opportunities, and threats. Though often associated with business strategy, the SWOT framework is equally valuable for nonprofits, offering a structured way to evaluate performance, set priorities, and align strategies with mission and vision. Conducting a SWOT analysis involves more than listing attributes; it requires inclusive participation, careful analysis, and a focus on actionable outcomes.

The process begins with clarifying the purpose of the SWOT analysis. For nonprofits, this is typically part of strategic planning, program development, or organizational assessment. The goal is to identify what the organization does well, where it struggles, what external trends it can leverage, and what risks it faces. Framing the exercise with a clear purpose ensures that the discussion remains relevant and that the findings can inform decision-making. For example, a nonprofit preparing to expand its services into a new community may conduct a SWOT analysis to evaluate readiness and external conditions.

To ensure accuracy and buy-in, conducting a SWOT analysis should involve diverse stakeholders. Board members, staff, volunteers, beneficiaries, and external partners all bring perspectives that enrich the process. Staff may highlight operational realities, board members may provide governance insights, and community members may share firsthand experiences of programs. A facilitated workshop is often the most effective format, allowing participants to brainstorm, discuss, and categorize ideas collaboratively. Surveys or interviews can supplement this process, particularly if the nonprofit seeks input from a broader constituency. Inclusivity is crucial, as it prevents blind spots and ensures that the analysis reflects the lived realities of the organization.

Strengths represent the internal assets that give the nonprofit an advantage. These might include a strong reputation in the community, dedicated volunteers, skilled staff, unique programs, or a solid donor base. Identifying strengths requires honest recognition of what sets the nonprofit apart from others. For instance, a community health clinic might cite its bilingual staff and trusted relationships with underserved populations as key strengths. Highlighting strengths provides a foundation for strategic planning, showing where the nonprofit can build and leverage its capacities. However, identifying strengths should not become an exercise in self-congratulation; it should focus on assets that are genuinely distinctive and strategically significant.

Weaknesses, by contrast, are internal limitations that hinder effectiveness. These may include inadequate funding diversity, weak technology infrastructure, governance challenges, or gaps in staff skills. Recognizing weaknesses requires humility and honesty, which can be difficult for organizations that fear exposing vulnerabilities. Yet failing to acknowledge weaknesses prevents nonprofits from addressing them. For example, a nonprofit may recognize that its reliance on a single funding source creates financial fragility, or that high staff turnover undermines program continuity. By candidly identifying weaknesses, nonprofits can target capacity-building efforts and avoid strategic missteps. Importantly, weaknesses should be seen not as failures but as areas for growth.

Opportunities focus on external conditions that the nonprofit can exploit to advance its mission. These might include emerging social trends, new funding streams, policy changes, or potential partnerships. Opportunities arise from the environment and require awareness of broader contexts. For example, a shift in public policy toward renewable energy might create funding opportunities for an environmental nonprofit. Similarly, demographic changes could expand the demand for services or open new avenues for outreach. Identifying opportunities requires nonprofits to look beyond their immediate operations and consider how external developments can be aligned with their mission.

Threats are external challenges that could harm the organization or its ability to fulfill its mission. These include economic downturns, competition from other nonprofits, political instability, or shifts in donor priorities. For example, a nonprofit reliant on government grants may face threats if public budgets are cut. A health-focused nonprofit may see its programs jeopardized by new regulations or rising costs of care. Identifying threats helps nonprofits anticipate risks and develop contingency plans. While threats cannot always be controlled, they can be mitigated through proactive strategies such as diversifying revenue or building stronger advocacy networks.

Once the four categories are articulated, the next step is to analyze the relationships among them. Strengths can be leveraged to seize opportunities; weaknesses must be addressed to prevent threats from becoming overwhelming. For instance, if a nonprofit's strength is a strong volunteer base, it might seize the opportunity of growing community interest in service by expanding volunteer programs. Conversely, if a weakness is limited technological capacity, the threat of digital fundraising becoming the norm must be taken seriously. This cross-analysis transforms the SWOT from a descriptive list into a strategic tool, guiding decision-making and prioritization.

Conducting a SWOT analysis is not only about identifying issues but also about translating them into action. The findings should feed directly into strategic planning, program development, or operational improvements. Strengths can be highlighted in communications with donors and stakeholders. Weaknesses can be targeted in capacity-building initiatives, such as training or governance reforms. Opportunities can shape new program initiatives or partnerships, while threats can inform risk management strategies. For example, if a nonprofit identifies declining youth engagement as a threat but recognizes social media expertise among staff as a strength, it might develop a new digital outreach campaign to attract younger supporters.

Documentation is another important part of the process. A written SWOT analysis provides a reference point for future planning and accountability. It ensures that the insights generated during workshops or discussions are not lost and that the organization can revisit them as circumstances evolve. Sharing the results with stakeholders, including staff, board members, and funders, reinforces transparency and builds trust. It also signals that the nonprofit is proactive in assessing its environment and adapting to change.

A SWOT analysis should not be treated as a one-time exercise. The environments in which nonprofits operate are dynamic, with shifting community needs, funding landscapes, and policy frameworks. Regularly revisiting the SWOT, perhaps every two to three years as part of strategic planning, ensures that the organization remains attuned to changes and can update its strategies accordingly. For example, an opportunity identified five years ago may no longer exist, while new threats may have emerged. By embedding SWOT into an ongoing culture of reflection, nonprofits can maintain resilience and relevance.

While the SWOT analysis is a powerful tool, it also has limitations. It is inherently subjective, relying on the perspectives and judgments of those who participate. Different stakeholders may disagree about whether something is a strength or a weakness, or whether an external trend represents an opportunity or a threat. Facilitators must manage these disagreements constructively, recognizing that diverse perspectives enrich the analysis. Another limitation is that SWOT does not provide solutions; it identifies factors but leaves strategy development to subsequent steps. To be effective, nonprofits must move beyond listing factors to interpreting them in light of mission and resources.

Despite these limitations, the value of SWOT lies in its simplicity and adaptability. It encourages nonprofits to take stock of themselves, to look outward as well as inward, and to link analysis to action. For small nonprofits with limited capacity, SWOT provides an accessible entry point to strategic planning. For larger organizations, it serves as a framework for organizing complex data and diverse perspectives. In both cases, it fosters reflection, dialogue, and alignment around shared priorities.

In conclusion, conducting a SWOT analysis for a nonprofit organization is a vital step in aligning internal capacities with external realities. By identifying strengths, weaknesses, opportunities, and threats, nonprofits gain a clearer understanding of their position and a roadmap for moving forward. The process requires inclusivity, honesty, and analysis, transforming data into strategies that advance mission and vision. While it is not a cure-all, SWOT provides a structured approach to self-assessment and strategic thinking, enabling nonprofits to remain resilient and effective in dynamic environments. When used thoughtfully and revisited regularly, it becomes more than an exercise in reflection; it becomes a tool for building impact, sustainability, and trust in the communities nonprofits serve.

Linking Strategy to Programs and Outcomes

Nonprofit organizations operate with the central goal of creating public value, whether by alleviating poverty, advancing education, improving health, protecting the environment, or promoting the arts. Unlike businesses that measure success through profits or governments that measure it through policy implementation, nonprofits measure their effectiveness by the extent to which they fulfill their missions. To ensure alignment between their overarching mission and their day-to-day activities, nonprofits must deliberately link strategy to programs and outcomes. This connection ensures that the organization's vision is translated into concrete actions that deliver measurable benefits to the communities it serves.

The starting point for linking strategy to programs and outcomes is the strategic plan. A strategic plan articulates an organization's long-term priorities, outlining where it wants to go and how it intends to get there. It builds on the mission and vision by setting clear objectives and identifying the resources required to achieve them. Without a strategic plan, nonprofits risk drifting into activities that are well-intentioned but disconnected from their core purpose. The strategic plan becomes the bridge between the abstract ideals of mission and the practical realities of implementation.

From the strategic plan, programs are developed as vehicles for carrying out the organization's objectives. Programs represent the specific initiatives, projects, or services through which the nonprofit pursues its goals. The design of these programs must be informed by strategy, ensuring that they directly address the priorities identified in the planning process. For instance, if a nonprofit's strategic goal is to improve literacy rates among children in low-income neighborhoods, its programs might include after-school tutoring, parent literacy workshops, and the distribution of free books. Each of these programs is a practical expression of the strategic objective. The connection ensures that resources are not wasted on activities that may be worthwhile in isolation but do not advance the nonprofit's defined priorities.

To link strategy effectively to programs, nonprofits must also establish clear theories of change or logic models. These frameworks articulate how specific activities are expected to lead to desired outcomes. A theory of change spells out the causal pathways between inputs, activities, outputs, and outcomes, providing a roadmap that connects everyday actions to broader impact. For example, in the literacy nonprofit, the logic model might outline that tutoring sessions (activity) lead to improved reading skills (short-term outcome), which in turn increase school performance and graduation rates (long-term outcome). This framework ensures that programs are not designed in isolation but are embedded within a broader strategic rationale.

Measurement is a critical component of linking strategy, programs, and outcomes. Nonprofits must define metrics that allow them to track whether their programs are achieving the intended results. These metrics should align with the strategic goals of the organization, creating a direct line of accountability. In the case of the literacy nonprofit, metrics might include the number of tutoring sessions delivered, reading level improvements among participants, or graduation rates over time. By collecting and analyzing this data, nonprofits can demonstrate that their programs are not only active but also effective in advancing strategic objectives. Measurement also provides feedback that can be used to refine programs, strengthen strategy, and communicate impact to funders and stakeholders.

Fundraising and resource allocation also illustrate the importance of linking strategy to programs and outcomes. Donors, grantmakers, and government funders increasingly expect nonprofits to demonstrate how their programs contribute to measurable results. Strategic alignment gives nonprofits credibility by showing that resources are directed toward evidence-based activities tied to long-term goals. When outcomes can be demonstrated, nonprofits strengthen their case for continued or expanded funding. For example, if a nonprofit can show that its tutoring programs lead to measurable literacy improvements, funders are more likely to invest in its expansion. In this way, linking strategy, programs, and outcomes not only enhances effectiveness but also strengthens sustainability.

Governance and leadership play an essential role in maintaining these connections. Boards of directors are responsible for ensuring that the nonprofit remains true to its mission and strategy, while executive leadership ensures that programs are designed and managed accordingly. Effective governance requires asking whether programs align with strategic priorities and whether outcomes demonstrate mission fulfillment. Leaders must resist the temptation of mission drift, which occurs when nonprofits pursue activities or funding opportunities that fall outside their strategic focus. While attractive in the short term, mission drift can dilute impact and confuse stakeholders. Linking programs to strategy and outcomes provides the discipline needed to maintain coherence.

At the operational level, staff and volunteers also play a crucial role in connecting strategy to outcomes. They must understand how their daily tasks contribute to the nonprofit's broader mission. Communication is key: leaders must articulate the strategic goals in ways that are accessible and relevant to staff at all levels. Training and orientation programs can reinforce these connections, ensuring that employees see how their work contributes to measurable outcomes. When staff understand the link between strategy, programs, and outcomes, they are more motivated and more effective in carrying out their roles.

The process of linking strategy to programs and outcomes is not static. Nonprofits operate in dynamic environments where community needs, funding landscapes, and political contexts change rapidly. Regular evaluation and strategic reflection are necessary to ensure that programs remain aligned with goals and that outcomes remain meaningful. For example, a health nonprofit might initially focus on direct service delivery but later recognize that systemic advocacy is a more effective way to achieve long-term outcomes. This evolution requires revisiting the strategic plan, redesigning programs, and redefining outcomes. Flexibility ensures that the organization remains relevant while maintaining alignment between mission and practice.

Stakeholder engagement further strengthens the connection between strategy, programs, and outcomes. Beneficiaries, community members, donors, and partners all have a stake in the nonprofit's work. Engaging these stakeholders in planning and evaluation ensures that programs are responsive to real needs and that outcomes are defined in ways that matter to those served. For example, measuring graduation rates may be important to funders, but beneficiaries may value improvements in self-confidence or access to supportive mentors. Incorporating multiple perspectives into program design and evaluation ensures that outcomes reflect both strategic objectives and community realities.

In conclusion, the effectiveness of a nonprofit depends on its ability to link strategy to programs and outcomes. Strategy provides direction, programs provide vehicles for action, and outcomes provide evidence of impact. The process requires deliberate planning, clear frameworks like logic models, rigorous measurement, and disciplined governance. It also requires ongoing adaptation and stakeholder engagement. When nonprofits successfully connect these elements, they not only demonstrate accountability but also maximize their capacity to create lasting change. By grounding programs in strategy and measuring outcomes with care, nonprofits transform mission-driven ideals into tangible improvements in the lives of the communities they serve.

Keeping the Plan Adaptable

Nonprofit organizations operate in environments that are often unpredictable, shaped by shifting community needs, fluctuating funding streams, evolving public policy, and unexpected global events. For this reason, the ability to adapt plans is as important as the ability to design them in the first place. A plan that is rigid may look sound on paper, but if it cannot adjust to new realities, it risks becoming irrelevant or even harmful to the organization's mission. Adaptability ensures that a nonprofit can remain effective, resilient, and responsive while staying anchored to its core purpose.

The foundation of adaptability is a clear mission and vision. When a nonprofit knows exactly what it exists to do and what long-term change it seeks, it can modify tactics and programs without losing direction. This clarity provides a compass that allows flexibility in methods while preserving integrity of purpose. For example, a nonprofit dedicated to improving educational outcomes for marginalized children may shift from in-person tutoring to online learning in response to a pandemic, but the ultimate mission remains the same. Anchoring adaptability in mission ensures that changes are strategic rather than reactive improvisations.

Another key factor in adaptability is the culture of the organization. A nonprofit that encourages open communication, experimentation, and learning is more likely to adjust effectively to change. Leaders play a critical role in setting this tone by promoting transparency and valuing feedback from staff, volunteers, and community members. When people throughout the organization feel empowered to share ideas and highlight challenges, the nonprofit can identify emerging issues more quickly and respond with agility. Conversely, when decision-making is overly hierarchical or communication channels are closed, adaptation is slowed, and the organization risks being blindsided by external shifts.

Regular monitoring and evaluation also contribute to adaptability. By tracking outcomes, reviewing data, and soliciting stakeholder feedback, nonprofits can see early warning signs when programs are not working as intended or when external conditions shift. This information enables course corrections before problems escalate. For example, a nonprofit providing workforce development programs might notice that enrollment drops sharply when offered only during daytime hours. By evaluating participation trends, the organization can adjust to offer evening sessions, better aligning with participant needs. Systematic reflection and adjustment create a cycle of continuous improvement that strengthens both adaptability and impact.

Financial planning is another critical area where adaptability is required. Nonprofits are often vulnerable to funding volatility, particularly if they rely heavily on a single source of revenue. To remain flexible, nonprofits build diverse funding portfolios, combining grants, individual donations, earned income, and corporate partnerships. Diversification reduces dependence on any one stream and allows the organization to withstand sudden losses. Adaptive nonprofits also establish reserves or contingency funds, providing a buffer during downturns or emergencies. A financially resilient organization can shift resources quickly to new priorities without jeopardizing its operations.

Collaboration further enhances adaptability. By partnering with other organizations, government agencies, and community groups, nonprofits can share resources, exchange information, and expand their capacity to respond to change. For instance, during a natural disaster, nonprofits that have pre-existing relationships with local agencies can coordinate relief efforts more effectively than those acting alone. Partnerships create networks of support that allow nonprofits to pivot more quickly in times of crisis. They also help avoid duplication of efforts, ensuring that adaptations are efficient and strategic.

Technology has become an increasingly important tool for nonprofit adaptability. Digital platforms allow organizations to gather data, communicate with stakeholders, deliver programs, and raise funds in new ways. Nonprofits that embrace technology can pivot more smoothly when circumstances shift. The COVID-19 pandemic illustrated this point vividly, as organizations that were able to transition programs to virtual formats maintained continuity of service, while those that lacked digital infrastructure struggled. Investing in flexible technology systems and digital literacy equips nonprofits to adapt not only in crises but also in evolving everyday contexts.

While adaptability is essential, it must be balanced with consistency. Constantly shifting directions can confuse stakeholders, weaken credibility, and undermine trust. Effective nonprofits strike this balance by maintaining steady long-term goals while adjusting short-term tactics. This balance ensures that the organization remains reliable and mission-focused even as it responds to change. Communicating these adjustments clearly to donors, beneficiaries, and partners reinforces trust, demonstrating that adaptations are deliberate, thoughtful, and aligned with the nonprofit's core commitments.

In conclusion, nonprofits keep their plans adaptable by anchoring them in mission, fostering a culture of openness and learning, regularly monitoring outcomes, diversifying funding, cultivating partnerships, and embracing technology. Adaptability does not mean abandoning strategy but refining it to remain responsive in dynamic environments. By combining flexibility with mission-driven consistency, nonprofits remain resilient and effective, capable of meeting both expected and unforeseen challenges while continuing to advance the public good.

Summary

One of the foundational tasks of strategic plan development is to conduct a sufficiently in-depth needs assessment. If subsequent planning work is based on an initially sketchy analysis, then it is entirely likely that the organization will not be properly aligned with the community it was built to serve, which increases the risk of failure. Consequently, of all the planning activities noted in this chapter, nonprofit founders should be most diligent in pursuing a detailed needs assessment.

Chapter 4
Developing a Budget

Introduction

Nonprofits rarely have sufficient funding to support their missions, so they must create budgets and then slavishly follow them to avoid having a cash shortfall. In this chapter, we discuss how nonprofit and for-profit budgets differ, and then delve into the details of how to construct a budget.

The Difference Between Nonprofit and For-Profit Budgets

Budgeting is one of the most important financial planning activities for any organization, regardless of its sector. It provides a framework for allocating resources, setting priorities, and tracking performance. Yet while the mechanics of budgeting may appear similar across different types of entities, the underlying assumptions, goals, and outcomes differ significantly between nonprofit and for-profit organizations. The contrast reflects the distinct missions of these two sectors: for-profits exist to generate financial returns for owners or shareholders, while nonprofits exist to pursue public benefit and reinvest all surpluses back into their mission. Understanding these differences is essential for leaders, funders, and stakeholders in both sectors, as it highlights how financial planning is deeply intertwined with organizational purpose.

At the most fundamental level, the objectives of nonprofit and for-profit budgets diverge. A for-profit budget is designed primarily to maximize profitability, ensure growth, and provide returns to investors. The central focus is on revenues exceeding expenses in ways that create wealth for the owners. For example, a retail company may build its budget around increasing sales volume, controlling operating costs, and improving margins to achieve higher profits. In contrast, a nonprofit budget is designed to maximize mission impact within the constraints of available resources. Success is not measured by financial surplus but by the effectiveness and reach of programs. A nonprofit's budget reflects the careful balancing of revenues (such as donations, grants, and earned income) with expenditures that directly advance its mission. Any surplus must be reinvested into services, infrastructure, or reserves rather than distributed to private individuals.

The sources of revenue are another key distinction. For-profit budgets are typically built around predictable income from the sale of goods or services. While market fluctuations can affect revenues, businesses generally have control over their pricing strategies, marketing efforts, and product development to influence sales. Nonprofits, on the other hand, often rely on more uncertain revenue streams, including donations, grants, membership dues, and special events. These funding sources can be unpredictable, subject to donor priorities, economic cycles, and competitive grantmaking processes. As a result, nonprofit budgets often include contingency planning and conservative revenue projections, acknowledging the uncertainty inherent in their funding environment. This reliance on external support makes revenue diversification critical for nonprofits, whereas for-profits can often focus on deepening and expanding their core lines of business.

The structure of expenses further differentiates nonprofit and for-profit budgets. For-profit budgets allocate significant resources to activities that drive profitability, such as product development, marketing, and sales. While administrative expenses are necessary, they are often seen as overhead that should be minimized to improve margins. In nonprofits, expenses are categorized more explicitly into program costs, administrative costs, and fundraising costs. Program expenses, which directly relate to mission activities, are considered the highest priority, as donors and funders want assurance that their contributions have a tangible impact. Administrative and fundraising expenses are also essential, but they are often scrutinized by donors and watchdog groups. This creates pressure for nonprofits to keep overhead costs low, even when investments in infrastructure, staff development, or technology are necessary for long-term sustainability. Thus, while for-profits can justify higher overhead as investments in growth, nonprofits must carefully manage perceptions and justify every administrative expense in relation to mission advancement.

Another important difference lies in the treatment of surplus and deficit. In for-profit organizations, a surplus (profit) is the desired outcome, representing the financial return on investment. This profit can be reinvested into the business to support growth, distributed to shareholders as dividends, or held as retained earnings. In nonprofits, a surplus is not the primary goal but may occur when revenues exceed expenses. While surpluses are welcomed as indicators of financial health, they must be reinvested into the organization's programs, reserves, or capacity-building initiatives. A deficit, on the other hand, may be acceptable in a for-profit if it is part of a strategic investment to gain market share or launch new products. Investors may tolerate short-term losses in exchange for long-term profitability. For nonprofits, persistent deficits are more problematic, as they signal financial instability and may undermine donor confidence. While a nonprofit may deliberately run a deficit to use restricted funds or in response to an urgent need, repeated shortfalls can jeopardize its credibility and sustainability.

Budget flexibility also varies between the two sectors. For-profit organizations generally have more discretion in reallocating resources as opportunities or challenges arise. If a new market trend emerges, a business can shift its budget to capitalize on it, adjusting expenditures to align with evolving revenue strategies. Nonprofits often face constraints due to donor restrictions on funds. Many grants and donations are earmarked for specific programs, leaving nonprofits with limited flexibility to reallocate resources. This restriction requires nonprofits to budget carefully, balancing unrestricted funding (which can support general operations) with restricted funding (which must be used as specified). For-profits rarely face such limitations, giving them greater agility in responding to changing circumstances.

Performance measurement in budgeting also reveals significant contrasts. For-profits evaluate their budgets based on financial outcomes such as revenue growth, profit margins, return on investment, and shareholder value. Success is quantified in terms of financial performance, and budgets are adjusted to optimize these metrics.

Nonprofits evaluate budgets based on programmatic outcomes and mission impact. While financial stability is essential, the ultimate measure of success is whether programs achieve their intended social, cultural, or environmental outcomes. Budgets are therefore linked to performance indicators such as the number of clients served, improvements in community conditions, or advocacy achievements. Donors and funders increasingly expect nonprofits to demonstrate not only sound financial management but also measurable impact linked to their budgets.

Governance and accountability add another layer of difference. For-profit budgets are approved by executive leadership and, in many cases, overseen by boards representing shareholder interests. The emphasis is on maximizing shareholder value and ensuring compliance with legal and financial regulations. In nonprofits, budgets are typically approved by a board of directors that serves as a fiduciary body for the public trust. Board members must ensure that budgets align with the mission and that resources are stewarded responsibly. Nonprofits are accountable not only to regulators but also to donors, beneficiaries, and the public at large. This broader accountability framework influences how budgets are crafted, reviewed, and communicated. Transparency is especially critical, as donors expect to see how funds are allocated and how they contribute to mission outcomes.

The communication of budgets reflects these differences in accountability. For-profits may keep budgets largely internal, sharing only summary financials with shareholders and regulators. Nonprofits, by contrast, often use budgets as communication tools to build trust with external stakeholders. Grant proposals, fundraising campaigns, and annual reports frequently include budget information to demonstrate the responsible stewardship of funds. Nonprofits must frame their budgets in ways that reassure donors that their contributions are used efficiently and effectively. This emphasis on transparency makes nonprofit budgeting as much about storytelling and accountability as about financial planning.

In conclusion, nonprofit and for-profit budgets differ in their objectives, revenue sources, expense structures, treatment of surplus, flexibility, performance measures, governance, and communication. While for-profits focus on maximizing financial returns and shareholder value, nonprofits focus on maximizing mission impact and public benefit. For-profits enjoy greater control over revenue and expenses, while nonprofits face constraints due to uncertain funding and donor restrictions. For-profits measure success in financial terms, while nonprofits measure it in terms of outcomes and impact. These differences reflect the fundamental distinction between organizations that exist to generate private wealth and those that exist to serve the public good. Yet despite these differences, both sectors rely on budgeting as a critical tool for planning, accountability, and sustainability. For nonprofits, the challenge lies in using budgets not only to manage resources but also to tell a compelling story of mission-driven impact.

Startup Budget vs. Operating Budget

While all nonprofits must create a budget, the types of budgets they prepare vary depending on the stage of their organizational lifecycle. Two of the most important types are the startup budget and the operating budget. Though both serve as financial roadmaps, they differ significantly in scope, purpose, and focus. Understanding these differences is essential for nonprofit leaders who must balance the challenges of launching a new organization with the ongoing realities of day-to-day operations.

A startup budget is the financial plan created when a nonprofit is in its earliest stages. It outlines the resources required to launch the organization, establish its infrastructure, and begin offering programs or services. Because the nonprofit has no history of revenue or expenses at this point, the startup budget relies on projections and assumptions. It identifies what is needed to get the organization off the ground, such as incorporation fees, legal and accounting services, technology, office supplies, and initial program costs. For example, a nonprofit aiming to provide after-school tutoring may include in its startup budget expenses for curriculum development, volunteer recruitment, and marketing to attract participants. Revenue in a startup budget often comes from seed funding, small donations from founders and early supporters, or startup grants specifically designed to help new nonprofits.

The purpose of the startup budget is to answer the question: what resources do we need to establish this organization and begin fulfilling our mission? It is not designed to sustain long-term operations but to bridge the gap between conception and functionality. As such, it is often focused on one-time or irregular costs rather than recurring expenses. Technology purchases, branding, or initial staff recruitment are typical examples. The startup budget must also anticipate cash flow challenges, since revenue sources may not be immediately reliable or predictable. Careful planning ensures that the nonprofit has enough resources to survive its early months, when enthusiasm may be high but financial stability is fragile.

In contrast, an operating budget is the financial plan for the ongoing management of the nonprofit once it is established. It covers a defined period (usually one fiscal year) and projects both revenues and expenses associated with the organization's regular activities. Unlike the startup budget, which focuses on getting the organization launched, the operating budget is designed to sustain programs and operations over time. It includes recurring expenses such as staff salaries, rent, utilities, insurance, supplies, program delivery costs, fundraising activities, and administrative expenses. Revenue in the operating budget comes from ongoing sources, including grants, donations, membership dues, program service fees, and contracts.

The operating budget's purpose is to answer a different question: how will we allocate resources to sustain and expand our mission-driven activities over the next year? It emphasizes balancing revenues and expenses to maintain financial health. While a startup budget may be heavily weighted toward expenses with uncertain revenues, an operating budget must demonstrate stability and accountability, especially to donors, funders, and regulators. A well-prepared operating budget communicates credibility, showing that the nonprofit is capable of managing resources responsibly and delivering on its promises.

The differences between startup and operating budgets also extend to the way they are prepared. Startup budgets often require brainstorming and estimation because there is no historical data to draw from. Founders may research typical costs for similar organizations, consult experts, or use conservative assumptions to create realistic projections. Flexibility is key, as actual costs may differ from expectations once operations begin. In contrast, operating budgets rely heavily on historical data from previous years. Past revenue and expense patterns provide a basis for projections, allowing for greater accuracy. Adjustments are made for anticipated changes, such as new grants, expanded programs, or inflation. The preparation of operating budgets tends to be more systematic, involving staff, finance committees, and boards in a structured process.

Another distinction lies in the audience for these budgets. A startup budget is often shared with potential funders, investors, or donors as part of the case for support. It demonstrates that the founders have thought carefully about the resources required to launch and have a plan for initial financial stewardship. It reassures funders that the nonprofit is realistic about costs and is prepared to use early contributions effectively. The operating budget, on the other hand, is reviewed and approved annually by the board of directors and shared with funders in grant applications or annual reports. It is both a planning document and an accountability tool, demonstrating how the nonprofit allocates resources to achieve measurable outcomes.

The role of risk also differs between the two budgets. In a startup budget, the risk level is high because the organization is untested, revenue sources are uncertain, and expenses may be underestimated. Startups must plan conservatively and build contingencies to avoid running out of resources prematurely. For example, founders might include a reserve for unexpected legal fees or delays in receiving grants. In an operating budget, risk management focuses on ensuring sustainability by diversifying revenue, monitoring cash flow, and maintaining reserves. While risks remain, they are mitigated by experience, data, and established relationships with funders.

Over time, the startup budget evolves into the operating budget. Once the nonprofit is established, the one-time costs associated with launching are largely behind it, and recurring revenues and expenses dominate financial planning. However, the distinction remains important because nonprofits may revisit "startup-like" budgets when launching new programs or entering new markets. For example, a mature nonprofit expanding into a new city may create a startup budget for the expansion, even though it already has an operating budget for its existing activities. In this way, the startup budget is not limited to the founding stage but can also serve as a tool for planning growth initiatives.

Both startup and operating budgets ultimately serve the same larger purpose: ensuring that a nonprofit's resources are aligned with its mission. The startup budget ensures that the organization can be born and begin its work. The operating budget ensures that the organization can survive, grow, and thrive over time. Each reflects the realities of its context, whether uncertainty and fragility at the beginning or accountability and stability during ongoing operations. Together, they represent the financial trajectory of a nonprofit, from conception to sustainability.

In conclusion, while the startup budget and the operating budget share the common goal of guiding financial stewardship, they differ significantly in purpose, scope, preparation, and focus. The startup budget addresses the resources needed to launch an organization, emphasizing one-time costs, uncertain revenues, and high risk. The operating budget addresses the resources needed to sustain ongoing operations, emphasizing recurring expenses, reliable revenue, and accountability. Both are essential at different stages of a nonprofit's life, and both require careful planning, transparency, and alignment with mission. Understanding the differences allows nonprofit leaders to plan effectively, communicate clearly with stakeholders, and build organizations capable of both starting strong and sustaining their impact over time.

Forecasting Revenue Sources

Financial planning is central to the health and sustainability of nonprofit organizations. Unlike for-profit businesses, which often rely heavily on predictable sales of goods or services, nonprofits draw their revenues from diverse and sometimes uncertain sources such as donations, grants, membership dues, program service fees, and fundraising events. Forecasting these revenue streams is essential to ensure that nonprofits can meet their programmatic obligations, maintain stability, and plan for growth. Accurate forecasting allows leaders to allocate resources wisely, anticipate challenges, and reassure funders and stakeholders that the organization is financially sound. Yet the process requires balancing optimism with realism, relying on data while recognizing the volatility of philanthropic and government support.

The process of forecasting nonprofit revenue begins with understanding the organization's revenue mix. Nonprofits rarely rely on a single source of income, instead piecing together a portfolio that reflects their mission, size, and stage of development. A small community arts group may depend heavily on ticket sales and small donations, while a large health nonprofit may rely primarily on government contracts and major foundation grants. Identifying all potential revenue categories – donations from individuals, foundation or corporate grants, government funding, earned income from services, membership dues, and special events – is the first step in creating a forecast. Each source has its own characteristics of predictability, growth potential, and risk, and each requires a distinct approach to estimation.

Individual donations represent one of the most common and important revenue sources for nonprofits. Forecasting donations involves examining historical giving patterns, donor retention rates, and fundraising strategies. For example, if a nonprofit has an established base of annual donors, it can use past data to predict the likelihood of repeat giving, adjusting for factors such as economic conditions or changes in donor engagement. New fundraising campaigns or digital platforms may expand donor bases, but projections should be conservative until results are proven. Major gifts, such as those from wealthy individuals, add complexity, as they may significantly boost revenue in one year but not recur regularly. To forecast individual giving, nonprofits must analyze donor pipelines, track pledges, and consider the success rates of fundraising appeals.

Or, if a large amount of revenue comes from individual donors, it can make sense to itemize expected receipts from the largest donors, and then cluster all smaller expected donations into a single line item. Doing so focuses attention on contacting the largest existing donors to maintain high levels of contact, thereby improving the odds of receiving a continuing stream of donations from them. The following sample exhibit illustrates the layout of this format. Note that the individual donors listing is in order by size of expected donations, so the most attention is paid to those at the top of the list.

Sample Donor Revenue Budget

	Quarter 1	Quarter 2	Quarter 3	Quarter 4
Smith, Donald	$55,000	$-	$10,000	$45,000
Arbuckle, Mary	38,000	25,000	15,000	5,000
Davis, Eduardo	50,000	-	-	-
Emery, Francis	-	24,000	-	24,000
Bingo, Marco	-	-	40,000	-
McKenzie, Elwood	7,000	7,000	7,000	7,000
Druthers, Kinsey	-	25,000	-	-
All other donors	70,000	35,000	60,000	85,000
Totals	$220,000	$116,000	$132,000	$166,000

Grants from foundations and corporations are another significant revenue stream, but forecasting them requires a nuanced approach. Unlike individual donations, which may be solicited annually, grants often depend on application cycles, competitive processes, and shifting funding priorities. A nonprofit may forecast revenue based on pending proposals, historical success rates, and knowledge of funder interests. For example, if a nonprofit has historically received two grants out of every five applications submitted, it can use that ratio to project likely revenues for the coming year. However, since grantmakers frequently shift their focus areas, nonprofits must stay informed about trends in philanthropy to avoid overestimating their chances. Including both secured grants and reasonable projections of pending applications in forecasts provides a balanced view of expected revenues.

If an organization relies upon specific grants to generate most of its revenue, one budgeting method is to itemize expected receipts by grant, as noted in the following exhibit. Budgeting can be especially difficult for a nonprofit when it is uncertain of the sources of support that it will need in the upcoming budget period. If so, one option is to create a Resource Development line item, which is used to budget for sources of support that are not yet apparent. This subcategory is shown in the following exhibit, where resource development comprises the bulk of all budgeted revenue.

Sample Revenue Budget by Grant

Contract	Quarter 1	Quarter 2	Quarter 3	Quarter 4
Existing Grants:				
HHS #01327	$175,000	$175,000	$25,000	$--
HHS #AC124	460,000	460,000	460,000	25,000
HHS #BG0047	260,000	280,000	280,000	260,000
Subtotal	$895,000	$915,000	$765,000	$285,000
Resource Development:				
DOA Farm Analysis	$--	$--	$150,000	$300,000
BLM Lease Analysis	--	210,000	600,000	550,000
NGS Survey Review	10,000	80,000	80,000	100,000
Subtotal	$10,000	$290,000	$830,000	$950,000
Totals	$905,000	$1,205,000	$1,595,000	$1,235,000

Government funding can be one of the most stable yet complex revenue sources for nonprofits, especially those in health, education, or social services. Forecasting government revenue depends on contracts, grants, and reimbursements that often span multiple years. Because government budgets are influenced by political cycles and policy decisions, nonprofits must monitor legislative developments closely. Multi-year contracts can provide predictability, but reimbursements tied to service delivery require accurate projections of program demand. For example, a nonprofit providing foster care services may forecast revenue based on the number of children it expects to serve, adjusted for state funding levels. The risk of sudden cuts in government budgets underscores the importance of conservative forecasting and contingency planning.

Earned income, or revenue generated through the sale of goods and services, is another increasingly important category for nonprofits. Forecasting earned income resembles forecasting in for-profit businesses, requiring the analysis of demand, pricing, competition, and costs. For instance, a museum might forecast ticket sales by examining historical attendance, adjusting for special exhibitions, seasonal trends, or marketing efforts. Similarly, a training nonprofit might project course fees based on anticipated enrollment and pricing models. While earned income can provide stability and independence, it also exposes nonprofits to market risks, requiring careful evaluation of capacity and demand. Forecasting in this area should be based on realistic market assessments rather than aspirational expectations.

If a nonprofit runs one or more programs, an alternative is to itemize expected revenues by program, with additional detail located in a supporting schedule. An example for several programs follows.

Sample Program Revenue Budget

	Quarter 1	Quarter 2	Quarter 3	Quarter 4
Program A revenue	$905,000	$1,205,000	$1,595,000	$1,235,000
Program B revenue	880,000	920,000	1,115,000	970,000
Totals	$1,785,000	$2,125,000	$2,710,000	$2,205,000

Membership dues represent a specialized revenue source for organizations such as professional associations, advocacy groups, or cultural institutions. Forecasting membership revenue requires analyzing trends in recruitment, renewal rates, and pricing structures. For example, if a nonprofit has a renewal rate of 80 percent and 1,000 members, it can reasonably project that 800 members will renew. Adjustments can then be made for anticipated growth or decline in new members. External factors, such as the perceived value of membership or the strength of competing organizations, must also be considered. Membership dues can provide steady income if managed well, but forecasting requires continuous tracking of member engagement and satisfaction.

Fundraising events, while often high-profile, are one of the most difficult revenue sources to forecast. Events depend heavily on variables such as attendance, sponsorships, ticket sales, and donor generosity. Weather, competing events, or economic downturns can all affect outcomes. To forecast event revenue, nonprofits should rely on historical data from past events, adjusting for changes in scale, pricing, or sponsorships. Conservative projections are essential, as events frequently cost more and raise less than anticipated. Many organizations supplement event forecasts with contingency plans, ensuring that a disappointing event does not destabilize the overall budget.

If a nonprofit earns revenues from several or all of the sources just described, it can make sense to derive a master revenue budget that aggregates all of the various revenue sources, with each source summarized in a single line item. For example, the following exhibit aggregates all of the revenue totals from the preceding sample exhibits.

Sample Master Revenue Budget

	Quarter 1	Quarter 2	Quarter 3	Quarter 4
Contract revenue	$905,000	$1,205,000	$1,595,000	$1,235,000
Program revenue	1,785,000	2,125,000	2,710,000	2,205,000
Donor revenue	220,000	116,000	132,000	166,000
Totals	$2,910,000	$3,446,000	$4,437,000	$3,606,000

Tip: There can be great uncertainty in the projected revenue figures. If so, consider conducting a periodic recasting of the budget to see if the projections have changed, and altering expenditures to be in proper alignment with expected revenues.

Forecasting nonprofit revenue also requires attention to timing and cash flow. Unlike for-profits that may receive steady monthly sales income, nonprofit revenues often arrive in uneven bursts, such as during year-end giving or grant disbursements. Forecasts must account not only for total annual revenues but also for when funds will be received. This ensures that nonprofits can manage their cash flow and avoid shortfalls that disrupt operations. For example, if a nonprofit expects a large grant in September, it must ensure that it has sufficient interim funding to cover expenses during the preceding months. Linking revenue forecasts to cash flow projections provides a more accurate picture of financial health.

Technology and data analysis have made forecasting more sophisticated. Nonprofits can now use donor management systems, financial software, and predictive analytics to track trends and model scenarios. For example, software can analyze donor behavior to predict which supporters are most likely to increase their contributions or lapse. Similarly, program demand data can help forecast revenue that is tied to service delivery. While technology cannot eliminate uncertainty, it enhances accuracy and allows nonprofits to test different assumptions, preparing for best-case, worst-case, and most likely scenarios.

Yet forecasting revenue for nonprofits is as much an art as a science. While data and analysis provide guidance, external factors such as economic conditions, cultural shifts, or global crises can disrupt even the most careful forecasts. The COVID-19 pandemic illustrated this dramatically, as nonprofits suddenly faced cancelled events, disrupted services, and shifting donor priorities. To remain resilient, nonprofits must combine careful forecasting with flexibility, building reserves and diversifying revenue streams to mitigate risk. Transparency in communicating forecasts and assumptions also builds trust with boards, donors, and stakeholders, reinforcing credibility even when revenues fall short of projections.

In conclusion, forecasting revenue sources for a nonprofit requires a comprehensive understanding of diverse income streams, from individual donations and grants to government contracts, earned income, membership dues, and events. Each source has its own dynamics of predictability, risk, and potential, requiring tailored methods of estimation. Effective forecasting balances optimism with realism, drawing on historical data, current trends, and careful assumptions. It must also consider timing, cash flow, and external conditions. More than a financial exercise, forecasting is a strategic process that enables nonprofits to plan programs, reassure funders, and maintain sustainability. When done thoughtfully, it transforms uncertainty into informed decision-making, equipping nonprofits to pursue their missions with confidence.

Expense Categories

Nonprofit organizations exist to advance missions that address social, cultural, environmental, or educational needs. While their purposes differ from those of for-profit businesses, nonprofits still face the same basic requirement of tracking revenues and expenses in order to remain financially viable. Effective expense management is essential for demonstrating accountability to donors, funders, and regulators while ensuring that resources are used efficiently to support mission-driven activities.

Nonprofits are subject to particular scrutiny about how they allocate expenses, as stakeholders often want assurance that the majority of funds are being directed toward programs rather than overhead. To understand nonprofit financial management, it is important to examine the main expense categories, which typically include program services, administrative or management and general expenses, and fundraising costs. Each category reflects a different aspect of the organization's operations and carries unique implications for accountability and sustainability.

Program Services

The largest and most important category of expenses for nonprofits is program services. These expenses encompass the costs directly associated with delivering the organization's mission-related activities and services. Donors, funders, and the public often view program expenses as the clearest indicator of whether a nonprofit is fulfilling its stated mission. For example, in a nonprofit dedicated to providing after-school tutoring, program expenses would include the salaries of tutors, educational materials, rent for classroom space, and the technology used to support instruction. For a healthcare nonprofit, program expenses might consist of medical supplies, staff time for patient care, and outreach activities in the community. The proportion of total expenses spent on programs is frequently highlighted in annual reports and evaluations, as stakeholders want to see that the organization prioritizes its beneficiaries.

Within program expenses, personnel costs are usually the largest component. Nonprofits, like businesses, rely heavily on human capital to deliver services. Salaries and benefits for program staff, contractors, or consultants fall under this category, reflecting the fact that skilled labor is central to mission execution. Additional program-related costs include supplies, travel, training, and equipment that directly support the nonprofit's activities. Some organizations also incur program-specific overhead, such as insurance for the facilities used in delivering services. Accurate tracking of these costs ensures that program expenses are properly distinguished from general overhead, giving funders a clear picture of how resources are allocated.

Management and Administration

The second major category of nonprofit expenses is administrative, often referred to as management and administration expenses. These are the costs associated with running the organization as a whole, rather than delivering specific programs. Examples include office rent and utilities, salaries and benefits for executive staff and administrative personnel, accounting and legal services, insurance, and information technology infrastructure. These expenses provide the backbone that allows the organization to operate effectively, ensuring compliance with laws, managing finances responsibly, and supporting strategic planning. While administrative expenses are sometimes criticized as "overhead," they are in fact essential for organizational sustainability. Without proper financial management, governance, and compliance, nonprofits cannot deliver programs effectively or maintain donor trust.

Administration expenses often include investments in infrastructure that may not be directly visible to beneficiaries but are critical for long-term success. For example, upgrading accounting software or investing in human resources systems falls into this category. These investments improve efficiency, reduce risk, and ensure accountability. However, nonprofits must manage perceptions carefully, as high administration expenses can raise concerns among funders about inefficiency. Striking the right balance between keeping administration costs reasonable and ensuring that infrastructure is robust is one of the ongoing challenges for nonprofit leaders.

The following example illustrates the basic layout of a management and administration budget.

EXAMPLE

Newton Education compiles the following management and administration budget, which is organized by expense line item:

	Quarter 1	Quarter 2	Quarter 3	Quarter 4
Audit fees	$35,000	$0	$0	$0
Bank fees	500	500	500	500
Insurance	5,000	5,500	6,000	6,000
Payroll taxes	10,000	10,500	10,500	11,000
Property taxes	0	25,000	0	0
Rent	11,000	11,000	11,000	14,000
Salaries	140,000	142,000	144,000	146,000
Supplies	2,000	2,000	2,000	2,000
Travel and entertainment	4,500	8,000	4,000	4,000
Utilities	2,500	3,000	3,000	4,000
Other expenses	1,500	1,500	1,500	2,000
Total expenses	$212,000	$209,000	$182,500	$189,500

The preceding example reveals a common characteristic of most line items in the management and administration budget, which is that most costs are fixed over the short term, and so only vary slightly from period to period. The exceptions are pay increases and scheduled events, such as audits. Otherwise, the main reason for a sudden change in an expense is a step cost, such as increasing the headcount.

> **Tip:** If a nonprofit simply carries forward its management and administration costs into the budget from the previous year, it will not know if the organization is being efficient in its expenditures. To find out, consider separating these costs into their constituent parts, such as the cost of the accounting, treasury, and human resources departments, and calculate each of these costs as a percentage of total revenues. Then compare these percentages to the industry average or a best-in-class benchmark. The comparison may reveal that some parts of this budget are operating at excessively high cost levels.

Fundraising

The third major category of nonprofit expenses is fundraising. Fundraising costs represent the expenditures necessary to secure financial support for the organization. These costs are needed for the following activities:

- Grant proposals
- Direct solicitation of individuals and businesses for contributions
- E-mail solicitations through a mailing list of donors
- Passive solicitation via a nonprofit's website
- Seminars regarding estate planning
- Fundraising events, such as charity balls and art auctions
- Contacting employers regarding matching contributions

The fundraising budget contains somewhat different expense line items than are usually found in the management and administration budget. There is a greater emphasis on compensation, advertising, and travel expenditures. An example of this budget format appears in the following exhibit.

Fundraising Budget by Expense Type

Expense Type	Quarter 1	Quarter 2	Quarter 3	Quarter 4
Salaries and wages	$270,000	$275,000	$320,000	$380,000
Payroll taxes	22,000	27,000	35,000	41,000
Promotions	0	50,000	85,000	42,000
Advertising	20,000	22,000	22,000	28,000
Grant research	0	0	35,000	0
Travel and entertainment	40,000	20,000	80,000	70,000
Office expenses	15,000	15,000	21,000	21,000
Other	5,000	5,000	5,000	5,000
Totals	$382,000	$484,000	$723,000	$727,000

Fundraising expenses often vary depending on the size and scope of the nonprofit. Large organizations may have dedicated development departments, with significant salaries and overhead devoted to securing major gifts, corporate sponsorships, and government contracts. Smaller nonprofits may rely on special events or grassroots campaigns, which can carry high costs relative to revenues raised. Evaluating fundraising effectiveness involves comparing costs to revenues generated. For instance, a direct mail campaign might cost $50,000 but generate $200,000 in donations, yielding a strong return on investment. Transparency in reporting these costs helps build donor confidence by showing that fundraising is managed strategically rather than wastefully.

Like administration expenses, fundraising costs are sometimes subject to scrutiny, as stakeholders want to know that their contributions are being used primarily for mission-related activities rather than raising more money. However, effective fundraising is essential for nonprofit survival. Without ongoing investments in donor cultivation and grant acquisition, most nonprofits would be unable to sustain their programs.

When reviewing the fundraising budget, there are several that call for detailed analysis. The first is the relationship between the expenditures *for* the fundraising staff and corresponding revenues generated *by* that staff. Consider the following factors when deciding whether this expenditure is reasonable:

- *Historical trend.* If the fundraising staff has historically been able to generate a certain amount of contributions per person, it should be quite difficult for them to exceed this productivity level in the new budget year, so be wary of large presumed productivity increases.
- *Diminishing returns.* It is increasingly difficult to extract more donations from existing target groups, so question such revenue increases where the related expenses do not increase to an even greater extent.

The second area to investigate is the justification for promotional expenditures. The fundraising staff should provide an analysis of the estimated number of target contributors reached, and the conversion rate for those contributors. This is a difficult analysis area, since projections are difficult to verify.

General Expense Classifications

Beyond these three broad categories (program, administration, and fundraising) nonprofits also face other types of expenses that cut across categories. Personnel costs, as mentioned earlier, are usually the largest single expense for nonprofits, often accounting for 60 to 80 percent of budgets. These costs include salaries, wages, payroll taxes, health insurance, retirement contributions, and other benefits. Whether staff are engaged in programs, administration, or fundraising, their compensation must be allocated appropriately to the correct category. Nonprofits that underinvest in staff risk burnout and turnover, while those that compensate competitively attract and retain the talent needed to deliver on their mission.

Occupancy costs represent another significant category. Rent, mortgage payments, utilities, maintenance, and insurance for office or program space fall into this group. For organizations that own facilities, such as theaters, museums, or community centers, occupancy costs can be substantial. These expenses are often shared across categories, with portions allocated to program, administrative, and fundraising functions based on usage. For example, utilities for a building housing both classrooms and administrative offices must be proportionally divided.

Supplies and equipment also constitute recurring expenses. These include everything from office supplies and educational materials to computers and vehicles. Technology expenses, in particular, have become increasingly important as nonprofits adopt digital tools for fundraising, program delivery, and administration. Investments in software, cybersecurity, and online platforms are now considered essential infrastructure costs, blurring the line between the program and administration categories.

Travel and training expenses further illustrate the diversity of nonprofit costs. Staff may need to travel for conferences, training, or direct service delivery, incurring costs for transportation, lodging, and meals. Professional development is also important, since it ensures that employees remain knowledgeable about best practices in their fields. These costs, while sometimes viewed as discretionary, are critical for maintaining program quality and organizational capacity.

Nonprofits must also account for compliance-related expenses. These include audit fees, licensing, permits, and costs associated with meeting government regulations. Funders and regulators often require audited financial statements, making audit expenses unavoidable for many organizations. Similarly, nonprofits providing health or social services may need to comply with complex state or federal licensing requirements, which add to their administration costs.

In conclusion, the main nonprofit expense categories can be broadly grouped into program services, management and administration, and fundraising costs. Program expenses represent the core of mission delivery, demonstrating to stakeholders that the nonprofit prioritizes its beneficiaries. Administration expenses ensure that the organization has the infrastructure and governance to operate effectively, while fundraising expenses provide the resources necessary to sustain operations over time. Within these categories, personnel, occupancy, supplies, technology, travel, and compliance costs all play important roles. Though program expenses often receive the most attention, the reality is that all categories are essential for organizational health. Effective nonprofits strike a balance, investing in infrastructure and fundraising to ensure sustainability while keeping program delivery at the heart of their operations. By managing and transparently reporting these expenses, nonprofits build trust, demonstrate accountability, and ensure that resources are used responsibly in pursuit of their missions.

Cash Flow Planning

Cash flow is the lifeblood of any organization, and for nonprofits it is especially critical. Unlike for-profit businesses that often enjoy more predictable income streams from the sale of goods and services, nonprofits rely on diverse and frequently irregular revenue sources such as grants, donations, membership dues, government contracts, and special events. At the same time, nonprofits must meet steady expenses for staff salaries, rent, utilities, program delivery, and fundraising. This mismatch between when revenue arrives and when expenses must be paid can create serious financial stress. Cash flow planning is therefore a vital part of nonprofit financial management, ensuring that organizations have enough liquidity to meet obligations, maintain stability, and deliver mission-driven services without interruption.

Cash flow planning differs from budgeting, though the two are related. A budget sets out projected revenues and expenses over a fiscal year, focusing on whether income will cover costs overall. Cash flow planning, however, tracks the timing of money moving in and out of the organization. A nonprofit may appear solvent on paper because annual revenues exceed expenses, yet it may still struggle if its revenues are concentrated in certain months while expenses are spread evenly throughout the year. For example, many nonprofits receive large donations in December, when year-end giving peaks, but payroll, rent, and utilities are due every month. Without careful cash flow planning, these organizations may face shortages in the first half of the year despite a healthy annual budget.

The first step in nonprofit cash flow planning is understanding revenue patterns. Different revenue streams behave in different ways, and nonprofits must identify the timing and reliability of each. Individual donations, for instance, may peak around holidays or after targeted campaigns. Foundation grants may arrive in lump sums, often after long application processes. Government contracts may reimburse expenses only after services are delivered, creating delays between spending and income. Earned revenue from program fees may provide steadier flows but could be seasonal. By analyzing past financial statements, nonprofits can map out when money typically comes in and forecast the timing of future inflows. Recognizing that revenue is not evenly distributed allows managers to anticipate periods of abundance and scarcity.

On the expense side, nonprofits must catalog all recurring and periodic obligations. Salaries and benefits are typically the largest and most predictable expense, occurring on a biweekly or monthly basis. Rent, utilities, insurance, and debt service also fall into the category of fixed expenses. Program-related costs, by contrast, may vary depending on activities and grant cycles. Fundraising events may generate large expenses upfront, with revenues being realized later. By mapping expenses alongside revenues, nonprofits can visualize potential gaps between inflows and outflows. This comparison forms the basis of a monthly cash flow projection.

A cash flow projection usually covers a 12-month period and is updated regularly. It begins with the cash balance at the start of the period, adds expected revenues by source, and subtracts expected expenses by category. The result is an estimate of the cash balance at the end of each month. When projected balances turn negative, it signals a cash flow gap that must be addressed through adjustments, reserves, or financing. For example, if a nonprofit projects a negative balance in July because a major grant is not expected until September, it can plan in advance by delaying discretionary expenses, drawing on reserves, or arranging a short-term line of credit. The projection thus transforms potential crises into manageable challenges.

> **Tip:** To improve accuracy, cash flow projections must be realistic and conservative. Overestimating revenues or underestimating expenses creates a false sense of security and can lead to serious shortfalls. Nonprofits should base projections on confirmed grants and pledges, not speculative income. For uncertain revenues, it is better to include them as potential rather than guaranteed. Expenses should reflect actual costs, including overhead and indirect expenses, which are sometimes overlooked. By erring on the side of caution, nonprofits prepare for the worst while benefiting when revenues exceed expectations.

Cash flow planning also requires strategies to smooth out mismatches between inflows and outflows. One strategy is building and maintaining operating reserves. An operating reserve is an unrestricted pool of funds set aside to cover short-term cash shortages or unexpected expenses. Best practice suggests that nonprofits maintain reserves equal to three to six months of operating expenses, though this target varies by size and sector. Reserves provide flexibility, allowing nonprofits to continue operations during revenue delays or emergencies without resorting to drastic cuts. However, building reserves requires discipline, as nonprofits may face pressure to spend all available funds on programs immediately. Educating boards and donors about the importance of reserves is essential to secure their support.

Another strategy is diversifying revenue sources. Nonprofits that rely heavily on a single grant or contract are vulnerable to cash flow disruptions if payments are delayed. By cultivating a mix of donations, grants, earned income, and events, organizations reduce their dependence on any one source and increase the likelihood of steady inflows. For example, a nonprofit that supplements foundation grants with membership dues and training fees may experience fewer cash flow shocks than one dependent entirely on grant disbursements. Diversification does not eliminate uncertainty, but it spreads risk across multiple streams.

Short-term financing can also help manage cash flow challenges. Many banks offer lines of credit to nonprofits, providing temporary funds to cover expenses until revenues arrive. For instance, if a nonprofit is waiting for government reimbursement, it might draw on a line of credit to meet payroll, repaying it once the funds are received. While borrowing should not be a long-term solution, it can provide a safety net when cash flow gaps are unavoidable. Nonprofits must weigh the cost of interest and fees against the risks of failing to meet obligations, but when managed responsibly, short-term financing can preserve stability.

Active communication with funders can further support cash flow planning. Some grantmakers and donors are willing to adjust payment schedules, provide advance payments, or offer unrestricted funding if nonprofits articulate their needs clearly. For example, a foundation may agree to disburse a grant in quarterly installments rather than one lump sum, thereby better aligning cash inflows with expenses. Donors may also be more inclined to provide general operating support if they understand the financial pressures nonprofits face. Transparent communication builds trust and can lead to more flexible funding arrangements that ease cash flow management.

Cash flow planning is not only about survival but also about strategic growth. By understanding their financial cycles, nonprofits can time new initiatives to coincide with periods of stronger cash flow. For instance, a nonprofit may launch a new program in the fall if it knows that revenues peak in late summer. Similarly, capital campaigns or major investments can be scheduled during periods when reserves are strong. In this way, cash flow planning becomes a proactive tool for aligning financial capacity with mission opportunities.

Technology and financial management systems play an increasingly important role in cash flow planning. Accounting software can generate real-time reports on revenues, expenses, and balances, providing greater visibility into financial health. Forecasting tools allow nonprofits to model different scenarios, testing the impact of optimistic, pessimistic, and most likely assumptions. These tools enhance accuracy and allow organizations to prepare contingency plans. For example, a nonprofit might model the effects of a 10 percent drop in donations, enabling it to identify cost-saving measures in advance.

Governance also matters in cash flow planning. Boards of directors are responsible for overseeing financial stability and ensuring that cash flow risks are managed appropriately. Finance committees often review cash flow projections, reserves, and liquidity ratios, providing guidance to staff. Strong governance ensures that financial planning is not left solely to administrators but is integrated into strategic decision-making. Boards that understand cash flow dynamics are better equipped to support staff during challenges and to make informed choices about growth and investment.

Ultimately, cash flow planning is about aligning financial realities with mission-driven goals. Nonprofits exist to create social value, but they cannot do so effectively without sound financial management. Planning for cash flow ensures that the organization can meet its obligations, retain staff, deliver services, and maintain credibility with funders and the public. It transforms uncertainty into foresight, equipping nonprofits to respond to challenges without compromising their mission.

In conclusion, cash flow planning is an essential practice for nonprofits, distinct from but complementary to budgeting. It focuses on the timing of revenues and expenses, recognizing that even financially healthy organizations can face liquidity crises without careful planning. Through tools like cash flow projections, strategies such as building reserves and diversifying revenue, and mechanisms like short-term financing and funder communication, nonprofits can navigate the volatility of their funding environments. By incorporating technology, governance oversight, and a focus on mission alignment, cash flow planning not only safeguards stability but also supports strategic growth. In a sector where financial pressures are constant and resources scarce, effective cash flow planning enables nonprofits to weather uncertainty and continue serving their targeted communities.

Summary

It is critical for a nonprofit to maintain and monitor a budget, since nonprofits rarely have sufficient cash reserves to soften the impact of excessively low revenues or high expenses. This means that the management team should build a review of the budget versus actual report into its monthly (if not weekly) management meetings. If this analysis indicates that there will be a funding shortfall, the team must take action at once to remedy the situation. Ideally, any actions taken should have been foreseen through periodic modeling sessions that estimated the impact of various scenarios on the financial situation of the nonprofit.

Chapter 5
Developing a Board of Directors

Introduction

An essential element of a nonprofit organization is its board of directors, who serve as stewards of the organization's mission, resources, and long-term sustainability. In this chapter, we discuss the legal duties of a nonprofit's board members, how to recruit and develop a board, how to set up guiding policies for this group, and several related matters.

The Legal Duties of Board Members

Board members play a pivotal role in setting strategic direction, overseeing management, and ensuring accountability to the public, donors, and regulators. Unlike shareholders in for-profit corporations, nonprofit board members do not receive financial returns on their service; rather, they assume responsibilities grounded in public trust and fiduciary obligation. Because nonprofits benefit from tax-exempt status and rely on contributions from donors, they are held to high standards of integrity and oversight. The law recognizes this by imposing specific duties on board members, most commonly expressed as the duty of care, the duty of loyalty, and the duty of obedience. Together, these duties define the framework within which board members must act and provide guidance for ethical and legal decision-making.

Duty of Care

The duty of care requires board members to act with the same level of diligence, competence, and prudence that a reasonably careful person would exercise in similar circumstances. In practice, this means that board members must be attentive, informed, and actively engaged in their governance roles. They are expected to attend meetings regularly, review financial reports and organizational documents, and participate in discussions and decisions with an understanding of the issues at hand.

The duty of care obligates board members to make decisions based on adequate information and thoughtful deliberation. For example, when considering whether to approve a new program, the board must review relevant data, assess risks, and ask probing questions about feasibility and sustainability. Similarly, when reviewing financial statements, board members must ensure that revenues and expenses are accurately reported and that the organization remains solvent. The failure to exercise appropriate care can expose a nonprofit to mismanagement, financial instability, or even legal liability.

Courts often apply the "business judgment rule" to evaluate whether board members have met their duty of care. This rule gives deference to board decisions as long as they are made in good faith, with due diligence, and without conflicts of interest. However, it also underscores the expectation that board members cannot simply rubber-stamp management proposals or remain passive. Active engagement and informed oversight are required.

Duty of Loyalty

The duty of loyalty requires board members to put the interests of the nonprofit above their own personal or professional interests. Because nonprofits exist to serve the public good, board members must avoid situations in which their private interests conflict with those of the organization. This duty is critical for preserving public trust and ensuring that decisions are made for the benefit of the nonprofit rather than for individual gain.

Conflicts of interest are the most common challenge to the duty of loyalty. For example, if a board member owns a company that bids on a contract with the nonprofit, the member must disclose the relationship and recuse themselves from related decisions. Even the appearance of a conflict can damage credibility with donors and regulators, so transparency is essential. Most nonprofits adopt written conflict-of-interest policies requiring the disclosure of financial and personal interests, and establishing procedures for handling potential conflicts.

The duty of loyalty also prohibits self-dealing, in which board members use their position to secure benefits for themselves, family members, or associates. This could include approving excessive compensation, using nonprofit assets for personal purposes, or steering contracts to related parties without proper oversight. In severe cases, self-dealing can lead to regulatory penalties, the loss of tax-exempt status, or personal liability for board members. Upholding the duty of loyalty ensures that the nonprofit remains mission-focused and that its resources are safeguarded for public benefit.

Duty of Obedience

The duty of obedience requires board members to ensure that the nonprofit adheres to its mission, complies with applicable laws, and follows its governing documents. This duty reflects the understanding that nonprofits operate under a social contract: they are granted tax-exempt status and donor support in exchange for pursuing purposes that serve the public good. Board members are thus responsible for keeping the organization aligned with its stated mission and accountable to legal and ethical standards.

At the most basic level, the duty of obedience requires compliance with laws and regulations governing nonprofits. This includes federal tax laws, state nonprofit corporation statutes, employment laws, and fundraising regulations. For example, board members must ensure that the organization files its annual Form 990 with the IRS, maintains proper employment practices, and registers for charitable solicitation where required. Any failure to comply with legal requirements can result in penalties, reputational damage, or even dissolution of the nonprofit.

The duty of obedience also requires adherence to the organization's mission as expressed in its articles of incorporation and bylaws. Board members may not authorize activities that stray from the stated mission, even if those activities are profitable or otherwise beneficial. For instance, if a nonprofit was created to provide literacy programs, its board cannot divert resources to unrelated ventures, such as running a restaurant, without formally amending its mission. This obligation protects donors, who give with the expectation that their contributions will be used for specific purposes, and ensures that the nonprofit remains focused and accountable.

Collective Implications of the Legal Duties

Together, the duties of care, loyalty, and obedience form the fiduciary responsibilities of nonprofit board members. Fiduciary responsibility means acting in trust for the benefit of others; in this case, the public and the communities the nonprofit serves. These duties establish the legal baseline for board service, but they also set ethical expectations for stewardship, accountability, and transparency.

Meeting these duties requires a combination of individual integrity and collective governance. Individual board members must be diligent, honest, and mission-focused, while boards as a whole must establish policies, procedures, and oversight mechanisms that institutionalize these standards. For example, adopting regular financial audits, establishing a conflict-of-interest policy, and conducting periodic strategic reviews all support the board's ability to fulfill its legal duties.

Practical Applications

In practice, the legal duties of nonprofit board members influence every aspect of governance. Financial oversight is a central responsibility, requiring boards to approve budgets, monitor cash flow, and review audits. Program oversight is equally important, as boards must ensure that activities align with the nonprofit's mission and produce meaningful outcomes. Fundraising responsibilities also fall within the scope of board duties, with members often expected to contribute personally and to support development efforts. Each of these roles is guided by the underlying legal duties: careful decision-making (duty of care), prioritization of organizational interests (duty of loyalty), and adherence to mission and law (duty of obedience).

These duties also shape how boards interact with executive leadership. Boards delegate day-to-day management to executive directors or CEOs, but they retain ultimate accountability. The duty of care requires boards to select qualified executives and evaluate their performance. The duty of loyalty requires boards to support executives while avoiding favoritism or undue influence. The duty of obedience requires boards to ensure that executives carry out programs consistent with mission and compliance requirements. In this way, the legal duties of the board extend to its supervisory role over management.

Consequences of Breach

Any failure to fulfill legal duties can have serious consequences for nonprofit board members and their organizations. Breaches of the duty of care may result in mismanagement, financial loss, or liability for negligence. Breaches of the duty of loyalty, such as self-dealing, may lead to legal sanctions, IRS penalties, or reputational harm. Breaches of the duty of obedience may result in the loss of tax-exempt status, donor lawsuits, or regulatory action. While nonprofit board members are often shielded from personal liability under state laws and indemnification policies, they can still face legal and reputational risks if they fail to uphold their fiduciary obligations.

Conclusion

The legal duties of nonprofit board members (care, loyalty, and obedience) define the framework of responsible governance. They require diligence in decision-making, integrity in avoiding conflicts of interest, and fidelity to mission and law. These duties reflect the unique role of nonprofits in serving the public good and the trust placed in them by donors, regulators, and communities. By fulfilling these obligations, board members ensure that nonprofits remain accountable, sustainable, and effective. Beyond legal compliance, these duties embody the spirit of stewardship that lies at the heart of nonprofit leadership. For board members, embracing these responsibilities is not only a legal mandate but also a moral commitment to advancing the mission of the organization and safeguarding its role in society.

Recruiting Board Members

Recruiting diverse and skilled directors to the board of a nonprofit is a critical process that directly impacts the organization's effectiveness, sustainability, and ability to serve its mission. A nonprofit board is more than a governance structure; it is a source of leadership, expertise, and accountability. To assemble a strong board, nonprofits must consider both the competencies required to guide the organization and the importance of reflecting the diversity of the communities they serve. This requires careful planning, intentional outreach, and a sustained commitment to equity and inclusion.

One of the primary goals of recruiting skilled directors is to ensure that the nonprofit has access to the range of talents necessary for success. Nonprofit boards are charged with oversight of finances, legal compliance, strategic planning, fundraising, and the overall advancement of the mission. Recruiting individuals with expertise in accounting, law, marketing, fundraising, technology, human resources, and the nonprofit's field of service ensures that the board can collectively make informed decisions. For example, an arts organization may need board members with knowledge of nonprofit finance, grant writing, and arts administration, while a health-focused nonprofit may need directors with backgrounds in public health, medicine, and government relations. The ideal board is not composed of generalists alone but of individuals who bring complementary skill sets, creating a well-rounded leadership team.

Beyond technical expertise, nonprofits increasingly recognize the importance of diversity in board composition. Diversity encompasses not only race, gender, and ethnicity but also age, socioeconomic background, professional experience, geography, and lived experience related to the nonprofit's mission. A diverse board brings multiple perspectives to problem-solving and reduces the risk of groupthink. When a nonprofit works with underserved communities, having directors who share cultural or experiential similarities with those communities strengthens the board's credibility and fosters trust. Furthermore, funders, donors, and regulators are increasingly attentive to whether nonprofits practice inclusivity at the governance level, which means that diverse recruitment is both an ethical and strategic necessity.

Recruiting diverse and skilled directors is not without challenges. Nonprofits often rely on existing board networks to identify candidates, but this can reinforce homogeneity by bringing in individuals from similar backgrounds. To break this cycle, organizations must expand their outreach efforts. Posting board opportunities publicly, working with community organizations, and tapping into affinity groups for underrepresented professionals can widen the pool of candidates. Some nonprofits partner with board-matching programs or professional associations that specialize in connecting diverse leaders with governance opportunities. In doing so, they not only find candidates with needed skills but also increase representation.

Clarity in recruitment is another key factor. Nonprofits must be transparent about the expectations of board service, including time commitments, fundraising responsibilities, committee participation, and fiduciary duties. When these expectations are not communicated clearly, mismatches can occur that discourage participation or weaken board performance. Creating a formal board recruitment plan, often led by a governance or nominations committee, ensures that each recruitment effort addresses specific gaps in skills or representation. For example, if the board recognizes a lack of financial expertise, it can deliberately seek out candidates with CPA or CFO backgrounds. If the board notes underrepresentation of younger voices, it can create a pathway for emerging leaders, perhaps through associate board programs that prepare individuals for eventual full board service.

Once diverse and skilled directors are recruited, retention and engagement become critical. New directors must be onboarded effectively, with orientation sessions that explain the nonprofit's mission, strategic plan, financial structure, and governance policies. Mentorship programs, where seasoned directors guide new members, can build confidence and foster inclusion. Moreover, a nonprofit must ensure that all voices are valued in board deliberations. Too often, diverse directors are recruited but not empowered, leading to tokenism rather than meaningful participation. Creating a board culture where input from all members is actively solicited and respected ensures that diversity translates into stronger governance.

Another important consideration in recruitment is balancing professional expertise with passion for the mission. A director may bring extensive skills in finance or law, but if they lack commitment to the cause, their contributions may be limited. Conversely, individuals with deep mission-related experience but little governance knowledge can still be valuable when paired with training and support. The strongest boards integrate directors who combine technical skill with genuine dedication, ensuring that decisions are guided by both professional judgment and mission-driven values.

Fundraising responsibilities often complicate board recruitment. Many nonprofits expect directors to contribute personally and to leverage their networks for financial support. While this expectation is important for sustaining the organization, it can unintentionally exclude candidates from underrepresented backgrounds who may not have access to wealthy networks. To reconcile this, nonprofits can adopt flexible fundraising policies that allow directors to contribute through advocacy, in-kind support, or outreach, rather than focusing solely on personal financial capacity. This broadens participation and ensures that diversity goals are not undermined by rigid fundraising demands.

Finally, successful recruitment requires a long-term perspective. Building a diverse and skilled board is not a one-time effort but an ongoing process. Regular board evaluations, both of individual members and of the collective body, can reveal gaps in skills or representation that inform future recruitment. Succession planning is equally important; by identifying potential leaders early, nonprofits can ensure continuity in governance while steadily improving diversity and expertise. Over time, this creates a self-reinforcing cycle where the board becomes a powerful driver of organizational excellence.

In conclusion, recruiting diverse and skilled directors to the board of a nonprofit is essential for strong governance and mission fulfillment. Skilled directors bring the technical expertise needed for financial oversight, strategic planning, and compliance, while diverse directors contribute the perspectives and lived experiences that make the board responsive to its community. Achieving this balance requires intentional outreach, clear expectations, inclusive policies, and sustained effort. A nonprofit that invests in building such a board not only strengthens its governance but also models the equity, accountability, and inclusivity that lie at the heart of effective nonprofit leadership.

Board Committees and Governance Structures

A central aspect of nonprofit governance is the board of directors, which serves as the governing body responsible for strategic oversight and fiduciary duties. Within the board, committees and governance structures play a vital role in distributing responsibilities, enabling detailed attention to complex matters, and strengthening organizational decision-making. By establishing committees and defining governance frameworks, nonprofits create systems that enhance efficiency, manage risks, and support long-term sustainability.

Committees are smaller working groups within the board, formed to focus on specialized areas of oversight and responsibility. They allow directors to use their skills and expertise to address specific functions without overburdening the entire board with detailed matters. For example, financial oversight requires specialized knowledge that may not be shared equally by all directors. By assigning such work to a finance or audit committee, the board ensures that experts lead in-depth reviews and report back with recommendations. Committees thus streamline governance and enhance the quality of board deliberations.

Among the most common committees is the executive committee, which is often composed of the board chair, vice chair, secretary, treasurer, and sometimes other key directors. This committee acts on behalf of the full board between meetings, particularly in urgent matters where immediate decisions are necessary. However, while the executive committee can provide efficiency, it must be carefully structured to avoid undermining the authority of the full board. Clear guidelines about its powers and limitations preserve the balance between responsiveness and accountability.

Another critical committee is the finance committee, which oversees budgeting, financial reporting, and resource allocation. This committee ensures that the nonprofit maintains fiscal discipline and complies with applicable accounting standards. Often, the finance committee collaborates with staff to prepare budgets and review performance against financial goals. A related body, the audit committee, is particularly important for larger nonprofits. The audit committee ensures the integrity of financial statements, supervises the external audit process, and monitors internal controls. Together, these committees safeguard the financial health of the organization and assure stakeholders that resources are managed responsibly.

The governance or nominations committee is another essential part of nonprofit board structure. Its responsibilities include identifying, recruiting, and onboarding new directors, as well as evaluating the board's performance. This committee ensures that the board has the right mix of skills, diversity, and commitment to the mission. By regularly assessing board composition, it helps prevent stagnation and promotes adaptability. The governance committee may also oversee compliance with bylaws, board policies, and best practices in nonprofit governance, making it central to the board's long-term effectiveness.

Fundraising and development committees also play a significant role in many nonprofits. Since nonprofits rely heavily on donations, grants, and sponsorships, the board must actively participate in resource development. The fundraising committee coordinates board members' efforts to cultivate donor relationships, organize events, and expand networks. While staff may lead operational fundraising activities, the committee ensures that the board fulfills its role in supporting the organization's financial sustainability. In some nonprofits, this committee also works closely with the marketing and communications team to align donor outreach with messaging.

Program committees are sometimes created to oversee the nonprofit's core activities and ensure alignment with strategic priorities. For example, an educational nonprofit may establish a committee to review curriculum effectiveness or assess program impact. These committees help boards stay connected to the mission and ensure accountability for results. However, care must be taken not to cross into management territory, as staff are responsible for operational execution. The role of program committees should be advisory and oversight-oriented, focusing on outcomes and mission alignment.

Special or ad hoc committees may also be formed to address temporary issues, such as strategic planning, capital campaigns, or mergers. These committees provide flexibility, allowing the board to address emerging needs without overloading standing committees. Once the task is complete, the committee dissolves. This approach ensures that board structures remain dynamic and responsive.

While committees are vital, they are only part of the broader governance framework. Governance structures define the distribution of responsibilities between the board, committees, and staff leadership. At the heart of nonprofit governance is the principle that the board governs while staff, led by the executive director or CEO, manages. Clear delineation of roles prevents micromanagement and ensures that directors focus on strategy and oversight rather than day-to-day operations. Written policies, bylaws, and committee charters reinforce these boundaries and provide consistency.

Effective governance also depends on accountability mechanisms. Boards must adopt conflict-of-interest policies, financial controls, and regular performance evaluations for both directors and staff leadership. Committees can support these efforts, but ultimate accountability rests with the full board. Transparency to donors, regulators, and the public is a fundamental requirement, meaning that governance structures must ensure compliance with reporting requirements and ethical standards.

Board governance structures often reflect the size and complexity of the nonprofit. Small organizations may have only a few committees or even operate without formal committees, relying on the full board to address all issues. Larger nonprofits, by contrast, may have multiple committees and subcommittees, reflecting the complexity of their programs, finances, and stakeholder relationships. Regardless of size, the goal is to strike a balance between efficiency and inclusivity, ensuring that important decisions receive adequate attention and diverse perspectives.

Diversity and inclusion in governance structures are increasingly emphasized as part of best practices. Committees and board leadership should reflect the communities the nonprofit serves, ensuring that governance decisions are informed by a variety of perspectives. Diverse committees also enhance creativity, problem-solving, and credibility. Governance structures must therefore prioritize equity in leadership opportunities and avoid concentrating power in small, homogenous groups.

In conclusion, nonprofit board committees and governance structures are essential tools for ensuring effective oversight, accountability, and mission alignment. Committees enable boards to distribute responsibilities, leverage expertise, and provide deeper focus on financial, governance, fundraising, and program matters. Governance structures define the boundaries between board and staff responsibilities, uphold accountability, and ensure compliance with ethical and legal standards. When carefully designed and implemented, these systems empower nonprofit boards to govern effectively, adapt to challenges, and sustain their organizations in pursuit of their missions.

Board Policies and Accountability

A nonprofit entity's board policies and accountability mechanisms are fundamental to its credibility, effectiveness, and long-term sustainability. Unlike for-profit corporations, nonprofits operate with a mission-driven purpose and hold resources in trust for the public good. This unique role requires high levels of governance integrity, which is achieved through clear board policies and robust systems of accountability. Together, these structures safeguard the nonprofit's reputation, ensure compliance with legal obligations, and align the organization's activities with its mission.

Board policies provide the framework that guides director behavior and organizational decision-making. These written rules and guidelines help the board operate consistently, fairly, and transparently. They establish expectations for director roles, set ethical standards, and define the processes through which decisions are made. Common policies include conflict-of-interest rules, codes of conduct, whistleblower protections, and guidelines on financial oversight. Such policies are not merely formalities; they create a culture of accountability where directors understand both their authority and their limits.

A central policy in nonprofit governance is the conflict-of-interest policy. Nonprofits must ensure that board members act in the best interest of the organization rather than personal gain. This policy requires directors to disclose any potential conflicts, such as financial ties to vendors, relatives employed by the nonprofit, or personal involvement in competing organizations. The board then evaluates these disclosures to prevent biased decision-making. By formalizing how conflicts are identified and managed, the nonprofit reinforces stakeholder trust and demonstrates a commitment to integrity.

SAMPLE CONFLICT OF INTEREST POLICY

The purpose of this policy is to protect the integrity and reputation of the organization by ensuring that decisions made by the Board of Directors are free from personal or financial conflicts of interest. Directors are expected to act in good faith, with loyalty to the organization, and in the best interests of its mission.

A conflict of interest arises when a director's personal, professional, or financial interests interfere, or appear to interfere, with the interests of the organization. Examples include situations where a director or a member of their immediate family has a financial stake in a business that is being considered for a contract with the organization, or when a director stands to benefit personally from decisions made by the board.

All directors must disclose any actual or potential conflicts of interest as soon as they arise. Disclosures should be made in writing to the Chair of the Board and recorded in the minutes of board meetings. When a conflict is disclosed, the director must abstain from voting or otherwise participating in discussions or decisions related to the matter. The remaining disinterested directors will determine whether a conflict exists and how it should be managed in the best interests of the organization.

The organization will require each director to complete and sign an annual disclosure statement identifying any business, professional, or personal relationships that may give rise to a conflict of interest. It is the responsibility of each director to update the disclosure form during the year if circumstances change.

Any director who fails to disclose a conflict of interest or who violates this policy may be subject to disciplinary action, including possible removal from the board. This policy is intended not to prevent relationships or transactions with related parties, but to ensure that such transactions are conducted with transparency, fairness, and in compliance with applicable laws.

By adopting this policy, the Board of Directors affirms its commitment to ethical governance and to serving the organization's mission with integrity and accountability.

Another cornerstone is the code of conduct or ethics policy. This establishes the standards of professionalism, respect, and transparency that directors must uphold. It covers matters such as confidentiality, respectful boardroom behavior, and adherence to mission-driven values. A strong code of conduct helps prevent reputational harm and creates a shared sense of responsibility. For nonprofits that depend on volunteers and donors, visibly upholding high ethical standards can make the difference between thriving and losing support.

SAMPLE CODE OF CONDUCT POLICY

The Board of Directors recognizes that its members are entrusted with the responsibility of safeguarding the mission, assets, and reputation of the organization. In carrying out this duty, each director agrees to uphold the highest standards of integrity, professionalism, and accountability.

Directors shall act in good faith and in the best interests of the organization, placing the nonprofit's mission above personal or professional gain. They will avoid conflicts of interest, disclose any potential conflicts promptly, and recuse themselves from related decisions when necessary. Confidential information gained through board service will not be disclosed or used for personal advantage.

Board members are expected to attend meetings regularly, prepare adequately, and participate constructively in discussions. Respectful communication, open dialogue, and collaborative decision-making shall guide all interactions, whether with fellow directors, staff, volunteers, or stakeholders. Directors will support the decisions of the board as a whole, even when they may differ personally, and will avoid undermining board actions outside official meetings.

Each director will comply with applicable laws, regulations, and organizational policies. They will exercise fiduciary responsibility by overseeing financial matters diligently, ensuring resources are used responsibly, and monitoring risks appropriately. Board members will also serve as ambassadors of the organization, promoting its mission in the community and assisting with fundraising and outreach where possible.

This Code of Conduct reflects the commitment of the board to ethical governance and accountability. Directors who fail to adhere to these standards may be subject to review and possible removal, in accordance with the organization's bylaws.

Financial oversight policies are equally important. Nonprofit boards carry fiduciary duties of care, loyalty, and obedience, requiring them to protect organizational assets and ensure that their use aligns with the mission. Policies that require annual budgets, regular financial reports, and independent audits create transparency around financial health. Internal control policies, such as dual signatures on checks or restrictions on credit card use, prevent fraud and misuse of funds. Through these measures, the board demonstrates accountability to donors, grantmakers, and the public.

Whistleblower policies further strengthen accountability by providing safe channels for reporting misconduct. These policies protect staff, volunteers, and even board members who raise concerns about financial irregularities, discrimination, or legal violations. By encouraging transparency and shielding whistleblowers from retaliation, the board promotes an organizational culture where problems are surfaced and addressed early. Such policies align with legal expectations under statutes like the

Sarbanes-Oxley Act, which, while primarily directed at corporations, has influenced nonprofit best practices.

SAMPLE WHISTLEBLOWER POLICY

[Organization Name] is committed to maintaining the highest standards of conduct and ethics. As part of this commitment, the organization expects its directors, officers, employees, and volunteers to report any suspected violations of law, organizational policy, or ethical standards without fear of retaliation.

This policy is intended to encourage and enable individuals to raise concerns so that the organization can address and correct inappropriate conduct and actions. It applies to all areas of operation, including financial practices, fundraising, governance, program activities, and employment matters.

Any individual who in good faith reports a suspected violation will not suffer harassment, retaliation, or adverse employment or volunteer consequences. Retaliation against anyone who raises a concern in good faith is strictly prohibited and will be treated as a serious violation of this policy.

Concerns may be reported to the Executive Director or Board Chair. If the concern involves either of these parties, the report may be directed to another officer or designated board member. Reports should be made as soon as possible and should include as much detail as possible to facilitate proper investigation.

All reports will be treated as confidential to the extent possible, consistent with the need to conduct a thorough investigation. The organization will take appropriate corrective action if misconduct or violations are found to have occurred.

Accountability also depends on policies that govern the board's own functioning. Attendance policies, term limits, and evaluation procedures hold directors responsible for active and meaningful participation. Term limits, for instance, prevent stagnation and open opportunities for fresh perspectives. Regular board self-assessments or peer evaluations encourage continuous improvement and help identify gaps in skills or diversity. These practices reinforce the principle that board service is a serious responsibility, not an honorary title.

Transparency policies extend accountability beyond the boardroom. Many nonprofits adopt guidelines for sharing annual reports, financial statements, and impact assessments with the public. This openness builds credibility with donors and beneficiaries, assuring them that resources are being used effectively. Governance policies may also require the board to disclose executive compensation, fundraising practices, and program outcomes, reinforcing compliance with both IRS requirements and donor expectations.

The accountability framework is incomplete without aligning board policies with the nonprofit's mission. Directors are bound by a duty of obedience, which requires them to ensure that activities remain consistent with the organization's founding purpose. Mission drift can undermine donor confidence and jeopardize an organization's tax-exempt status. To prevent this, boards adopt strategic planning policies that require the periodic review of mission statements, program alignment, and long-term goals. These policies ensure that governance decisions remain focused on advancing the nonprofit's core purpose.

Ultimately, accountability is about creating trust with stakeholders; donors, clients, staff, regulators, and the community. Board policies formalize the principles of integrity, transparency, and responsibility. They serve as guardrails that keep directors aligned with fiduciary duties and legal requirements. At the same time, they provide a basis for evaluating board performance and holding individual directors accountable for their conduct.

In conclusion, a nonprofit entity's board policies and accountability mechanisms form the backbone of responsible governance. Conflict-of-interest rules, codes of conduct, financial oversight procedures, and whistleblower protections ensure integrity and transparency. Attendance, term limit, and evaluation policies strengthen board performance, while transparency policies reassure external stakeholders. By adopting and enforcing these policies, nonprofit boards uphold their fiduciary duties, align activities with the mission, and build the trust necessary for long-term success. Accountability is not only a legal requirement but also an ethical commitment that sustains the nonprofit's role in serving the public good.

Board Development and Succession Planning

Nonprofit board development and succession planning are essential practices that ensure the long-term effectiveness, stability, and sustainability of an organization's governance. Because nonprofit boards hold fiduciary responsibility for mission fulfillment, financial oversight, and strategic direction, they must not only recruit skilled and diverse directors but also prepare for leadership transitions. Without thoughtful development and succession planning, nonprofits risk gaps in leadership, the loss of institutional knowledge, and diminished effectiveness. By investing in ongoing training, evaluation, and leadership pipelines, nonprofits build resilient boards capable of guiding the organization through both challenges and growth.

Board development refers to the continuous process of strengthening directors' skills, knowledge, and engagement. It begins with recruitment, where organizations deliberately seek individuals whose expertise, backgrounds, and values align with the nonprofit's mission. Once recruited, new directors must undergo structured orientation programs that introduce them to the organization's history, mission, strategic priorities, bylaws, and financial condition. Effective onboarding equips new members to contribute quickly and confidently while fostering a sense of shared responsibility. Development, however, extends far beyond orientation. Nonprofits that thrive encourage board members to engage in ongoing education, such as workshops on governance best practices, seminars on nonprofit finance, or retreats that strengthen strategic thinking. By continuously deepening directors' knowledge, organizations prevent complacency and keep the board adaptive to changing external conditions.

Evaluation is another critical component of board development. Periodic assessments of both the board as a whole and individual directors help identify strengths, weaknesses, and opportunities for improvement. These evaluations may review attendance, participation in committees, fundraising contributions, or adherence to governance responsibilities. Constructive feedback allows directors to reflect on their contributions and commit to improvement. More importantly, evaluations reveal gaps in board skills or diversity that can inform future recruitment efforts. Boards that take development seriously understand that growth is an ongoing process and not a one-time achievement.

Succession planning complements development by preparing for inevitable leadership transitions. Just as staff leadership succession is vital for organizational continuity, board succession ensures stability in governance. Key positions such as the board chair, treasurer, and committee chairs carry significant responsibility, and abrupt departures can disrupt the board's effectiveness. A proactive succession plan identifies potential future leaders early, nurtures their skills, and creates a clear pathway for assuming leadership roles. This not only reduces uncertainty but also fosters confidence among stakeholders that the nonprofit has continuity at the governance level.

A strong succession plan starts with term limits. While some nonprofits resist them, term limits prevent stagnation, create space for fresh perspectives, and force boards to think proactively about leadership transitions. As directors approach the end of their terms, boards can begin grooming successors through committee assignments, mentoring, and exposure to leadership responsibilities. For example, a vice chair may be deliberately prepared to transition into the chair role, ensuring a smooth transfer of responsibilities. Committees such as the governance or nominations committee often oversee this process, developing a pipeline of leaders to prevent last-minute scrambles.

Succession planning also includes preparing for unplanned departures. Illness, career changes, or other personal circumstances can lead to sudden vacancies in leadership positions. Nonprofits that plan for contingencies, such as by designating interim leaders or maintaining an emergency succession protocol, protect themselves from instability. These plans should be documented, reviewed regularly, and communicated clearly to avoid confusion during transitions.

Diversity and inclusion are critical in both board development and succession planning. Nonprofits serve increasingly complex and diverse communities, and their boards must reflect that reality to maintain legitimacy and relevance. Development initiatives should actively build cultural competence, while succession planning should prioritize leaders from varied backgrounds and experiences. By doing so, nonprofits avoid replicating homogenous leadership patterns and ensure that future boards are better equipped to represent their stakeholders.

Another aspect of succession planning involves aligning leadership transitions with the organization's strategic direction. For instance, if a nonprofit anticipates expanding its fundraising capacity, it may prioritize grooming leaders with development expertise. If advocacy becomes a growing priority, succession planning may emphasize directors with public policy experience. In this way, succession planning is not just about replacing leaders but about ensuring that the board evolves in step with organizational needs.

Finally, both board development and succession planning foster a culture of accountability. Directors understand that their roles are not permanent but part of a continuum of governance. Leaders are expected to prepare the next generation and leave the board stronger than they found it. This mindset prevents the entrenchment of power and supports organizational resilience.

In conclusion, nonprofit board development and succession planning are not optional practices but essential strategies for effective governance. Development ensures that directors remain engaged, knowledgeable, and capable of fulfilling their fiduciary duties, while succession planning secures continuity in leadership and protects against instability. Together, these processes build strong governance structures that adapt to change, reflect diverse perspectives, and advance the organization's mission over time. Nonprofits that invest in these practices demonstrate foresight, accountability, and commitment to their long-term sustainability, ensuring that they remain effective stewards of the public trust.

Summary

The recommendations noted in this chapter will not necessarily apply to every nonprofit. A small nonprofit that is just starting out may find that it cannot yet attract additional board members, and so must preserve its founding group of board members for an extended period of time. However, as the organization grows in size and complexity, more of the recommendations noted here will apply, such as the need for regular board turnover, the creation of policies, and the use of committees to deal with specialized matters. In effect, ongoing changes to the organization as a whole will drive the extent to which its board of directors is organized and functions.

Chapter 6
Assembling a Workforce

Introduction

Staffing a nonprofit is an especially difficult task, since it involves a mix of paid employees and volunteers, and a financial environment in which it can be difficult to provide high levels of compensation. A further difficulty is that the organization is driven by something other than the profit motive, which calls for different types of motivation. In this chapter, we discuss the difficult task of balancing paid staff and volunteers, recruitment and training strategies, retention and motivation, and several related issues.

Balancing Paid Staff and Volunteers

Balancing paid staff and volunteers is one of the most significant organizational challenges and opportunities for a nonprofit. Both groups are essential to mission delivery, but they bring different roles, expectations, and motivations. Paid staff provide professional expertise, continuity, and accountability, while volunteers embody community engagement, donor goodwill, and mission-driven passion. If managed carefully, the integration of staff and volunteers creates a dynamic, efficient, and sustainable workforce. If neglected, however, tensions can arise that undermine morale and weaken effectiveness. Nonprofits therefore need deliberate strategies, clear policies, and a culture of respect to harmonize the contributions of both paid staff and volunteers.

The Importance of Paid Staff in Nonprofits

Paid staff form the professional backbone of nonprofit organizations. They are typically responsible for executing day-to-day operations, managing finances, maintaining compliance, and implementing programs. Unlike volunteers, who may commit limited hours or bring specialized skills intermittently, staff members are accountable for consistent performance. Their presence ensures that organizational knowledge is preserved and that operations run smoothly regardless of volunteer turnover.

Staff roles often include executive leadership positions such as executive directors, financial managers, program coordinators, and development officers. These positions require specialized training and professional expertise that volunteers may not be able to provide on a reliable basis. For example, grant writing, budget management, or human resources oversight demand professional accountability. Paid staff are also critical for ensuring compliance with laws and regulations, from IRS reporting requirements to labor standards. Their responsibility is not just to keep the nonprofit running but to create an environment where volunteers can contribute effectively.

The Role of Volunteers in Nonprofits

Volunteers, on the other hand, bring energy, passion, and community credibility. They often serve as ambassadors for the nonprofit, spreading its mission and attracting donors, supporters, and clients. Volunteers provide labor that extends organizational reach, especially in service delivery, fundraising events, and advocacy efforts. For smaller nonprofits with limited budgets, volunteers are indispensable for carrying out work that would otherwise be unaffordable.

Volunteers are not simply unpaid staff; they are community members who give their time because they believe in the mission. This unique motivation enhances authenticity and legitimacy. For example, a food bank may employ paid staff to coordinate logistics and compliance, but rely on volunteers to pack and distribute food. In such contexts, volunteers demonstrate community ownership of the nonprofit's mission and deepen its connection with beneficiaries.

Potential Tensions Between Staff and Volunteers

Despite the complementary roles of staff and volunteers, tensions can arise if boundaries and expectations are unclear. Staff may perceive volunteers as untrained or inconsistent, while volunteers may see staff as overly bureaucratic or detached from grassroots realities. Conflicts can occur when volunteers feel excluded from meaningful decision-making or when staff resent volunteers encroaching on professional roles.

Additionally, compensation differences may create resentment if volunteers believe that staff members are paid excessively, or if staff feel that volunteers are undermining their job security. Without clear role definitions, overlap between staff and volunteer duties can lead to confusion, the duplication of effort, and inefficiency. Managing these dynamics requires proactive leadership and communication.

Strategies for Balancing Paid Staff and Volunteers

A successful nonprofit recognizes the unique contributions of both groups and establishes systems to align them. One strategy is the creation of clear job descriptions for both staff and volunteers. Defining responsibilities prevents duplication and ensures that tasks are assigned based on expertise, availability, and mission impact. For example, staff might handle administrative and compliance-heavy tasks, while volunteers focus on service delivery, community outreach, and supplemental support.

Another strategy is fostering mutual respect. This requires a cultural commitment to valuing both groups equally. Staff must acknowledge that volunteers bring passion and community connections, while volunteers must respect the professional expertise and accountability of staff. The executive director plays a central role in setting this tone, emphasizing that both staff and volunteers are essential team members working toward the same mission.

Training and orientation are also key to balance. Just as staff undergo onboarding and professional development, volunteers should receive orientation about the nonprofit's mission, policies, and expectations. Training helps volunteers perform their roles effectively and reduces frustration for staff who rely on them. Similarly, staff should be trained in volunteer management skills, such as coaching, motivating, and recognizing volunteers' contributions. This mutual investment in learning builds stronger partnerships.

Communication structures enhance alignment between staff and volunteers. Regular meetings, updates, and feedback sessions ensure that both groups understand the nonprofit's goals and progress. Volunteers should be included in appropriate planning discussions and given opportunities to share their perspectives. Staff, in turn, should communicate clearly about policies, boundaries, and the importance of adhering to organizational standards. Open dialogue prevents misunderstandings and reinforces shared purpose.

Recognition is another critical component. Nonprofits must acknowledge the contributions of both paid staff and volunteers to maintain morale and motivation. Staff recognition often takes the form of compensation, benefits, and performance evaluations, while volunteers are motivated by non-monetary recognition. Certificates, thank-you events, public acknowledgments, or personal notes of appreciation go a long way in sustaining volunteer commitment. When recognition is consistent, it reinforces the idea that both groups are valued equally, even if in different ways.

Balancing Resources Between Staff and Volunteers

A nonprofit must also consider how it allocates financial and organizational resources between staff and volunteers. Budgets may prioritize salaries for staff but should also allocate resources to support volunteer programs, such as training, supervision, and recognition initiatives. Neglecting volunteer resources can diminish effectiveness and discourage participation. At the same time, nonprofits must ensure that staff are adequately compensated to attract and retain professional talent. Balancing these investments demonstrates the organization's commitment to sustaining both workforce components.

Technology can support this balance as well. Volunteer management software helps track hours, match volunteers to roles, and recognize contributions, while HR systems help staff manage compliance and performance. Integrating these systems creates a unified approach that underscores the equal importance of staff and volunteers in organizational planning.

Case Examples of Balancing Staff and Volunteers

Consider a community health clinic. Paid staff such as doctors, nurses, and administrators ensure that medical and regulatory standards are met. Volunteers assist by welcoming patients, providing translation services, or organizing fundraising events. The combination allows the clinic to deliver professional-quality care while remaining deeply connected to the community.

Similarly, a large nonprofit like Habitat for Humanity balances skilled staff project managers with armies of volunteers who build homes. Staff ensure safety, compliance, and technical oversight, while volunteers contribute labor and community spirit. Together, they achieve outcomes neither group could accomplish alone.

Long-Term Sustainability Through Balance

Ultimately, balancing paid staff and volunteers is about sustainability. A nonprofit that over-relies on volunteers risks burnout and inconsistency, while one that neglects volunteers risks losing community support and legitimacy. Successful nonprofits treat staff and volunteers as interdependent, not interchangeable. By fostering collaboration, investing in training, and building mutual respect, they create a workforce that is greater than the sum of its parts.

In conclusion, nonprofits balance paid staff and volunteers by recognizing the complementary strengths of each, preventing conflicts through clear policies, and fostering a culture of respect. Staff provide professionalism and continuity, while volunteers supply passion and community engagement. Through training, communication, and recognition, both groups can thrive together. A well-balanced approach not only enhances operational efficiency but also strengthens the nonprofit's connection to its mission and stakeholders. The harmony between staff and volunteers is not just a management issue; it is a core driver of nonprofit success and sustainability.

Recruitment and Training Strategies

Recruitment and training strategies are central to the success of a nonprofit organization, because its mission depends heavily on the people it attracts and develops. Unlike for-profit enterprises, nonprofits often operate with constrained budgets, heightened accountability to donors and stakeholders, and a reliance on volunteers alongside paid staff. These dynamics make recruitment and training especially important, as the organization must maximize the contributions of every individual while aligning them with the mission and values of the nonprofit. A comprehensive approach requires deliberate strategies for attracting, selecting, onboarding, and continuously developing both staff and volunteers, thereby ensuring that the workforce is prepared to advance the organization's goals in a sustainable way.

Recruitment begins with clarity about the roles needed within the nonprofit. This requires careful workforce planning, which identifies the skills and capacities required to meet current and future objectives. For example, an organization that is expanding its fundraising initiatives may need professionals skilled in grant writing, donor relations, and digital marketing, while one focused on service delivery may need program coordinators and outreach staff. By articulating the exact competencies and values it seeks, the nonprofit positions itself to attract candidates who are both capable and mission-driven. Position descriptions play a central role here, not just listing duties but also communicating the organization's culture and purpose, which are often the strongest motivators for nonprofit staff and volunteers.

Sourcing candidates is another critical step in recruitment. Nonprofits often rely on a blend of traditional and mission-specific channels to reach potential recruits. Job boards, local universities, and professional associations provide access to general talent pools, while nonprofit-specific platforms and volunteer networks can attract individuals who are motivated by service. Word of mouth, community outreach, and board member referrals also remain important, as many candidates are drawn by personal connections and alignment with the cause. Social media has become a particularly powerful tool, allowing nonprofits to showcase their impact stories, highlight staff and volunteer experiences, and reach audiences already engaged with their mission. For volunteer recruitment in particular, tapping into local civic groups, faith-based organizations, and schools provides a steady pipeline of committed individuals.

Once candidates are identified, selection processes must balance professionalism with mission fit. Nonprofits typically cannot offer the same financial incentives as for-profit organizations, so assessing values alignment becomes especially important. Structured interviews, behavioral assessments, and scenario-based exercises can reveal whether candidates are prepared to work within resource constraints, collaborate across diverse teams, and respond flexibly to challenges. For volunteers, the screening process may be simpler but should still include an evaluation of motivations, availability, and reliability. Background checks may be necessary for roles that involve vulnerable populations. The goal is to ensure that both staff and volunteers are not only capable but also energized by the organization's mission.

Onboarding is where recruitment transitions into training, and nonprofits must pay special attention to this stage. A thoughtful onboarding program introduces new hires and volunteers to the nonprofit's mission, values, programs, and expectations, setting the tone for their engagement. It should include an orientation that explains the organization's history, governance, and impact, helping individuals see the broader significance of their roles. For staff, onboarding may also include policy training on compliance, financial stewardship, and reporting, given the unique accountability structures of nonprofits. For volunteers, orientation can focus more on specific tasks, safety protocols, and community engagement guidelines. In both cases, a clear and welcoming onboarding process fosters early retention and productivity.

Beyond onboarding, ongoing training is essential for both effectiveness and motivation. Nonprofit staff often wear multiple hats, making cross-training and skill development especially valuable. Training programs may address technical competencies, such as fundraising systems, case management software, or program evaluation techniques, as well as soft skills like leadership, communication, and cultural competency. Given budget constraints, nonprofits often leverage creative approaches, such as peer mentoring, job shadowing, online learning platforms, and partnerships with other organizations to provide training opportunities at low cost. Volunteers also benefit from ongoing training, which not only sharpens their skills but deepens their connection to the mission. For example, volunteers at a literacy nonprofit might receive workshops on tutoring techniques, child development, and cultural awareness, which enhance both their effectiveness and satisfaction.

An important element of nonprofit training strategies is leadership development. Succession planning is particularly critical in nonprofits, where executive turnover can create instability. Training programs for emerging leaders help ensure that the organization has a pipeline of individuals prepared to step into leadership roles. This may involve offering stretch assignments, leadership workshops, and mentoring relationships that expose staff to governance, strategy, and financial management. Volunteers, too, can be developed into leadership positions, such as volunteer coordinators or board members, providing a pathway for deeper engagement and ensuring continuity in mission-driven leadership.

Recruitment and training also intersect with diversity, equity, and inclusion (DEI) goals. Nonprofits serve diverse communities and must reflect this diversity in their workforce to maintain credibility and effectiveness. Recruitment strategies should actively reach out to underrepresented groups, ensuring that job postings are accessible, inclusive, and free of bias. Training programs should include DEI components that build awareness, reduce unconscious bias, and equip staff and volunteers to work respectfully with diverse populations. By embedding DEI in recruitment and training, nonprofits strengthen their organizational culture and increase their ability to meet the needs of the communities they serve.

Retention is another dimension closely tied to recruitment and training. Nonprofits cannot afford high turnover, as it drains resources and disrupts service delivery. Investing in training helps retain staff by demonstrating a commitment to their growth, while structured volunteer development keeps individuals engaged for longer periods. Recognition programs, regular feedback, and opportunities for advancement reinforce this commitment. Moreover, when training is coupled with meaningful work assignments and visible impact, it fosters a strong sense of purpose that is one of the most powerful retention tools available to nonprofits.

Evaluation and adaptation are essential to ensure that recruitment and training strategies remain effective. Nonprofits should regularly assess the success of their recruitment channels, track turnover rates, and gather feedback from staff and volunteers about the onboarding and training processes. Program evaluations and performance reviews can highlight skill gaps, prompting adjustments in training content. Similarly, analyzing recruitment outcomes can reveal whether certain approaches yield higher-quality or more committed candidates. By treating recruitment and training as evolving processes rather than static policies, nonprofits remain responsive to changing needs and external challenges.

In sum, a nonprofit's recruitment and training strategies are more than administrative functions; they are mission-critical investments. Successful recruitment ensures that the right individuals (those who are competent, committed, and values-aligned) join the organization. Effective training transforms those individuals into capable contributors, leaders, and ambassadors for the mission. Together, these strategies build a workforce that is motivated, skilled, and adaptable, capable of sustaining the nonprofit's operations and advancing its vision despite the inherent challenges of the sector. When thoughtfully designed and continuously refined, recruitment and training strategies provide nonprofits with one of their most important assets: a human foundation strong enough to achieve lasting social impact.

Retention and Motivation

Retention and motivation are central concerns for nonprofit organizations, since their ability to deliver on mission is directly tied to the commitment and performance of both paid staff and volunteers. Unlike for-profit businesses, nonprofits often operate with limited financial resources, constrained administrative capacity, and accountability to diverse stakeholders including donors, beneficiaries, and regulators. These realities mean that traditional incentives such as high salaries or bonuses are often unavailable, leaving nonprofits to rely on other approaches to keep their workforce engaged. Retention and motivation are particularly challenging in a nonprofit environment because staff and volunteers are motivated by a complex blend of personal values, career goals, and the desire to make a meaningful impact. Understanding the drivers of retention and the obstacles to motivation allows nonprofits to develop strategies that maintain stability, reduce turnover, and strengthen organizational effectiveness.

One of the most pressing issues affecting retention among nonprofit staff is compensation. Salaries in the nonprofit sector are often lower than those in the private sector for comparable roles, leading to an environment where highly skilled employees may leave for better-paying opportunities. This creates a cycle of turnover that disrupts programs and burdens the organization with constant recruitment and onboarding. For mission-driven employees, the lower compensation may be tolerable in the short term, but over time financial pressures can erode even the strongest commitment to the cause. Nonprofits must therefore grapple with the challenge of offering competitive compensation within limited budgets, often turning to benefits such as flexible work schedules, professional development opportunities, and workplace culture to offset financial limitations.

Volunteers face a different set of retention challenges. Since they are unpaid, their motivation relies entirely on intrinsic and non-financial factors. Volunteers often start with strong enthusiasm for the mission, but their engagement can wane if their contributions feel undervalued or if the organization fails to make effective use of their time. Poorly defined roles, lack of adequate training, and insufficient communication can leave volunteers frustrated and disengaged. When volunteers feel that their work is not making a difference or that their time is wasted, they are likely to leave, which can create reputational challenges for the nonprofit and strain service delivery. Therefore, managing volunteers requires as much care and planning as managing paid staff, even though the relationship is structured differently.

Another issue influencing retention and motivation for both groups is the emotional intensity of nonprofit work. Many nonprofits operate in fields such as health care, poverty alleviation, environmental activism, or social justice, which involve direct exposure to human suffering or societal challenges. While these experiences can be motivating and provide a strong sense of purpose, they can also contribute to burnout and compassion fatigue. Paid staff may feel overwhelmed by the demands of delivering services with limited resources, while volunteers may experience disillusionment if the scale of the problems feels insurmountable. Without intentional strategies to support emotional well-being, burnout can become a leading cause of turnover in nonprofits, reducing the organization's capacity to achieve its mission.

Organizational culture also plays a significant role in retention and motivation. Nonprofits often pride themselves on having values-driven cultures, but if the day-to-day environment fails to reflect those values, staff and volunteers may lose faith in the organization. For example, an organization that promotes inclusivity in its mission but fails to provide equitable treatment in its workplace may struggle to maintain morale. Similarly, if communication between leadership and frontline workers is weak, or if decision-making processes lack transparency, employees and volunteers may feel disconnected from the mission. Creating a culture of respect, recognition, and participation is essential for keeping people engaged, especially when financial compensation is not a primary driver.

Career development is another key factor for paid staff. Nonprofit organizations often have smaller structures with fewer opportunities for upward mobility, which can frustrate ambitious employees who want to advance their careers. The lack of clear career pathways may encourage staff to leave after gaining experience, using their nonprofit role as a stepping stone to positions in government or the private sector. This turnover can deprive nonprofits of institutional knowledge and leadership capacity. Addressing this issue requires creativity, such as offering lateral growth opportunities, project leadership experiences, or professional development programs that allow staff to expand their skills and see continued value in remaining with the organization even if promotions are limited.

For volunteers, motivation is closely linked to recognition and the ability to see the tangible impact of their contributions. Many nonprofits struggle to implement consistent volunteer recognition programs, sometimes because they are focused on pressing service needs and have limited administrative support. Without regular expressions of gratitude, whether through formal recognition events or informal thank-you messages, volunteers may feel invisible. In contrast, when organizations make a concerted effort to acknowledge the value of volunteer contributions and share stories of impact, volunteers are more likely to feel connected to the mission and motivated to continue their service. Recognition does not require significant financial resources but does require consistent attention and intentionality.

Another dimension of motivation is alignment between personal values and the nonprofit's mission. For both staff and volunteers, a sense of purpose is one of the strongest motivators to join and remain in the organization. However, when individuals perceive a gap between the mission and the actual operations of the nonprofit, motivation can quickly decline. This can happen when bureaucratic inefficiencies prevent meaningful impact, when fundraising priorities overshadow service delivery, or when leadership fails to live up to stated values. To address this, nonprofits must ensure that their internal practices are consistent with their external mission, creating authenticity that sustains long-term commitment among their people.

Retention also depends on the relationships within the organization. Supportive supervisors, collaborative colleagues, and opportunities to build community all enhance motivation and reduce turnover. Paid staff are more likely to stay in nonprofits where they feel supported by managers who provide constructive feedback, mentorship, and opportunities for growth. Volunteers are more likely to continue when they feel part of a community of like-minded individuals who share their passion for the cause. Social bonds, whether formal or informal, create a sense of belonging that strengthens motivation even when external challenges are present.

Nonprofits also face challenges in balancing demands and expectations. For staff, the expectation to do more with less can create a constant sense of overload, while volunteers may be asked to commit more time or responsibility than they are able to give. Managing these expectations is essential for retention. Clear communication about roles, realistic workload distribution, and flexibility in accommodating personal circumstances all help staff and volunteers feel that their contributions are manageable and valued. Without this balance, individuals may become overwhelmed or resentful, leading to disengagement.

Finally, retention and motivation are influenced by how nonprofits manage change and uncertainty. Nonprofits often operate in unstable funding environments, dependent on grants, donations, or government contracts that can fluctuate dramatically. This instability can create insecurity among staff, who may leave for more stable opportunities, and volunteers, who may lose confidence in the organization's ability to sustain its programs. Building transparency around financial realities, involving staff and volunteers in problem-solving, and developing adaptive strategies can mitigate the negative impact of uncertainty on motivation and retention.

In conclusion, the issues of retention and motivation for nonprofit staff and volunteers are multifaceted, shaped by financial limitations, emotional demands, organizational culture, and the alignment between personal values and mission. Paid staff struggle with challenges of compensation, career development, and workload, while volunteers face issues of recognition, meaningful engagement, and time management. Both groups are susceptible to burnout and disillusionment if their contributions are undervalued or if organizational practices fail to reflect stated missions and values. Addressing these challenges requires nonprofits to invest in supportive cultures, intentional recognition, professional and personal development opportunities, and authentic alignment with mission. Though financial resources may be limited, the careful cultivation of motivation and retention strategies enables nonprofits to maintain a committed workforce, ensuring the stability and effectiveness necessary to achieve long-term impact.

Building a Positive Organizational Culture

Building a positive organizational culture within a nonprofit organization is essential to sustaining its mission, retaining both staff and volunteers, and creating an environment where individuals feel valued and motivated. Unlike in the corporate world, where culture often develops around profit goals and competition, nonprofit culture must be anchored in the values of service, community, and collective impact. The tone of the culture influences every aspect of the nonprofit, from how employees engage with one another to how the organization is perceived by donors, beneficiaries, and the broader community. A strong, positive culture not only strengthens internal cohesion but also enhances the nonprofit's ability to achieve meaningful outcomes in the face of resource constraints and external challenges.

The foundation of a healthy nonprofit culture begins with clarity of mission and values. Every staff member and volunteer must understand not just what the organization does, but why it does it. This sense of shared purpose is the cornerstone of motivation in nonprofits, where financial incentives are often secondary to the desire to make a difference. Leadership must consistently reinforce this mission, weaving it into daily conversations, decision-making processes, and organizational storytelling. When individuals see how their work contributes directly to the larger goals of the nonprofit, they are more likely to feel connected, engaged, and proud of their roles. A positive culture thrives when people can draw meaning from their contributions and see tangible results from their collective efforts.

Leadership plays an especially influential role in shaping nonprofit culture. Leaders who are approachable, transparent, and values-driven establish trust and model the behaviors expected throughout the organization. For example, a leader who demonstrates humility, listens actively to staff, and is willing to acknowledge mistakes sets a tone of authenticity that others will follow. In contrast, a leadership style that emphasizes hierarchy or micromanagement can erode morale and create divisions. In nonprofits, where staff often wear multiple hats and resources are stretched thin, supportive leadership becomes even more critical. Leaders must create space for open dialogue, invite input into decisions, and recognize the contributions of both employees and volunteers. This inclusive approach fosters a sense of ownership and belonging, which are vital components of a positive organizational culture.

Another important aspect of building culture in nonprofits is the cultivation of respect and equity. Nonprofits serve diverse communities, and it is essential that their internal culture reflects the same commitment to diversity, equity, and inclusion that they promote externally. Creating equitable opportunities for advancement, ensuring fair treatment of all staff regardless of background, and addressing unconscious bias in hiring and decision-making processes are all critical steps. For volunteers, equity means ensuring that their time and talents are valued equally to those of paid staff, even though their roles are different. A culture that truly values diversity fosters innovation and builds stronger connections to the communities being served.

Communication is another key driver of nonprofit culture. Because many nonprofits operate in environments of financial uncertainty or changing priorities, transparent communication becomes essential to maintaining trust. Staff and volunteers should not be left in the dark about organizational challenges or strategic changes. Instead, leadership should provide regular updates, explain the rationale behind decisions, and create channels for questions and feedback. This transparency helps prevent the spread of rumors, reduces anxiety, and builds confidence that leadership is acting in the best interests of both the organization and its people. Effective communication also reinforces the sense that everyone is part of a team working toward a common goal.

Recognition and appreciation are also central to sustaining a positive culture. While financial rewards may be limited, the acknowledgment of effort and achievement costs little but yields significant returns in morale. Regularly thanking staff and volunteers, celebrating milestones, and highlighting contributions in newsletters or meetings helps individuals feel seen and valued. Volunteers in particular rely on these non-monetary forms of recognition to remain motivated and connected. Beyond formal recognition programs, cultivating a culture where peers recognize and support one another builds camaraderie and strengthens collective spirit.

Work-life balance and well-being must also be addressed in nonprofit culture. Because nonprofit work is often emotionally demanding and resource-constrained, burnout is a constant risk. An organization that values its people will promote reasonable workloads, provide access to wellness resources, and encourage time off to recharge. Leaders should set the example by respecting boundaries, avoiding unrealistic expectations, and encouraging self-care. When staff and volunteers feel that their well-being is prioritized, they are more likely to stay engaged and committed over the long term. In this way, a culture of care becomes not just a benefit to individuals but a strategy for organizational sustainability.

Building a positive culture also involves fostering collaboration and teamwork. Nonprofits often rely on interdepartmental cooperation and partnerships with external stakeholders, making collaborative skills essential. A culture that encourages knowledge sharing, collective problem solving, and mutual support creates resilience in the face of challenges. This collaborative spirit must extend beyond staff to include volunteers, board members, and community partners, ensuring that everyone feels like an integral part of the mission. By creating an environment where people feel they are working together rather than in isolation, nonprofits reinforce solidarity and collective achievement.

Finally, a nonprofit's organizational culture must be dynamic and adaptable. Social, economic, and political environments change constantly, and nonprofits must evolve in response. A positive culture embraces adaptability without losing sight of the organization's core mission and values. Encouraging innovation, learning from failures, and remaining open to new ideas ensures that staff and volunteers feel empowered to contribute creatively. Adaptability also requires ongoing reflection, where leadership regularly assesses whether the culture continues to support the mission and makes adjustments where needed. In this way, culture becomes a living element of the nonprofit, capable of sustaining long-term impact.

In conclusion, building a positive organizational culture in a nonprofit requires intentional effort across multiple dimensions, including mission clarity, leadership style, respect for diversity and equity, transparent communication, recognition, well-being, collaboration, and adaptability. When these elements are in place, staff and volunteers feel engaged, valued, and united in their purpose, even in the face of external challenges. A strong, positive culture does more than support internal harmony; it enhances the nonprofit's credibility, effectiveness, and resilience, ultimately allowing it to better serve its community and fulfill its mission.

Dealing with Turnover and Burnout

Turnover and burnout are persistent challenges for nonprofit organizations, reflecting both the demanding nature of the work and the sector's resource constraints. Because nonprofits often depend on a combination of paid staff and volunteers to sustain programs, disruptions caused by high turnover or declining motivation can directly affect service delivery, donor confidence, and long-term sustainability. Dealing with these issues requires a combination of proactive strategies aimed at prevention and responsive measures that address them when they arise. The approaches nonprofits adopt must balance their limited financial capacity with the need to create supportive environments where people can remain engaged without sacrificing their well-being.

Turnover in nonprofits is often linked to compensation and career development. Paid staff may leave when salaries are uncompetitive compared to other sectors, or when opportunities for advancement within the organization are limited. Volunteers, while not financially compensated, may disengage if they feel underutilized, unappreciated, or disconnected from the mission. To manage turnover, nonprofits invest in clear recruitment practices that set accurate expectations, so individuals know what to anticipate before committing. For staff, this means transparent discussions about compensation, responsibilities, and potential career pathways. For volunteers, it involves defining roles carefully, ensuring that their time is respected, and providing opportunities for meaningful engagement. Clarity from the outset helps reduce the mismatch between expectations and reality that often drives turnover.

Once individuals are part of the organization, retention depends heavily on creating a positive and supportive culture. Paid staff are more likely to stay when they feel valued, respected, and given opportunities to grow. Professional development programs, even if modest in scope, can signal some level of investment in employees' careers. Offering flexibility in work arrangements, such as remote work or adaptable schedules, also helps staff balance the demands of nonprofit work with their personal lives. For volunteers, retention efforts often focus on recognition and appreciation. Simple gestures, such as thank-you notes, public acknowledgment, or appreciation events, can go a long way in showing volunteers that their contributions are noticed and valued. When people feel connected to both the mission and the community within the nonprofit, their commitment tends to endure longer.

Burnout presents a deeper challenge because it arises from the emotional and physical toll of nonprofit work. Paid staff may face heavy workloads, inadequate resources, and the emotional strain of working closely with communities in need. Volunteers can also experience burnout, especially if they are repeatedly exposed to difficult circumstances or if their responsibilities expand beyond what they originally intended to give. To address burnout, nonprofits must prioritize well-being. This may include offering counseling or peer support groups, encouraging regular breaks, and promoting realistic workloads. Leadership plays a central role here, as managers who model healthy boundaries and actively check in with their teams create an environment where staff and volunteers feel permitted to care for themselves.

Preventing burnout also involves fostering resilience through teamwork and shared responsibility. When staff and volunteers feel supported by colleagues and know they are part of a collective effort, they are better able to cope with challenges. Regular communication about the impact of their work can also counteract feelings of futility, reminding individuals that their efforts matter. Celebrating small wins and sharing success stories help keep morale high, even when systemic challenges seem daunting. Additionally, nonprofits that create open channels for feedback are better positioned to identify signs of burnout early, allowing them to intervene before individuals disengage entirely.

Ultimately, dealing with turnover and burnout requires nonprofits to be intentional and adaptive. While they may lack the financial resources to compete with for-profit employers, they can foster environments rooted in mission, recognition, and care. By balancing expectations, investing in growth, valuing contributions, and protecting the well-being of their people, nonprofits can reduce the disruptions of turnover and burnout, ensuring that their staff and volunteers remain committed partners in advancing their mission.

Summary

Given the comparatively low resource levels of most nonprofits, it is essential to find and retain the right staff and volunteers. Being cost-effective in doing so is essential to the long-term financial viability of a nonprofit, which might otherwise squander large amounts of cash on training people who choose not to stay with the organization. The cost-effectiveness of assembling a workforce can be enhanced when a nonprofit focuses in particular on two areas, which are the initial review of job applicants and the selection of its executive director. Spending extra time evaluating job applicants is more likely to weed out people who will either not be effective or choose to leave the organization within a short period of time. Of even more importance is the selection of an executive director who is skilled in motivating staff and volunteers; conversely, bringing in an insensitive executive director may have a negative multiplier effect, as the person triggers the departure of multiple staff and volunteers – which may require years to replace. In short, focusing on just two areas can improve both the quality of the workforce and how long they work for the nonprofit.

Chapter 7
Fundraising Essentials

Introduction

Few nonprofits have the comfort of a steady stream of reliable revenue. Instead, they are more likely to have a difficult time digging for it, using a fundraising team to constantly probe all possible funding sources for commitments. In short, the typical nonprofit lives or dies by the amount of cash it can generate from a variety of sources. In this chapter, we cover the core fundraising strategies, the ethical issues associated with fundraising, and several related issues.

Core Fundraising Strategies

Fundraising lies at the heart of nonprofit sustainability, shaping the ability of an organization to advance its mission, support programs, and expand its impact. Because nonprofits rely on external financial resources rather than generating profits from market activities, fundraising becomes both a practical necessity and a strategic function. Effective fundraising involves far more than soliciting donations; it requires building long-term relationships with supporters, diversifying revenue streams, and aligning strategies with the mission and values of the organization. A nonprofit that adopts a thoughtful, multifaceted fundraising approach not only secures the resources needed to operate but also builds credibility and strengthens its connection to the community. Core fundraising strategies include individual giving, major gifts, grants, corporate partnerships, special events, planned giving, membership programs, and increasingly, digital and peer-to-peer fundraising campaigns. Each strategy comes with unique strengths and challenges, and successful nonprofits often employ a mix that balances immediate revenue with long-term sustainability.

One of the most fundamental strategies is individual giving, which constitutes the largest portion of charitable donations in many countries. This approach focuses on cultivating relationships with ordinary donors who contribute at varying levels, from modest monthly gifts to occasional larger contributions. Nonprofits typically develop annual campaigns that use direct mail, email, social media, and personal appeals to solicit donations from individuals. The key to success in individual giving lies in relationship building – thanking donors promptly, demonstrating the impact of their contributions, and creating a sense of belonging to the cause. Many nonprofits use donor databases to track giving histories, preferences, and engagement, allowing for personalized communication that fosters loyalty. Monthly giving programs, which encourage donors to commit to recurring contributions, are particularly valuable because they provide predictable revenue and deepen donor commitment over time.

> **Tip:** Many nonprofits set up their annual fund campaigns to encourage automated monthly deductions from donor bank accounts, or via credit card charges. Either approach can result in more total payments than would be made through a single annual payment, since donors do not feel the pain of a single, large payment. Also, these payments tend to be self-perpetuating, with no additional fundraising contacts needed unless a donor cancels a payment or the person's credit card expires.

EXAMPLE

The American Red Cross regularly conducts targeted fundraising campaigns to re-engage lapsed donors—individuals who previously donated but have not contributed within a certain period of time. The organization uses a combination of direct mail, email, phone outreach, and digital marketing to reconnect with past donors. Its campaigns include the following activities:

- *Personalized direct mail appeals.* The Red Cross sends personalized letters to lapsed donors, reminding them of their past generosity and emphasizing the impact of their contributions. These letters often include a heartfelt message from beneficiaries, success stories, and a call to action encouraging the donor to give again. By addressing donors by name and referencing their last donation, the organization creates a sense of personal connection.
- *Targeted email campaigns.* Using donor data, the Red Cross segments lapsed donors based on their previous giving amounts, frequency, and campaign preferences. They send customized email messages highlighting urgent needs, disaster relief efforts, or recent achievements made possible by past donations. These emails often include compelling images, testimonials, and a simple "Donate Now" button to streamline the giving process.
- *Phone outreach.* To make the re-engagement process more personal, the Red Cross employs volunteers or donor relations staff to call lapsed donors. These calls serve as a thank-you for past support while also informing donors about current programs that need urgent funding. Conversations often include updates on how donations have been used, reinforcing the donor's previous impact and inspiring them to give again.
- *Social media and retargeting ads.* The Red Cross also uses digital marketing strategies to re-engage lapsed donors. If a donor has previously interacted with the Red Cross website or social media pages, they may see retargeted ads encouraging them to renew their support. These ads may feature time-sensitive appeals, such as disaster relief efforts, matching gift opportunities, or limited-time fundraising challenges.
- *Special incentives.* To encourage lapsed donors to give again, the Red Cross occasionally offers matching gift opportunities, where a corporate partner agrees to double any donations made within a specified timeframe. They also use incentives like exclusive donor reports, invitations to special events, or recognition in donor newsletters to re-engage supporters.

Through these targeted efforts, the American Red Cross successfully reactivates thousands of lapsed donors each year. By combining personalized outreach, data-driven marketing, and compelling storytelling, the organization effectively reconnects with past supporters, fostering long-term donor retention and financial sustainability.

Tip: It is essential to build an email list of potential donors, so that you can periodically contact them regarding donations. This can be done in any of the following ways:

- Create a "Join Our List" box on your website (or consider installing a pop-up form)
- Include an email list link on all social media posts.
- Gather addresses in-person and at fundraising events.
- Incorporate email sign-ups into the donation process.

Major gifts represent another cornerstone of nonprofit fundraising. These gifts are typically made by wealthy individuals who have both the capacity and the inclination to contribute significant amounts. Securing major gifts requires a highly personal approach, often involving months or years of cultivation. Nonprofit leaders and development officers invest time in building trust, understanding the donor's values, and aligning them with specific organizational initiatives. Stewardship after the gift is equally important, as ongoing engagement ensures that the donor feels valued and may be inclined to give again in the future. Major gifts can transform an organization, funding capital projects, launching new programs, or stabilizing finances, but they also require careful management to avoid overreliance on a small number of donors.

Grant funding from foundations, government agencies, and other institutions provides another core fundraising avenue. Grants are often awarded to support specific projects, research, or services, and they typically require detailed applications and reporting. Nonprofits must align their proposals with funders' priorities, demonstrating measurable outcomes and organizational capacity. A strong grants strategy involves identifying the right opportunities, developing relationships with program officers, and building internal systems for compliance and reporting. While grants can be a significant source of revenue, they also come with restrictions and cannot usually be applied to general operating expenses. Thus, nonprofits must balance their reliance on grants with unrestricted funding sources to maintain flexibility.

Why Grant Applications Fail

The following are among the most common reasons why a grant application might fail:

- *Misalignment with the foundation's mission and priorities.* Foundations have specific focus areas, such as education, healthcare, or environmental conservation. If a nonprofit applies for a grant that does not closely align with these priorities, the application is unlikely to be successful. Even if a nonprofit's work is valuable, foundations prefer to fund organizations that directly support their strategic goals.
- *Lack of demonstrated impact or measurable outcomes.* Foundations want to fund projects that produce tangible, measurable results. If a nonprofit fails to provide clear data, benchmarks, or success stories, funders may doubt the project's effectiveness. A strong application includes specific goals, a plan for tracking progress, and evidence of past achievements.

- *Incomplete or noncompliant applications*. Many applications are rejected simply because they do not follow the foundation's guidelines. Missing documents, exceeding word limits, or failing to meet submission deadlines can lead to automatic disqualification. Carefully reviewing the application requirements and double-checking for completeness is essential before submission.

- *Unrealistic budget or financial instability*. A budget that lacks detail, overestimates costs, or seems unrealistic raises concerns for funders. Foundations want to see that a nonprofit can responsibly manage grant funds and sustain the project beyond the grant period. Financial instability, such as significant debt or dependence on a single funding source, may signal a high-risk investment to funders.

- *Lack of organizational capacity or experience*. Funders want assurance that a nonprofit has the staff, infrastructure, and expertise to execute the proposed project effectively. If an organization lacks a track record of managing similar initiatives, the foundation may question whether it can deliver results. Providing examples of past successes and strong leadership can help build confidence in the nonprofit's ability.

- *Overreliance on one-time grant funding*. Foundations prefer to support projects that have long-term sustainability beyond their initial funding. If a nonprofit does not outline a plan for securing future funding, funders may hesitate to invest. Demonstrating diverse revenue streams, partnerships, or other funding sources can strengthen an application.

- *Poorly established relationships with the funder*. Grantmaking is not just about submitting an application—it also involves building relationships with foundations. If a nonprofit applies for funding without prior engagement, such as attending events or speaking with program officers, the application may not stand out. Strong relationships can help nonprofits better understand funder expectations and increase their chances of success.

- *High competition for limited funds*. Even well-crafted proposals can be rejected due to the sheer volume of applicants. Some foundations receive far more applications than they can fund, forcing them to make difficult choices. In these cases, nonprofits should remain persistent, seek feedback, and continue applying to multiple funding sources.

By avoiding these common mistakes and refining their approach, nonprofits can improve their grant-writing success and build stronger partnerships with funders.

Corporate partnerships also play an important role in nonprofit fundraising. These relationships can take many forms, including sponsorships of events, cause-related marketing campaigns, employee giving programs, and direct donations. Corporations often seek partnerships that enhance their reputations and demonstrate social responsibility. For nonprofits, the value lies not only in financial support but also in access to networks, visibility, and in-kind contributions such as products or professional services. Building strong corporate partnerships requires nonprofits to demonstrate alignment between their mission and the corporation's brand values, ensuring that the relationship benefits both parties without compromising the nonprofit's integrity.

Special events are another widely used strategy, ranging from galas and charity auctions to community walks, concerts, or benefit dinners. These events serve a dual purpose: raising funds and raising awareness. They provide opportunities for donors, volunteers, and community members to come together in support of a cause, strengthening the organization's visibility and network. Successful events require careful planning to balance the costs of execution with the revenue generated. While large-scale events can be resource-intensive, smaller community-oriented gatherings can provide steady streams of support and foster deeper engagement. Increasingly, nonprofits combine in-person events with digital elements such as livestreaming or online auctions, broadening participation and revenue potential.

Planned giving, or legacy giving, is a strategy that encourages donors to include the nonprofit in their estate plans. This may involve bequests, charitable gift annuities, or trusts. Planned giving appeals to individuals who want to leave a lasting impact on a cause they care about, and it provides nonprofits with long-term sustainability. Cultivating planned giving requires sensitive conversations, often facilitated by development professionals who can explain options while respecting donors' personal and financial circumstances. Although the revenue from planned giving may not be immediate, its importance cannot be overstated, as it secures the organization's future.

Membership programs are another fundraising strategy, particularly for nonprofits such as museums, zoos, or advocacy organizations. Memberships provide individuals with a sense of belonging and tangible benefits, such as free admission, newsletters, or exclusive events. In return, the organization gains a predictable revenue stream and an engaged community of supporters. The challenge lies in balancing the costs of member benefits with the revenue generated, while continuously offering value that encourages renewals.

In the digital era, online and peer-to-peer fundraising have emerged as powerful tools. Online giving platforms allow nonprofits to reach supporters globally, often through campaigns tied to Giving Tuesday or other special appeals. Peer-to-peer fundraising harnesses the networks of individual supporters, who create personal fundraising pages and solicit donations from friends and family. These approaches expand reach, engage younger demographics, and generate excitement around causes. Social media campaigns that tell compelling stories, share videos, or highlight beneficiary testimonials have proven especially effective at motivating small, widespread donations. Nonprofits that embrace digital tools can reach audiences far beyond their traditional base, opening up new possibilities for fundraising growth.

Underlying all of these strategies is the importance of donor stewardship and relationship management. Fundraising is not simply about asking for money; it is about creating lasting partnerships. Nonprofits must prioritize thanking donors, communicating the impact of their contributions, and involving them in the life of the organization. Stewardship may include annual reports, impact stories, site visits, or opportunities to meet program beneficiaries. By demonstrating accountability and transparency, nonprofits strengthen donor trust and encourage repeat giving. Poor stewardship, on the other hand, can lead to donor attrition and reputational damage.

Diversification of fundraising strategies is critical to managing risk. Overreliance on a single revenue source, whether major donors, grants, or events, can leave a nonprofit vulnerable to sudden funding shortfalls. For example, a change in government funding priorities or the loss of a key donor can destabilize an organization. A balanced mix of fundraising strategies ensures greater resilience, allowing nonprofits to weather fluctuations and adapt to changing circumstances. This diversification also supports strategic planning, enabling organizations to align revenue streams with their long-term goals and mission priorities.

Finally, successful fundraising requires investment. While it may be tempting for nonprofits to minimize administrative costs, underinvesting in fundraising capacity can undermine long-term sustainability. Hiring skilled development professionals, maintaining robust donor databases, and investing in communications infrastructure all contribute to more effective fundraising. Donors increasingly recognize that strong infrastructure is necessary for impact, and organizations that communicate this effectively can justify such investments. By treating fundraising as a strategic function rather than an overhead burden, nonprofits build the capacity needed to secure sustainable resources.

In conclusion, core fundraising strategies for nonprofits encompass a wide range of approaches, from individual giving and major gifts to grants, corporate partnerships, events, planned giving, membership programs, and digital campaigns. Each strategy brings unique opportunities and challenges, and their effectiveness depends on how well they align with the nonprofit's mission, resources, and community. The most successful organizations recognize that fundraising is about building relationships, fostering trust, and demonstrating impact. By diversifying revenue streams and prioritizing stewardship, nonprofits can secure the resources necessary not only to survive but to thrive. In doing so, they position themselves to fulfill their missions more effectively and to create lasting change in the communities they serve.

Building Donor Relationships

Building strong donor relationships is one of the most vital functions within a nonprofit organization. While fundraising efforts often focus on securing gifts, the long-term health of a nonprofit depends far more on sustaining connections with donors over time. A gift is only the beginning of a relationship, and the nonprofit's responsibility extends beyond merely asking for support. This is where the related concept of stewardship becomes central. Stewardship involves the ongoing process of nurturing relationships, showing appreciation, ensuring accountability, and demonstrating the impact of contributions. Together, relationship building and stewardship form the backbone of sustainable fundraising, transforming one-time donors into loyal supporters and advocates for the organization's mission.

At the core of donor relationship building is trust. Donors, whether individuals, corporations, or foundations, want to know that their contributions will be used responsibly and effectively. A nonprofit builds this trust through transparency, open communication, and consistent alignment between its stated mission and its actions. This means sharing not only successes but also challenges, giving donors a realistic view of the organization's work. Trust is also cultivated when donors feel listened to and respected, rather than simply treated as sources of money. By engaging donors as partners in the mission, nonprofits lay the foundation for meaningful, enduring relationships.

One of the earliest stages in donor relationship building is cultivation, which involves the deliberate process of identifying potential supporters and introducing them to the organization's mission and values. This phase requires research and intentional outreach, ensuring that the nonprofit is connecting with individuals whose values and priorities align with its own. Cultivation often begins with storytelling – sharing the nonprofit's history, impact, and vision for the future in ways that resonate emotionally. Donors are more likely to give when they feel personally connected to the cause, and this connection is best fostered through authentic and compelling communication. Cultivation is not about asking for a gift immediately but about laying the groundwork for a donor to feel invested in the organization's mission.

Once a donor makes a contribution, the relationship must be strengthened through stewardship. Stewardship is far more than sending a generic thank-you letter. It involves a sustained commitment to demonstrating gratitude, showing how contributions are making a difference, and engaging the donor in meaningful ways. Effective stewardship recognizes that donors give not only money but also trust and, in many cases, their personal reputation when they recommend an organization to others. Stewardship honors that trust by keeping the donor informed, appreciated, and connected. This may take the form of personalized thank-you notes, phone calls from staff or board members, or opportunities to see the nonprofit's work firsthand. Importantly, stewardship should not be transactional; it is about building a relationship based on shared purpose and mutual respect.

A critical part of stewardship is reporting impact. Donors want to see evidence that their gifts are achieving results, whether that means meals served, scholarships awarded, patients treated, or habitats preserved. Regular updates, such as annual reports, newsletters, and impact stories, provide concrete demonstrations of effectiveness. Some nonprofits invite donors to events or site visits where they can observe programs in action, deepening their personal connection to the mission. By linking contributions directly to outcomes, nonprofits reinforce the idea that donors are partners in creating change. This sense of partnership motivates donors to continue giving and often to increase their level of support over time.

Donor relationships also flourish when nonprofits engage in two-way communication. Too often, organizations treat communication as a one-sided process, sending appeals and updates without inviting feedback. Building authentic relationships means listening to donors, understanding their interests, and incorporating their perspectives into organizational planning where appropriate. This might include surveys, small group meetings, or one-on-one conversations with major donors. When donors feel heard, they are more likely to remain committed. Furthermore, feedback can help nonprofits tailor their engagement strategies, ensuring that donors feel connected in ways that resonate with them personally.

Another dimension of relationship building is personalization. Donors differ in their motivations, capacities, and preferred methods of engagement. Some may be driven by a passion for a particular program, while others may be motivated by tax considerations or the desire to leave a legacy. Some prefer to receive updates through digital platforms, while others appreciate phone calls or in-person visits. A nonprofit that takes the time to understand these preferences can tailor its stewardship efforts accordingly, demonstrating respect for the donor's individuality. For example, a younger donor might be more engaged through interactive social media campaigns, while an older donor might value a printed annual report accompanied by a personal letter.

Board members also play a role in donor relationship building and stewardship. Because board members are often community leaders, they bring credibility and networks that can be invaluable in cultivating and stewarding donors. Their involvement in thanking donors, attending events, and sharing the organization's story adds a personal dimension to stewardship. When donors see that board members are personally invested in the nonprofit, their confidence in the organization deepens. Staff and board collaboration in stewardship ensures that donor relationships are supported at multiple levels of the organization, reinforcing a culture of appreciation.

Stewardship is not limited to financial contributions; it extends to recognizing and nurturing non-financial gifts as well. Donors often contribute time, expertise, or in-kind resources, and acknowledging these forms of support is just as important as recognizing monetary gifts. Volunteers who are appreciated for their time may later become financial donors, and donors who are treated as valued advisors may strengthen their commitment. Expanding stewardship to encompass the full range of contributions underscores the nonprofit's holistic respect for its supporters.

Sustained stewardship also requires consistency. A nonprofit may do well with immediate thank-you efforts but lose momentum over time. Donors should be engaged regularly, not only when the organization needs money. This ongoing attention shows that the relationship is valued for more than financial reasons. Periodic updates, invitations to events, or simple check-ins help maintain the connection between gifts. Even small gestures, such as sending a holiday card or acknowledging a donor's birthday, can reinforce the sense of relationship. Consistent stewardship builds loyalty, transforming donors into long-term partners.

An important aspect of donor relationships and stewardship is the concept of donor retention. Acquiring new donors is costly and time-consuming, while retaining existing donors is far more efficient and sustainable. Stewardship plays a decisive role in donor retention, as donors who feel appreciated and informed are more likely to give again. Research consistently shows that one of the top reasons donors stop giving is a lack of acknowledgment or communication from the organization. By investing in stewardship practices that emphasize gratitude and transparency, nonprofits increase the likelihood of repeat giving, ensuring more stable revenue streams.

Technology has become an increasingly important tool in donor relationship building and stewardship. Donor management systems allow nonprofits to track giving histories, preferences, and engagement, enabling personalized communication at scale. Email campaigns, social media updates, and online donor portals create ongoing opportunities for interaction. At the same time, technology must be balanced with personal touches to avoid making donors feel like numbers in a database. The most effective stewardship strategies combine the efficiency of technology with the warmth of human connection.

In conclusion, building donor relationships and practicing stewardship are intertwined processes that lie at the core of nonprofit sustainability. Relationship building begins with cultivating trust, aligning donor values with mission, and creating authentic connections. Stewardship sustains these relationships through gratitude, transparency, personalization, and ongoing engagement. Together, they transform one-time gifts into long-term partnerships, ensuring both financial stability and deeper community impact. By viewing donors not merely as sources of revenue but as vital partners in achieving social good, nonprofits create a culture of appreciation and accountability that strengthens their mission. Stewardship, then, is not an afterthought to fundraising but a fundamental practice that elevates donor relationships into enduring collaborations, securing the resources and trust needed to create lasting change.

Donor Value

Donor value is a key fundraising concept that refers to the total benefit a donor provides to a nonprofit organization over the lifetime of their engagement, typically measured in financial contributions, loyalty, advocacy, and personal involvement. It encompasses more than just monetary donations, including intangible factors such as the donor's influence, connections, volunteer efforts, and ability to attract other donors. Understanding donor value helps nonprofits recognize that each donor relationship carries different levels of strategic significance, enabling the organization to prioritize resources, time, and effort most effectively.

By assessing donor value, a nonprofit can tailor its standard of donor care. Rather than treating all donors uniformly, effective nonprofits provide varying levels of attention, recognition, stewardship, and personalization based on each donor's overall value to the organization. This approach does not imply treating lower-value donors poorly or neglecting them; rather, it means focusing extra energy, resources, and personalized attention on those donors who bring the greatest sustained benefit to the organization's mission. Such targeted stewardship ensures that high-value donors receive the deeper engagement and personalized attention necessary to maintain and grow their support. At the same time, this approach allows nonprofits to efficiently steward lower-value donors using scaled and automated approaches, ensuring they remain informed and connected while managing limited organizational resources effectively.

Determining donor value involves analyzing several important factors beyond merely a donor's financial contribution amount. Financial generosity, frequency of giving, and consistency over time are key indicators of high donor value, but equally important are considerations such as advocacy potential, influence within the community, and willingness to actively promote the organization's mission to others. Nonprofits must assess a donor's potential lifetime value, considering their capacity and likelihood of future increased support, recurring giving commitments, legacy giving opportunities, and non-financial engagement, such as volunteerism, introductions to new donors, or promoting the organization through professional or social networks. By comprehensively evaluating donors according to these dimensions, nonprofits identify those donors who represent substantial strategic value.

Once donor value is assessed, nonprofits can adjust their standards of donor care accordingly, employing a carefully segmented approach that is tailored to the specific value each donor group represents. Donors demonstrating the highest levels of lifetime value and strategic importance require greater, more personalized stewardship and relationship management. For these donors, nonprofits should deliver customized communication, individualized attention, exclusive involvement opportunities, personalized updates, invitations to special events, and direct interactions with senior organizational leadership. These actions convey genuine respect and appreciation for their generosity and sustained commitment, building stronger emotional connections that reinforce loyalty and encourage continued, growing support.

For instance, a high-value donor might receive personal phone calls or handwritten thank-you notes from the executive director after every major contribution, be invited to private events featuring intimate discussions about the organization's impact, or receive customized reports explicitly outlining the difference their generosity has made. Special recognition opportunities, such as membership in exclusive donor societies, naming opportunities, or lifetime giving awards, also reinforce to these high-value donors that their significant contributions are deeply valued. Personalized stewardship at this level helps cultivate emotional bonds and secure sustained, long-term commitment, ultimately maximizing the donor's lifetime value and benefit to the organization.

Mid-level donors, while still critically important, may receive slightly less intensive care. Nonprofits can use strategic communication that feels individualized but may involve greater reliance on targeted emails, personalized mailings, or invitations to donor appreciation events designed specifically for mid-tier contributors. Mid-level donors benefit from periodic personalized interactions, occasional personal outreach from key staff, and clear, relevant updates on program successes that are funded by their contributions. These gestures reinforce ongoing engagement, nurture relationships, and strategically position mid-level donors for potential future progression to higher giving tiers.

Lower-value donors, who may contribute smaller amounts less frequently or demonstrate less direct engagement, still require respectful, appreciative, and consistent stewardship, but with fewer resources allocated to them individually. Effective nonprofit practice at this level typically involves scalable, cost-effective strategies such as group-oriented email newsletters, digital impact updates, social media communications, and automated acknowledgment letters. Organizations must ensure that lower-value donors feel recognized, informed, and genuinely appreciated, but should allocate fewer individualized staff interactions at this level. This ensures careful and strategic use of limited organizational resources, while maintaining a positive donor experience that is capable of fostering long-term engagement and potential future upgrades in giving levels.

As donor relationships evolve over time, nonprofits must consistently reassess and adjust their standards of donor care according to changing donor value. Regular tracking and analysis of donor giving patterns, response rates, engagement behaviors, and other metrics enable nonprofits to identify when a donor's value may be increasing or decreasing. Nonprofits must remain responsive and flexible, increasing stewardship and personalization when a donor shows increased generosity or heightened engagement, while appropriately adjusting the resource allocation if donor involvement wanes. This continual reassessment helps ensure that donor care remains relevant, impactful, and strategically appropriate at every stage of the donor lifecycle.

However, nonprofits must approach differentiated donor care thoughtfully, balancing the strategic allocation of resources with the ethical obligation to show gratitude, respect, and genuine appreciation to all donors, regardless of giving level. Differentiation in care should never result in disrespect, neglect, or a lack of appreciation for smaller or lower-value donors. Every donor relationship matters, and effective nonprofits understand the potential for donors to grow in their value over time. Even lower-value donors represent important opportunities for future development, referrals, volunteer engagement, and community advocacy. Therefore, nonprofits must adopt strategies that balance efficiency with genuine, respectful appreciation and engagement at every level.

In conclusion, donor value is a vital consideration guiding nonprofits in determining the appropriate level of donor care and stewardship. By strategically differentiating stewardship practices based on comprehensive assessments of donor value, nonprofits can effectively prioritize their resources, maximize donor retention, deepen relationships, and ensure long-term sustainability. This donor-centric approach creates stronger emotional connections, enhances donor loyalty, increases retention rates, and ultimately maximizes the lifetime value each donor provides to the organization.

EXAMPLE

Cedar Hill Community Hospital Foundation serves as the fundraising arm of a regional nonprofit hospital system that provides comprehensive medical care, advanced health services, and community wellness programs. The Cedar Hill Foundation periodically calculates donor value, assessing the lifetime potential value that each donor represents to the organization.

To illustrate how Cedar Hill calculates donor value, consider a representative donor named Mrs. Jennifer Thompson. Jennifer made her first contribution five years ago, donating $1,000 following exceptional treatment that her husband received at the hospital. Over the next four years, she contributed annually, with donations varying between $500 and $2,000. She also began volunteering, serving on the hospital foundation's special events committee, and recruited several friends who subsequently became donors.

When Cedar Hill Community Hospital Foundation calculates Jennifer's total donor value, they examine multiple critical elements, including her historical giving behavior, potential lifetime value, non-monetary involvement, and referral value. The initial step involves calculating her historical donor value. In Jennifer's case, Cedar Hill compiles her past giving amounts:

- Year one: $1,000
- Year two: $500
- Year three: $1,500
- Year four: $2,000
- Year five: $1,000

Total historical donor value for Jennifer over five years equals $6,000.

Next, Cedar Hill calculates Jennifer's average annual gift, an important metric often used in estimating future donor value. Over five years, she contributed a total of $6,000, meaning her average annual donation is calculated as:

$$\$6,000 \div 5 \text{ years} = \$1,200 \text{ per year}$$

Having established Jennifer's average gift, Cedar Hill then estimates her potential future life-time donor value. They consider her age, income, philanthropic propensity, relationship history with the organization, and affinity for their mission. Suppose Jennifer, currently aged 55, expresses ongoing strong interest in the hospital's mission. Cedar Hill estimates conservatively that she may actively support them at a similar rate for at least another 15 years. Using her average annual giving amount of $1,200, they project her potential future contributions as follows:

$$\$1,200 \times 15 \text{ years} = \$18,000 \text{ projected future lifetime value}$$

Combining historical giving ($6,000) with estimated future giving ($18,000), Jennifer's total lifetime monetary donor value is therefore projected at approximately $24,000.

However, the Foundation recognizes that true donor value extends beyond monetary contributions alone. Therefore, they assess and quantify the additional non-financial contributions Jennifer makes, particularly her volunteer service. Over five years, Jennifer volunteers approximately 40 hours per year, totaling 200 hours. Cedar Hill assigns an estimated financial value to volunteer hours using the nationally recognized standard value (e.g., approximately $30/hour, a common value used by nonprofits to reflect volunteer contributions):

$$200 \text{ hours} \times \$30/\text{hour} = \$6,000 \text{ estimated volunteer contribution value}$$

Additionally, Cedar Hill considers the value Jennifer generates through advocacy, referrals, and introductions to other potential donors. Jennifer has referred three new donors to Cedar Hill, each contributing $2,500 in total thus far, totaling $7,500 in referral-based donor value to date. Cedar Hill conservatively estimates Jennifer may continue making occasional referrals in coming years, potentially adding another $5,000 in future referral-based value.

Summing these various elements provides Cedar Hill with a comprehensive calculation of Jennifer's overall donor value, both monetary and non-monetary:

- Historical monetary giving: $6,000
- Projected future monetary giving (next 15 years): $18,000
- Volunteer service value (200 hours): $6,000
- Referral-based giving value (actual and projected): $12,500

This brings Jennifer's total estimated comprehensive donor value to approximately $42,500.

This thorough calculation significantly influences the Foundation's stewardship and donor care strategy for Jennifer. Given her high overall donor value, Cedar Hill provides her with personalized, high-touch donor stewardship, including invitations to exclusive donor events, periodic personal phone calls or visits from senior foundation leadership, and targeted communications tailored specifically to her interests and preferences.

By calculating donor value in this detailed manner, Cedar Hill Community Hospital Foundation strategically identifies donors whose lifetime engagement warrants enhanced attention, personalized stewardship, and additional resources. Such careful calculations of donor value inform strategic planning and resource allocation, guiding the nonprofit's approach to donor relations and ensuring that valuable supporters remain engaged and committed for the long term.

Online Fundraising and Crowdfunding

Online fundraising and crowdfunding have transformed the way nonprofit organizations secure resources to fulfill their missions. Where traditional fundraising methods often centered on in-person events, direct mail, or one-on-one donor cultivation, digital technologies have expanded the reach and efficiency of fundraising efforts. Today, nonprofits can connect with supporters across the globe, telling their stories through online platforms and inspiring individuals to give directly from their smartphones or computers. This shift has democratized philanthropy, allowing people of all ages and income levels to participate in charitable giving. At the same time, it has created new opportunities and challenges for nonprofits, requiring them to rethink their strategies, communication styles, and engagement methods to succeed in the digital landscape.

Online fundraising encompasses a wide variety of digital strategies, including donation portals on nonprofit websites, social media campaigns, email appeals, text-to-give programs, and peer-to-peer fundraising platforms. These tools allow nonprofits to reach audiences far beyond their immediate geographic communities. A small organization working in a rural area, for instance, can attract supporters from across the world if its message resonates. The accessibility and convenience of online giving lower barriers to participation, enabling donors to give with just a few clicks. For nonprofits, online fundraising also provides data and analytics that help track donor behavior, measure campaign effectiveness, and refine strategies over time.

Crowdfunding has emerged as one of the most distinctive forms of online fundraising. Unlike traditional campaigns, which typically rely on established donors or institutional grants, crowdfunding leverages broad networks of individuals who each contribute relatively small amounts toward a specific goal. Platforms such as GoFundMe, GlobalGiving, and Kickstarter for nonprofit projects provide the infrastructure for these campaigns, while social media helps spread the message. Crowdfunding is especially effective for time-bound projects, emergency relief efforts, or campaigns that lend themselves to compelling storytelling. Donors are attracted to the immediacy and specificity of crowdfunding goals, such as raising funds to build a school, provide clean water to a village, or cover medical expenses for a community member in need.

The strength of online fundraising and crowdfunding lies in storytelling. Nonprofits that succeed in this space craft narratives that connect emotionally with potential donors. Photos, videos, and testimonials from beneficiaries humanize abstract causes, making them relatable and urgent. For example, a nonprofit working on animal rescue may post videos of animals being rehabilitated, while a health organization may share stories of individuals whose lives have been transformed through medical care funded by donations. The digital medium allows these stories to be shared widely and rapidly, often going viral when they resonate strongly. In this way, storytelling not only secures immediate donations but also raises awareness and builds long-term community support.

Social media platforms amplify the reach of online fundraising and crowdfunding efforts. Nonprofits can use Facebook, Instagram, TikTok, LinkedIn, and Twitter to share updates, highlight progress, and create interactive campaigns. Facebook and Instagram in particular have integrated fundraising tools that allow users to create birthday fundraisers or donate directly through the platform. These features turn supporters into advocates, extending the nonprofit's reach to their networks of friends and followers. Peer-to-peer fundraising takes this concept even further, as individuals create their own mini-campaigns on behalf of the nonprofit, encouraging their personal networks to donate. This not only raises funds but also expands awareness exponentially, as each participant becomes an ambassador for the cause.

Despite the opportunities, online fundraising and crowdfunding also present challenges. One issue is the saturation of digital spaces with countless appeals for donations. Donors are bombarded with requests, making it difficult for any single campaign to stand out. To address this, nonprofits must invest in creativity, developing campaigns that are visually appealing, emotionally engaging, and easy to share. Another challenge is donor trust. Online donors may hesitate to give if they are uncertain whether the nonprofit is legitimate or whether the funds will be used effectively. Nonprofits must therefore prioritize transparency, providing clear information about their mission, financial accountability, and the specific use of funds raised through campaigns.

Retention is another challenge in online fundraising. While digital platforms are effective at attracting first-time donors, many of these donors give once and never return. Nonprofits must therefore integrate stewardship practices into their online strategies, following up with thank-you messages, impact reports, and ongoing communication. Personalized emails, social media shoutouts, and updates about how donations are making a difference can transform one-time donors into recurring supporters. The key lies in making donors feel like valued partners rather than anonymous contributors. This requires the thoughtful integration of traditional relationship-building techniques into digital contexts.

Online fundraising and crowdfunding also provide nonprofits with valuable data. Digital platforms collect information on donor demographics, giving amounts, campaign performance, and engagement levels. Nonprofits can analyze this data to identify patterns, segment donors, and tailor future campaigns. For example, analytics might reveal that younger donors respond more to video content shared on Instagram, while older donors are more responsive to email appeals. This information allows nonprofits to optimize their efforts, allocating resources to the most effective channels and messages. However, data management requires technical capacity and attention to privacy concerns, as donors expect their information to be secure and used responsibly.

Crowdfunding, while powerful, requires careful planning. A successful campaign often demands significant preparation, including setting realistic goals, creating compelling multimedia content, and developing a marketing plan for outreach. Launching the campaign is only the beginning; ongoing engagement throughout the campaign period is crucial. Regular updates on progress, recognition of donors, and reminders to share the campaign keep momentum going. Many successful crowdfunding efforts employ deadlines and visible progress bars, which create urgency and encourage participation. After the campaign, follow-up stewardship is essential to maintain credibility and foster long-term relationships with new supporters.

The cost-effectiveness of online fundraising and crowdfunding is another advantage, especially for smaller nonprofits. Compared to the expenses of hosting a gala or producing direct mail campaigns, digital campaigns can often be launched with relatively low overhead. However, they do require investment in digital infrastructure, such as a user-friendly website, secure payment systems, and staff or consultants with expertise in digital marketing. Organizations that neglect these investments risk poorly executed campaigns that fail to inspire confidence or generate results.

Looking forward, online fundraising and crowdfunding are likely to become even more central to nonprofit strategies. Advances in technology, such as mobile payment apps, artificial intelligence-driven donor personalization, and virtual reality storytelling, will open new possibilities for engagement. Younger generations, who are digital natives, expect nonprofits to have strong online presences and to provide seamless giving experiences. They also value transparency and impact reporting, which digital tools can deliver effectively. To remain competitive, nonprofits must continue to innovate, experiment with new platforms, and integrate digital fundraising into their broader development strategies.

In conclusion, online fundraising and crowdfunding have reshaped the nonprofit sector by making giving more accessible, immediate, and participatory. They provide nonprofits with powerful tools to reach global audiences, tell compelling stories, and mobilize broad-based support for specific projects and causes. While challenges such as donor saturation, retention, and trust must be addressed, the benefits of digital fundraising are undeniable. With careful planning, transparency, creativity, and stewardship, nonprofits can harness the full potential of online fundraising and crowdfunding. These strategies not only generate resources but also build communities of engaged supporters, ensuring that nonprofits can continue to advance their missions in an increasingly digital world.

Tip: Remarketing is a digital marketing strategy used to re-engage visitors who have previously interacted with a website but left without completing a desired action, such as making a donation. Their interaction can be tracked through digital tools such as Google Ads, Facebook Pixel, or email automation platforms. Once identified, a visitor can be included in a remarketing audience. From there, the nonprofit can deploy targeted marketing efforts to bring them back, such as email campaigns, social media ads, and display ads. In essence, remarketing keeps a nonprofit's mission in front of potential donors and reinforces the reasons why they initially engaged with the site.

Ethics and Legal Issues in Fundraising

Nonprofit fundraising is central to the survival and growth of organizations that serve the public good. Because nonprofits rely heavily on donations from individuals, corporations, foundations, and governments, the way in which they solicit and manage these funds carries enormous ethical and legal weight. Donors entrust nonprofits with financial resources on the assumption that they will be used responsibly, transparently, and in alignment with the organization's mission. Any breach of that trust can result in reputational harm, the loss of funding, and even legal consequences. The ethics and legal issues surrounding nonprofit fundraising therefore form a delicate balance between maximizing resources and ensuring integrity, accountability, and compliance.

Ethics in fundraising goes beyond simply following the law. It involves adhering to standards of honesty, respect, and fairness in donor relationships and fundraising practices. The Association of Fundraising Professionals has promulgated widely recognized ethical guidelines, emphasizing transparency, accountability, and the primacy of donor intent. Ethical fundraising requires nonprofits to represent their mission truthfully, avoid misleading claims about the use of funds, and ensure that solicitations are free of coercion or manipulation. For example, overstating the percentage of donations that go directly to programs, or exaggerating the impact of contributions, undermines trust and violates ethical norms even if it skirts the boundaries of legality.

One of the most important ethical issues in nonprofit fundraising is donor intent. When donors give money, they often earmark it for specific purposes, such as scholarships, disaster relief, or research. Ethically and legally, nonprofits must honor these restrictions and ensure that the funds are applied as promised. Misusing restricted funds, even inadvertently, constitutes a breach of trust and can lead to lawsuits or regulatory intervention. For unrestricted donations, nonprofits still carry an ethical responsibility to ensure that funds are managed prudently and in ways that directly support the mission. Transparency in communicating how donations are allocated (whether to programs, operations, or fundraising expenses) is essential to maintaining donor confidence.

Another key ethical issue is donor recognition and influence. Nonprofits must strike a balance between showing appreciation for major donors and maintaining independence in decision-making. Accepting large gifts from individuals or corporations whose values conflict with the mission can create ethical dilemmas. For instance, a health-focused nonprofit might face scrutiny if it accepts donations from a tobacco or alcohol company. Similarly, allowing donors to dictate organizational policies or programs risks compromising mission integrity. Ethical fundraising requires organizations to establish clear gift acceptance policies that outline what types of contributions they will or will not accept and under what conditions. These policies protect the nonprofit from undue influence while ensuring consistency in decision-making.

Legal issues in nonprofit fundraising vary depending on jurisdiction, but several common areas require attention. One of the most basic is compliance with charitable solicitation laws. In many states and countries, nonprofits must register with regulatory authorities before soliciting donations from the public. These laws are designed to protect donors from fraud and ensure accountability. A failure to register properly can result in fines, penalties, or the suspension of fundraising activities. Moreover, nonprofits that solicit across state or national lines must understand and comply with multiple regulatory frameworks, which can be complex and resource-intensive.

Tax law also plays a central role in nonprofit fundraising. In the United States, for example, donations to organizations with 501(c)(3) status are tax-deductible, but only if the nonprofit complies with specific requirements. Nonprofits must provide accurate donation receipts, particularly for large gifts or in-kind contributions, so that donors can claim their deductions legally. The mismanagement of receipts, exaggeration of gift values, or failure to disclose quid pro quo arrangements (where donors receive goods or services in exchange for contributions) can result in IRS penalties and the loss of tax-exempt status. Similarly, nonprofits must avoid excessive lobbying or political activities, as engaging in these beyond permissible limits can jeopardize their tax-exempt designation.

The issue of transparency in financial reporting bridges both ethics and legality. Nonprofits are generally required to file annual reports or tax forms, such as the IRS Form 990 in the United States, which disclose revenue, expenses, and executive compensation. These reports are public documents and serve as key tools for accountability. Nonprofits have both a legal duty and an ethical obligation to ensure accuracy and honesty in these reports. Inflating program expenses or obscuring fundraising costs may mislead donors into believing their gifts are used more efficiently than they actually are. Ethical fundraising requires candor about administrative and fundraising expenses, even if such disclosures make the organization less competitive in attracting donations.

Another important legal issue involves donor privacy and data protection. Online fundraising, crowdfunding, and digital donor management systems collect vast amounts of personal data, including credit card information, contact details, and giving histories. Nonprofits are legally obligated to safeguard this data and comply with privacy laws such as the General Data Protection Regulation (GDPR) in the European Union or state-specific laws like the California Consumer Privacy Act (CCPA). Ethically, nonprofits must also respect donor preferences regarding communication and data use. Sharing or selling donor lists without consent violates both trust and, in some cases, the law. Establishing clear privacy policies and secure data systems is therefore critical to both compliance and ethical stewardship.

The rise of professional fundraisers and consultants also raises ethical and legal considerations. It is generally considered unethical for fundraisers to work on commission, as this creates incentives to pressure donors or prioritize short-term gains over long-term relationships. Some jurisdictions even prohibit commission-based compensation for fundraisers. Nonprofits must ensure that their contracts with fundraising professionals align with ethical standards and comply with applicable laws. Transparency about how much is spent on fundraising, including fees for outside consultants, is also essential to maintaining donor trust.

Accountability in stewardship further highlights the intersection of ethics and legality. Donors expect nonprofits to provide regular updates on how their contributions are making an impact. Failure to do so may not always be illegal, but it is ethically problematic. Moreover, misrepresenting outcomes or fabricating success stories to attract or retain donors crosses into fraud, with serious legal consequences. Nonprofits should therefore commit to honest, evidence-based reporting, even when results fall short of expectations. This honesty builds long-term credibility, even if it risks disappointing donors in the short term.

Conflicts of interest also present ethical challenges in fundraising. For example, if a board member stands to benefit financially from a contract with a donor or vendor, the integrity of fundraising decisions can be questioned. Most nonprofit governance structures require the disclosure of such conflicts and recusal from related decision-making. Ethically, nonprofits must go beyond minimum compliance, cultivating a culture of transparency where potential conflicts are addressed openly. By doing so, they protect both their reputation and their ability to attract funding.

In addition to these concerns, cultural sensitivity is increasingly recognized as an ethical dimension of nonprofit fundraising. Appeals that exploit stereotypes, use sensationalized images of suffering, or perpetuate unequal power dynamics between donors and beneficiaries may raise money in the short term but undermine dignity and respect in the long run. Ethical fundraising calls for campaigns that honor the voices and agency of those served, presenting them as partners in change rather than passive recipients of charity. This approach aligns fundraising with the values of equity and justice that many nonprofits espouse.

In conclusion, ethics and legal issues in nonprofit fundraising are deeply intertwined, requiring organizations to navigate a complex landscape of regulations, accountability standards, and moral obligations. Legally, nonprofits must comply with solicitation laws, tax requirements, financial reporting standards, and data privacy rules. Ethically, they must prioritize honesty, respect donor intent, safeguard independence, and communicate transparently about the use of funds and impact achieved. Beyond compliance, nonprofits that embrace high ethical standards build enduring trust, which is the most valuable currency in fundraising. By aligning their practices with both the letter of the law and the spirit of ethical responsibility, nonprofits ensure not only their financial sustainability but also their credibility and legitimacy as agents of social good.

Diversifying Funding Streams

Diversifying funding streams is one of the most important financial strategies a nonprofit can pursue to ensure its long-term stability, sustainability, and resilience. Nonprofits exist to serve communities, advance causes, and fill societal gaps often overlooked by government and private industry. Yet, their ability to achieve these missions is highly dependent on financial resources. Too often, they rely heavily on one or two major sources of income, such as government grants, a handful of large donors, or annual fundraising events. While these sources may provide short-term security, overdependence exposes nonprofits to significant risk. If a grant is not renewed, a donor withdraws support, or an event underperforms, the nonprofit's programs and services may be jeopardized. Diversification of funding is not merely a financial safeguard; it is also a way to strengthen independence, foster innovation, and deepen community engagement.

One of the primary reasons nonprofits must diversify their funding is the inherent unpredictability of revenue sources. Government funding, for example, is often subject to shifting political priorities, budget cuts, and changes in administration. A nonprofit that relies predominantly on federal or state contracts can find itself vulnerable to forces beyond its control. Similarly, corporate sponsorships may be withdrawn if companies face financial pressures or alter their philanthropic strategies. Even individual giving can fluctuate depending on broader economic conditions, as donors may reduce contributions during recessions or personal financial hardship. By cultivating multiple funding streams, a nonprofit mitigates the risk of sudden financial shortfalls. The loss of one stream can be offset by the stability of others, allowing the organization to continue operations without severe disruption.

Diversification also supports organizational independence. When a nonprofit depends too heavily on one source of funding, it may feel pressured to shape its programs or priorities around the expectations of that funder, rather than staying true to its mission. For example, a nonprofit reliant on a government grant may be constrained by restrictive reporting requirements or narrow program guidelines. Similarly, a major donor might attempt to influence organizational decisions in exchange for financial support. A more diversified funding base allows nonprofits to maintain greater autonomy, ensuring that mission and community needs remain at the center of their decision-making rather than external pressures. Independence enhances credibility with stakeholders and strengthens the nonprofit's reputation as a mission-driven entity.

From a strategic perspective, diversified funding also encourages innovation and adaptability. Different funding sources open doors to new partnerships, ideas, and constituencies. For instance, earned income strategies such as social enterprises or fee-for-service programs allow nonprofits to develop entrepreneurial approaches that generate unrestricted revenue. Online fundraising and crowdfunding campaigns engage younger, tech-savvy audiences, while membership programs create a loyal community of supporters. Grants, sponsorships, and events each bring unique opportunities for visibility and collaboration. By exploring varied revenue streams, nonprofits can innovate not only in fundraising but also in program delivery, finding creative ways to link mission with revenue generation.

Another benefit of diversifying funding is the strengthening of donor relationships and community trust. A nonprofit that engages multiple groups of stakeholders creates a broader base of support. This inclusivity fosters a sense of shared ownership of the mission. Donors are more likely to contribute when they see others investing as well, and a diversified funding profile signals organizational stability and professionalism. It reassures stakeholders that the nonprofit is not overly dependent on one source of support and can weather financial challenges. This confidence can, in turn, attract new donors and partners, creating a positive cycle of support.

Financial sustainability is perhaps the most tangible outcome of diversification. Nonprofits with multiple funding streams are better positioned to build reserves, manage cash flow, and plan for the long term. Rather than lurching from one fundraising crisis to another, they can develop strategic plans with confidence, knowing that their revenue is not tied to a single vulnerable source. Diversified funding allows for flexibility in addressing emerging needs, expanding programs, or investing in capacity-building. It transforms fundraising from a reactive scramble into a proactive, strategic function that supports growth and resilience.

In conclusion, the need for nonprofits to diversify funding streams cannot be overstated. Reliance on a single or limited source of income exposes organizations to financial instability, external influence, and mission drift. By cultivating a balanced mix of revenue sources, including individual giving, grants, corporate partnerships, events, earned income, and digital fundraising, nonprofits can protect themselves against revenue volatility while enhancing independence, credibility, and innovation. Diversification not only secures financial sustainability but also strengthens the organization's relationship with its community, ensuring that it can continue to serve its mission regardless of external challenges. In a world of economic uncertainty and evolving donor expectations, diversified funding is not a luxury but a necessity for any nonprofit seeking to thrive over the long term.

Summary

Of the many priorities facing a nonprofit, fundraising is perhaps the most essential. Without a reasonably steady inflow of cash, it will be extremely difficult for any nonprofit to fulfill its mission. Consequently, having a competent fundraising team is essential to the organization's success. This team should focus on multiple revenue sources, long-term relationships with donors, and funding sources that can be used to pay for the administrative functions of the organization, rather than just its programs. With such a capability in place, any nonprofit has a fighting chance at serving its targeted community for an extended period of time.

Chapter 8
Risk Management

Introduction

The financial situation of many nonprofits can safely be described as "lean," where any unexpected loss could shut them down. These entities have few cash reserves, and so even a modest unexpected loss could have dire consequences. However, there are ways to protect a nonprofit from this situation. In this chapter, we discuss the process of identifying risks, altering operations to mitigate most of them, and using insurance to offset the remaining issues. The result should be a significantly more stable nonprofit.

Identifying Operational and Strategic Risks

Identifying operational and strategic risks is a crucial element of managing a nonprofit organization. While nonprofits differ from for-profit enterprises in their missions and objectives, they share the same exposure to uncertainty, disruption, and the potential for failure if risks are not anticipated and managed. What makes risk identification especially important for nonprofits is the delicate balance they must maintain between fulfilling their mission, stewarding donor resources responsibly, and remaining compliant with regulatory requirements. Because nonprofits often operate with limited financial reserves and rely on external funding sources, even minor risks can have outsized impacts. Recognizing and analyzing both operational and strategic risks equips nonprofit leaders to protect an organization's sustainability.

Operational risks are those that affect the day-to-day functioning of a nonprofit. They often involve internal systems, processes, and resources that enable the organization to deliver programs and services. A common operational risk lies in financial management. Nonprofits frequently depend on restricted funds, grants, and donations, and poor oversight of these resources can lead to misallocation, cash flow crises, or even allegations of fraud. Weak internal controls, inadequate accounting systems, or insufficient staff training exacerbate these risks. An organization that fails to pay attention to its financial processes may find itself unable to meet payroll, fund programs, or comply with donor requirements, thereby eroding trust and jeopardizing future support.

Human resources also represent a significant operational risk. Many nonprofits rely heavily on a combination of paid staff and volunteers. High staff turnover, inadequate succession planning, and a lack of volunteer management can disrupt continuity and diminish organizational capacity. Nonprofits may also struggle to attract and retain qualified employees due to limited compensation budgets, leaving them vulnerable to skill gaps in critical areas such as program evaluation, technology, or compliance. For volunteers, the absence of clear roles, training, and recognition can lead to disengagement, damaging both morale and the organization's ability to deliver services. Furthermore, risks related to workplace culture, discrimination, or harassment can expose the nonprofit to legal liability while undermining its mission-driven values.

Technology and data management create another layer of operational risk. As nonprofits increasingly rely on donor databases, online fundraising platforms, and digital communication tools, they become vulnerable to cybersecurity threats, data breaches, and system failures. Donor data must be protected to comply with privacy laws and to preserve trust. Outdated technology can hamper efficiency and limit the ability to analyze data for strategic decision-making, while overreliance on a single system without adequate backups can leave the organization paralyzed in the event of a failure. Nonprofits must also contend with the challenge of integrating technology into operations when budgets and staff expertise are limited, often leaving them lagging behind best practices.

Program delivery risks are central to operational concerns. Nonprofits exist to provide services, advocate for causes, or support communities, and any disruption to program delivery threatens their reason for existence. Risks in this area may include insufficient funding to sustain programs, ineffective program design, lack of measurable outcomes, or dependency on external partners whose failures ripple into the nonprofit's operations. For example, a nonprofit offering health services may depend on local government funding or partnerships with clinics, and if these partners fail to deliver, the nonprofit's programs may collapse. Failure to monitor and evaluate program effectiveness also carries reputational risk, as donors increasingly demand evidence of impact.

Legal and regulatory compliance is an additional operational concern. Nonprofits must navigate a complex web of tax regulations, charitable solicitation laws, employment laws, and reporting requirements. Noncompliance can lead to fines, loss of tax-exempt status, or reputational damage that undermines donor confidence. Risks are heightened when compliance responsibilities are concentrated in a small staff or when board members lack adequate training in fiduciary duties. Even well-meaning nonprofits can stumble if they do not invest in compliance systems and education, exposing themselves to avoidable operational disruptions.

While operational risks are internal and immediate, strategic risks are broader in scope, relating to the long-term direction, positioning, and sustainability of the nonprofit. One of the most significant strategic risks is overreliance on a narrow funding base. A nonprofit that depends too heavily on one government grant, a single corporate sponsor, or a handful of major donors places its future in jeopardy should those revenue sources disappear. The risk is not only financial but also strategic, as dependency can create pressure to align programs with funder priorities rather than community needs or organizational mission. Diversification of funding streams is therefore a strategic imperative, but it requires foresight and investment.

Mission drift represents another major strategic risk. Nonprofits may be tempted to chase funding opportunities that do not align perfectly with their mission, especially when faced with financial pressure. While this may provide short-term relief, it can erode organizational focus, dilute impact, and confuse stakeholders about the nonprofit's identity. Mission drift undermines credibility and can alienate donors and beneficiaries alike. Strategic discipline, grounded in clear values and objectives, is essential to resisting this risk.

Reputation risk is closely tied to strategy as well. A nonprofit's credibility is one of its most valuable assets, and any perception of mismanagement, inefficiency, or misconduct can be devastating. Negative media coverage, scandals involving board members or executives, or dissatisfaction among beneficiaries can damage a nonprofit's reputation and cause donors to withdraw their support. In an age of social media, even small missteps can escalate quickly into crises. Nonprofits must proactively manage their reputations by ensuring transparency, demonstrating accountability, and fostering open communication with stakeholders.

External environmental changes also pose strategic risks. Nonprofits operate in contexts shaped by political, economic, social, and technological forces. Policy changes can eliminate funding streams or impose new restrictions on operations. Economic downturns reduce donations and increase the demand for services, placing nonprofits in a double bind. Social changes, such as shifting donor demographics or evolving community needs, can render programs outdated or less relevant. Technology advances create opportunities but also require adaptation, and nonprofits that fail to keep pace risk losing their competitive edge in attracting donors and engaging communities.

Leadership and governance risks are also strategic in nature. Boards of directors are responsible for setting direction, providing oversight, and ensuring accountability. Weak governance structures, disengaged board members, or a lack of strategic vision leave nonprofits vulnerable to stagnation or mismanagement. A lack of succession planning for executive leadership compounds the problem, as transitions can destabilize the organization. Strong, engaged governance is vital to identifying and addressing risks before they escalate, and a weak board can itself become a strategic liability.

Strategic risks also emerge in the area of partnerships and collaborations. Many nonprofits rely on alliances with other organizations, government entities, or businesses to expand their reach and impact. While partnerships can be beneficial, they also create risks if goals are misaligned, expectations are unclear, or partners fail to uphold their commitments. A nonprofit's reputation can be damaged by association with a poorly performing partner, or its resources may be stretched thin in collaborations that do not yield results. Careful vetting and clear agreements are essential to managing these risks.

Identifying both operational and strategic risks requires intentional processes. Nonprofits must embed risk assessment into their culture and governance structures. This includes regular reviews of financial systems, program performance, technology infrastructure, and compliance obligations, as well as broader assessments of external trends, funding landscapes, and mission alignment. Risk identification should not be viewed solely as a defensive activity but as a proactive tool for strengthening organizational resilience and advancing mission impact. By anticipating risks, nonprofits can develop contingency plans, diversify their revenue sources, strengthen governance, and invest in staff and systems that reduce vulnerability.

In conclusion, operational and strategic risks are an inevitable part of nonprofit life. Operational risks, such as financial mismanagement, human resources challenges, technological vulnerabilities, program disruptions, and compliance fail-ures, threaten the day-to-day functioning of the organization. Strategic risks, including funding dependency, mission drift, reputational harm, external environmental shifts, governance weaknesses, and problematic partnerships, threaten long-term sustaina-bility and relevance. The identification of these risks is not a one-time exercise but a continuous process that requires vigilance, honesty, and foresight. By systematically identifying, analyzing, and preparing for operational and strategic risks, nonprofits safeguard their ability to serve communities, maintain donor trust, and achieve their missions over the long term.

Liability Risks for Directors and Officers

Liability risks for the directors and officers of nonprofit organizations are a serious concern, even though many people assume that the nonprofit status of an entity offers broad legal protection. Directors and officers play critical roles in guiding the organi-zation, setting policy, overseeing finances, and ensuring compliance with laws and ethical standards. Their responsibilities place them in positions of trust, and with that trust comes potential personal liability if they are found to have failed in their duties. While the nonprofit structure does provide some statutory protections, directors and officers are not immune from lawsuits or regulatory actions. Understanding the scope of liability risks helps nonprofit leaders take the necessary steps to minimize their exposure while fulfilling their governance responsibilities.

One of the primary areas of risk arises from fiduciary duties. Directors and offic-ers of a nonprofit are bound by three fiduciary duties (as described in an earlier chap-ter): the duty of care, the duty of loyalty, and the duty of obedience. The duty of care requires them to make informed decisions in the best interests of the organization, exercising the same prudence that a reasonable person would in similar circumstances. If directors fail to properly oversee finances, ignore red flags about misconduct, or approve contracts without due diligence, they could face liability for negligence. The duty of loyalty obligates directors to place the interests of the nonprofit above personal or financial gain. Conflicts of interest, such as directing contracts to businesses owned by board members or their relatives, can lead to both ethical breaches and legal liabil-ity. The duty of obedience requires directors to ensure that the organization remains true to its mission and complies with applicable laws and governing documents. Fail-ure to adhere to the nonprofit's stated purpose or violation of state or federal laws could result in personal liability for directors who sanctioned or ignored the behavior.

Employment-related issues present another significant liability risk. Nonprofit or-ganizations, like their for-profit counterparts, must comply with employment laws covering discrimination, harassment, wrongful termination, and wage and hour regu-lations. Directors and officers can be named personally in lawsuits alleging discrimi-natory practices, hostile work environments, or retaliatory actions against whistle-blowers. Even if they are not directly involved in day-to-day personnel decisions, board members may be held accountable if they fail to adopt proper policies, provide adequate oversight, or respond appropriately to complaints. With nonprofits often operating under resource constraints, the lack of dedicated human resources expertise can heighten these risks.

Financial oversight is also an area where liability exposure is high. Nonprofits depend on donor contributions, grants, and sponsorships, and directors are responsible for ensuring that these funds are properly managed. Mismanagement of restricted funds, misuse of grant money, or failure to file required financial reports can all lead to legal action. For example, directors may be held personally liable for unpaid payroll taxes, as the Internal Revenue Service can pursue individuals who are responsible for ensuring tax compliance. Similarly, a failure to comply with charitable solicitation laws, such as state registration requirements, can expose directors to penalties. While intentional fraud is less common, even unintentional missteps in financial management can result in costly investigations and reputational harm that implicate the board.

Another risk stems from regulatory compliance, particularly related to maintaining tax-exempt status. Nonprofits must adhere to strict rules prohibiting private inurement, excessive lobbying, and political campaigning. If directors approve activities that jeopardize the organization's tax-exempt status, they could be personally liable for penalties. For example, engaging in partisan political activities could trigger IRS sanctions and expose directors to liability for approving expenditures outside the legal limits. Directors must also ensure compliance with state laws governing nonprofit governance, reporting, and transparency. Ignorance of these requirements does not protect them from liability if regulators determine that governance failures occurred under their watch.

Litigation risk is another dimension that directors and officers must confront. Nonprofits are not immune from lawsuits, and directors can be named personally as defendants in cases alleging negligence, breach of duty, or mismanagement. Beneficiaries of services may bring claims if they feel harmed by the nonprofit's actions, vendors may sue over contract disputes, and donors may initiate litigation if funds are misused. While courts often apply the "business judgment rule" to protect directors who act in good faith and with reasonable care, this protection does not extend to gross negligence, fraud, or willful misconduct. Litigation, even when directors are ultimately not held liable, can be financially and emotionally draining, underscoring the importance of proactive risk management.

Reputational harm adds a further layer of liability risk. While not always resulting in personal financial exposure, reputational damage can have serious consequences for directors and officers. Allegations of mismanagement, conflicts of interest, or the misuse of funds can tarnish professional reputations and limit future opportunities for board service or employment. Directors who are associated with scandals, even indirectly, may find themselves facing personal scrutiny from donors, community members, and regulators. The risk to reputation is often as significant as legal liability, since it can deter qualified individuals from serving on nonprofit boards.

To mitigate liability risks, many nonprofits secure Directors and Officers (D&O) liability insurance. This insurance provides coverage for defense costs and damages in cases where directors and officers are sued for alleged wrongful acts in their capacity as board members or executives. While insurance does not cover intentional misconduct or fraud, it does provide an essential safety net for individuals who act in good faith but nonetheless become embroiled in litigation. Beyond insurance, strong governance practices are crucial in reducing risk. These include adopting clear conflict-of-interest policies, maintaining accurate records, providing regular financial oversight, and ensuring compliance with legal and regulatory requirements. Training for directors and officers on their fiduciary duties and emerging legal issues also plays an important preventive role.

Ultimately, the liability risks facing directors and officers of nonprofits highlight the seriousness of board service. While serving on a nonprofit board can be deeply rewarding, it is not without responsibilities and potential exposure. Directors and officers must approach their roles with diligence, integrity, and a commitment to continuous oversight. By understanding their fiduciary duties, ensuring financial and legal compliance, addressing employment and governance risks, and securing adequate insurance, they can reduce liability while advancing the nonprofit's mission effectively. The stakes are high not only for the individuals serving but also for the communities and causes that rely on strong nonprofit leadership.

In conclusion, nonprofit directors and officers face liability risks that stem from fiduciary duties, employment practices, financial oversight, regulatory compliance, litigation, and reputational exposure. These risks are heightened by the unique resource constraints and public accountability that characterize the nonprofit sector. However, with proactive governance, clear policies, strong oversight, and adequate insurance, directors and officers can manage these risks while fulfilling their responsibilities to the organization and its stakeholders. Recognizing and addressing liability risks is not simply a defensive measure; it is an essential component of responsible nonprofit leadership, one that safeguards both the individuals involved and the mission they serve.

Types of Insurance Needed by Nonprofits

Insurance is a vital component of risk management for nonprofit organizations, even though many nonprofits focus primarily on program delivery and fundraising rather than operational protections. Because nonprofits operate in a wide variety of sectors (health, education, arts, social services, advocacy, and more) their risk profiles differ significantly. Yet all nonprofits face potential legal, financial, and operational exposures that could disrupt their mission or even threaten their survival. Insurance provides a safety net against these exposures, transferring the financial consequences of certain risks to an insurer while allowing the nonprofit to continue operations. Understanding the types of insurance nonprofits need is therefore essential to protecting their people, assets, and reputations.

The most fundamental insurance for any nonprofit is general liability insurance. Often called "slip and fall" coverage, general liability protects the organization against claims of bodily injury or property damage caused by its operations, premises, or activities. For example, if a donor attending a fundraising event slips on a wet floor, general liability insurance would cover medical costs and potential legal claims. It also covers situations where nonprofit staff or volunteers accidentally damage third-party property while carrying out organizational activities. Without this basic coverage, a single accident could drain a nonprofit's limited resources and divert funds away from mission-driven programs.

Closely related is property insurance, which protects the nonprofit's physical assets such as office buildings, furniture, equipment, and supplies. Even nonprofits that lease their space may need property insurance to cover the contents inside, as landlords' policies typically do not extend to tenants' belongings. Property insurance provides compensation in cases of fire, theft, vandalism, or natural disasters, enabling the nonprofit to replace or repair damaged assets quickly. For nonprofits that rely on specialized equipment, such as servers for data management or musical instruments for an arts program, property insurance is especially critical. Business interruption coverage, often included with property policies, compensates for lost revenue if operations are suspended due to covered events, ensuring that payroll and other obligations can still be met.

As just noted, D&O liability insurance is another core coverage, protecting board members and senior executives from personal liability arising from their governance decisions. Claims against these parties might involve the mismanagement of funds, conflicts of interest, or failure to comply with regulations. Even if lawsuits are baseless, the cost of defense can be substantial. D&O insurance provides coverage for legal expenses and settlements, giving board members confidence to serve without fear that their personal assets will be at risk. This type of coverage is particularly important for attracting qualified, experienced individuals to nonprofit boards.

Employment practices liability insurance (EPLI) addresses another major risk area: employee and volunteer relations. Nonprofits, like any employer, face potential claims of discrimination, harassment, wrongful termination, or retaliation. These claims can be especially damaging for nonprofits, as they not only involve legal costs but also pose reputational risks that may affect donor confidence. Even organizations with strong policies and training programs cannot eliminate the possibility of claims. EPLI provides coverage for defense costs and damages, helping nonprofits navigate the complexities of employment law while protecting their reputations. Some policies also cover claims brought by volunteers, which is significant since many nonprofits depend heavily on volunteer labor.

Professional liability insurance, sometimes called errors and omissions (E&O) insurance, is essential for nonprofits that provide professional services such as counseling, healthcare, or education. This type of coverage protects against claims of negligence, errors, or omissions in the course of delivering services. For instance, a client of a nonprofit counseling center could allege harm due to advice received, or a patient could claim malpractice in a health services program. Even if the nonprofit ultimately prevails, the legal costs of defending such claims could be devastating. Professional liability insurance ensures that organizations can continue providing critical services without being derailed by litigation.

For nonprofits that own or operate vehicles, commercial auto insurance is necessary. This coverage protects against liability for accidents involving organizational vehicles, as well as damage to the vehicles themselves. Importantly, nonprofits also need non-owned and hired auto liability insurance to cover situations where employees or volunteers use their personal cars for organizational business. If a volunteer driving to deliver meals is involved in an accident, the nonprofit could be held liable, even if the vehicle is not owned by the organization. Non-owned auto liability ensures that such exposures are addressed, protecting both the nonprofit and its volunteers.

Workers' compensation insurance is another essential type of coverage, mandated by law in most jurisdictions. It provides medical benefits and wage replacement to employees injured on the job, while also protecting the nonprofit from lawsuits arising from workplace injuries. For nonprofits with paid staff, this coverage is non-negotiable. Some jurisdictions also require coverage for volunteers, or at least recommend it as a best practice. Providing workers' compensation not only fulfills legal obligations but also demonstrates the nonprofit's commitment to caring for its workforce.

Nonprofits must also consider cyber liability insurance, given the increasing reliance on digital platforms for fundraising, donor management, and program delivery. Cyber liability policies cover expenses related to data breaches, such as notification costs, credit monitoring for affected individuals, forensic investigations, and legal defense. They also address liability arising from the unauthorized release of donor or client data. Since nonprofits often collect sensitive personal and financial information, they are prime targets for cyberattacks, yet they frequently lack the sophisticated defenses of larger corporations. Cyber liability insurance provides a critical backstop against the financial and reputational fallout of such incidents.

Another important coverage is crime and fidelity insurance, which protects nonprofits against losses from employee or volunteer theft, fraud, or embezzlement. Unfortunately, nonprofits are not immune from internal misconduct, and their often lean internal controls make them vulnerable. A single act of financial fraud can devastate a small nonprofit's budget and erode donor trust. Fidelity coverage reimburses the organization for stolen funds or assets, ensuring that it can recover financially and maintain its operations.

Event insurance is also relevant for nonprofits that host fundraising galas, walks, festivals, or other gatherings. Special event policies provide liability coverage for accidents that occur during the event and may also cover cancellations due to unforeseen circumstances. Given that many nonprofits rely heavily on events for both revenue and visibility, protecting against the risks associated with large gatherings is essential. For example, if inclement weather forces the cancellation of a charity run, event insurance can cover the financial losses.

Some nonprofits may also require specialized insurance depending on their activities. For example, organizations working internationally may need travel insurance for staff and volunteers abroad, as well as political risk insurance to address instability in certain regions. Nonprofits running youth programs may need abuse and molestation coverage, which provides protection against claims of misconduct in sensitive environments. Environmental liability insurance may be relevant for nonprofits engaged in conservation work or those that own property where pollutants could be present. Tailoring coverage to the specific risk profile of the nonprofit ensures comprehensive protection.

Ultimately, the mix of insurance that a nonprofit needs depends on its size, scope, and activities. However, general liability, property, D&O, EPLI, professional liability, auto, workers' compensation, cyber, crime, and event insurance form the backbone of comprehensive coverage. Securing these policies requires thoughtful assessment of risks, often with the help of insurance brokers who specialize in the nonprofit sector. Nonprofits must also balance the cost of premiums with their limited budgets, making prioritization necessary. Yet the cost of being uninsured or underinsured in the face of a claim is often far greater than the investment in coverage.

In conclusion, insurance is a critical safeguard for nonprofits, protecting them from financial losses, legal exposure, and reputational damage. The types of insurance nonprofits need span from basic liability and property coverage to specialized policies addressing employment practices, professional services, cyber risks, and events. By carefully evaluating their activities and securing appropriate coverage, nonprofits can ensure that unforeseen risks do not derail their mission. Insurance is not simply an administrative expense but a strategic investment in resilience, sustainability, and the confidence of donors, staff, and the communities served. In an environment where resources are scarce and trust is paramount, comprehensive insurance coverage provides the stability that nonprofits need to focus on what matters most: advancing their mission and making a lasting impact.

Insurance Policy Terms and Conditions

When buying insurance, a nonprofit must be cognizant of the related contract terms and conditions, since they can greatly restrict the amount of coverage that a carrier is actually agreeing to. The net result of the following terms and conditions is that a carrier is limiting the extent of its maximum payout, avoiding certain high-loss events, and forcing buyers to participate to varying degrees in any losses incurred.

Indemnity

The terms of an insurance contract may state that the insurer will indemnify the insured party if there is a loss. An indemnity refers to a payment by the insurer for the monetary value of a loss, as defined by the related insurance contract. The amount of an indemnity does not exceed the monetary loss experienced by the insured party, since an excessive payment would be akin to a gambling win by the insured.

Deductibles

The typical insurance policy contains a deductible, which is an initial loss amount that must be absorbed by the insured party. There are several reasons why insurance companies impose a deductible, which are:

- *Frivolous claims avoidance*. The bulk of all losses incurred by an organization are quite small, and they would inundate insurers with these claims if the insurers were solely responsible for losses. The cost to investigate and pay these claims would be excessive. The deductible keeps these smaller claims from ever being filed.
- *Ownership of losses*. If insured entities can pass the full amount of losses on to their insurers, they have no reason to take action to avoid losses. By making

the insured parties responsible for smaller losses, there is a stronger incentive to avoid all types of losses.

Limit of Insurance

All insurance policies contain a limit of insurance, which is the maximum amount that the insurer will pay. This is needed by the insurer in order to avoid massive payouts due to catastrophic loss situations. Some of these limits of insurance are set quite low, so that the amounts paid out are inconsequential. If so, there may be little point in obtaining the insurance, since the amount of risk being passed off to the insurer is immaterial.

Coinsurance

There may be a coinsurance provision in an insurance policy. This provision is designed to penalize the insured party if it under-insures the value of property. Coinsurance is stated as a percentage. The following example illustrates the concept.

EXAMPLE

Evergreen Social Services owns its headquarters building, which has a replacement cost of $3,000,000. The organization's property insurance contains an 80% coinsurance clause, which means that the insured amount must be at least 80% of the replacement cost of the building, or $2,400,000. The actual amount insured is for $2,000,000. Since the insured value is less than 80% of its replacement value, a loss payout under the policy will be subjected to an under-reporting penalty.

The building subsequently suffers $500,000 of property damage. The amount paid to Evergreen by the insurer is calculated as follows:

$2,000,000 insured amount ÷ (80% coinsurance percentage × $3,000,000 replacement cost) × $500,000 loss

= $416,667

In essence, Evergreen pays an $83,333 penalty because it did not insure the full value of the property.

The most commonly-used coinsurance percentage is 80%. If the percentage is higher, the insurer is imposing a stricter standard on the insured entity to insure the full value of property.

Given the negative impact of the coinsurance provision, a nonprofit must routinely examine the values of its insured property to verify that adequate amounts of insurance are being carried. Otherwise, a loss could result in a significantly reduced payout by the insurer.

Exclusions

Insurance policies typically contain a lengthy list of exclusions. If losses are caused by one of these events, they are not covered by the insurance. The exact exclusions will vary by insurance policy, but may include the exclusions noted in the following table.

Sample Policy Exclusions

Earthquakes	Government seizure	War or sabotage
Flooding	Mold damage	Windstorm or hail
	Nuclear explosions or radiation	

Insurance Riders

An insurance rider is an adjustment to a basic insurance policy. A rider usually provides an additional benefit over what is described in the basic policy, in exchange for a fee payable to the insurer. A rider is not a standalone insurance product; it must be attached to a standard insurance policy. A rider is useful for tailoring an insurance policy to the precise needs of the insured entity. Examples of insurance riders are:

- *Life insurance.* An accelerated death benefit is added to the policy, so that a payout occurs when the policy holder is diagnosed with a terminal illness.
- *Directors and officers insurance.* A "tail" is added to the policy, so that the directors and officers receive coverage for several years following the normal termination of the policy.
- *Property insurance.* Additional coverage is provided for flooding, earthquakes, and fire damage, which may not be addressed by the basic policy.

Perils

Insurers may attempt to underwrite only a specific set of risks that they identify in the coverage; this is called named perils coverage. Since this type of coverage can exclude many types of risks, one should instead strive for all-perils coverage. Realistically, the cost of all-perils coverage may be so high that it is not attainable; if so, obtaining insurance devolves into an analysis of how to obtain the largest amount of named perils coverage for the lowest price.

Endorsements

Endorsements are attachments to a contract that either add to or restrict coverage. In essence, each endorsement is designed to adapt a boilerplate policy to the specific needs of the insured party.

Insurance Claim Problems

An insured party can have problems collecting from an insurer when there is a con-current cause of loss. This means that more than one peril was involved in a loss. For example, in a property claim, damage might have been caused by a combination of flooding and a windstorm. If so, coverage might have been provided for the windstorm peril but not the flooding peril. When coverage only applies to a sub-set of the perils causing damage, settlement of the related claim could be lengthy. A likely outcome is a negotiation between the insurer and insured party to arrive at a reduced settlement amount.

Another claim problem can arise when the insurance coverage provided by two insurers overlaps, so that either one could pay a claim. In this case, payment will even-tually occur, but may be delayed until the insurers reach an agreement regarding the proportions to be paid by each party.

Risk Mitigation Policies and Procedures

Risk mitigation is a fundamental responsibility for nonprofit organizations, given their often-limited resources, reliance on donor support, and accountability to multiple stakeholders. While risk cannot be eliminated entirely, nonprofits can implement pol-icies and procedures that reduce the likelihood of adverse events and minimize their impact. Effective risk mitigation requires both operational safeguards and strategic frameworks that protect the organization's people, finances, assets, and reputation. The following discussion examines the key policies and procedures nonprofits should adopt to build resilience and ensure that risks do not undermine their mission.

A cornerstone of nonprofit risk mitigation is the establishment of strong govern-ance policies. The board of directors plays a central role in overseeing the organiza-tion's strategic direction and fiduciary responsibilities. Policies that define board re-sponsibilities, conflict-of-interest standards, and ethical codes of conduct provide the foundation for good governance. A well-crafted conflict-of-interest policy ensures that board members disclose personal or financial interests that could compromise impartial decision-making. Similarly, adopting codes of ethics reinforces the non-profit's values and sets behavioral expectations for board members, staff, and volun-teers. Governance policies also include clear procedures for evaluating executive lead-ership, ensuring accountability at the highest level of management. By embedding oversight into governance structures, nonprofits reduce risks of mismanagement, mis-sion drift, and reputational harm.

Financial management policies are another critical area of risk mitigation. Non-profits are particularly vulnerable to financial mismanagement and fraud because they often rely on donations and grants, which must be stewarded with transparency. Poli-cies should include requirements for internal controls such as the segregation of du-ties, ensuring that no single individual has control over all aspects of financial trans-actions. Procedures for approving expenditures, reconciling accounts, and conducting periodic audits safeguard against errors and fraud. Budgeting and cash flow manage-ment policies provide a framework for aligning resources with program priorities and monitoring financial health. Investment policies, where applicable, should specify how funds may be invested to balance growth and safety. These financial safeguards not only reduce the risk of loss but also strengthen donor confidence and regulatory compliance.

Human resources policies are essential in managing risks associated with staff and volunteers. Employment-related claims are among the most common and costly risks for nonprofits. Adopting policies on equal employment opportunity, anti-discrimination, harassment prevention, and workplace safety ensures compliance with labor laws and fosters a positive work environment. Clear procedures for recruitment, performance evaluation, and disciplinary action help reduce liability by ensuring fairness and consistency. Volunteer management policies are equally important, as volunteers are integral to many nonprofits' operations. These policies should cover screening, training, supervision, and recognition, ensuring that volunteers are engaged appropriately and understand their responsibilities (see the following exhibit). Risk is further mitigated by maintaining clear job descriptions, documenting performance, and providing access to grievance mechanisms.

SAMPLE POLICIES RELATED TO VOLUNTEERS

1. Volunteer Screening and Background Checks
- Require applications, interviews, and references for all volunteers.
- Conduct background checks for volunteers working with vulnerable populations (children, elderly, disabled).
- Document screening processes to demonstrate due diligence.

2. Volunteer Code of Conduct
- Define expected behavior, including professionalism, confidentiality, and nondiscrimination.
- Establish rules for social media use when representing the organization.
- Require acknowledgment of the code as part of onboarding.

3. Confidentiality and Data Protection Policy
- Ensure volunteers understand their obligations to protect donor, client, and organizational data.
- Limit volunteer access to sensitive information to a "need-to-know" basis.

4. Training and Orientation Policy
- Provide orientation on the nonprofit's mission, policies, and procedures.
- Train volunteers on safety, emergency protocols, and role-specific responsibilities.
- Require periodic refresher training for long-term volunteers.

5. Supervision and Accountability Policy
- Assign staff supervisors to oversee volunteer work.
- Require regular check-ins and performance reviews for long-term assignments.
- Create reporting channels for concerns or grievances.

6. Health and Safety Policy
- Provide workplace safety training tailored to volunteer roles.
- Enforce use of protective equipment when needed.

- Establish incident reporting and accident response procedures.

7. Non-Discrimination and Harassment Policy
- Apply the same workplace harassment and discrimination protections to volunteers as employees.
- Create a process for volunteers to report inappropriate conduct confidentially.

8. Insurance and Liability Policy
- Maintain general liability and volunteer accident insurance coverage.
- Require volunteers to sign waivers acknowledging risks associated with their role.
- Define coverage limits and exclusions clearly in volunteer materials.

9. Conflict of Interest Policy
- Require volunteers in leadership or advisory roles to disclose potential conflicts.
- Establish recusal procedures for volunteers engaged in decision-making.

10. Volunteer Dismissal Policy
- Define grounds for dismissal (e.g., misconduct, repeated absence, policy violations).
- Ensure dismissal procedures are consistent, documented, and fair.

Policies addressing compliance and legal obligations also play a major role in risk mitigation. Nonprofits must comply with federal, state, and local regulations, including those related to tax-exempt status, charitable solicitations, employment law, and data protection. Compliance policies establish systems for monitoring legal requirements and ensuring timely filings such as IRS Form 990 or state registration documents. Document retention policies specify how long records must be kept and the procedures for secure disposal, reducing the risk of regulatory penalties or legal complications. Whistleblower policies encourage staff and volunteers to report misconduct without fear of retaliation, creating a culture of accountability that identifies risks early. By proactively addressing compliance, nonprofits reduce the risk of fines, investigations, or loss of tax-exempt status.

Insurance policies and related procedures are also critical tools for mitigating risk. Policies governing insurance should include regular reviews of coverage levels, assessment of organizational changes that affect risk exposure, and procedures for promptly reporting claims. By embedding insurance into risk management, nonprofits ensure they can withstand financial shocks that could otherwise cripple operations.

Operational procedures addressing health, safety, and crisis management are equally important. Many nonprofits deliver services directly to vulnerable populations or organize public events, creating risks of accidents, injuries, or emergencies. Policies on workplace safety, emergency preparedness, and crisis response ensure that the organization can respond effectively to incidents. These may include evacuation plans, first aid protocols, and procedures for handling incidents such as natural disasters, pandemics, or security threats. Training staff and volunteers in these procedures ensures readiness and minimizes harm. Beyond physical safety, crisis communication policies establish guidelines for managing media inquiries, donor communications, and social media responses during a crisis. A proactive communication strategy mitigates reputational risks and reassures stakeholders that the organization is managing the situation responsibly.

Information technology and data protection policies have become increasingly important in an era of digital fundraising and online donor management. Nonprofits collect sensitive information, including donor financial data, client records, and employee files. Cybersecurity policies should outline procedures for protecting this data through encryption, secure passwords, firewalls, and regular system updates. Access control policies limit who can view or modify sensitive data, reducing the risk of internal breaches. Data retention and privacy policies ensure compliance with laws such as the General Data Protection Regulation (GDPR) or state-specific privacy acts. In the event of a breach, incident response procedures should guide immediate action, notification of affected parties, and corrective measures. By protecting data, nonprofits safeguard both their operational capacity and their reputations. See the following exhibit for a detailed list of these policies.

SAMPLE POLICIES RELATED TO INFORMATION TECHNOLOGY

Core IT Policies

- **Acceptable Use Policy** – Defines appropriate use of computers, email, internet, and other IT resources.
- **Bring Your Own Device Policy** – Governs personal devices used for nonprofit work.
- **Remote Work & Telecommuting Policy** – Establishes secure access requirements for offsite staff and volunteers.
- **Cloud Services Policy** – Provides rules for using cloud platforms (Google Workspace, Microsoft 365, Dropbox, etc.).
- **Mobile Device Policy** – Covers security settings, encryption, and approved apps for smartphones/tablets.
- **Hardware and Software Management Policy** – Addresses procurement, installation, licensing, and decommissioning of hardware and software.
- **Email & Communication Policy** – Regulates nonprofit email use, professional communication, and anti-phishing practices.
- **Password Management Policy** – Requires strong passwords, multi-factor authentication, and periodic changes.

Data Protection Policies

- **Data Classification & Handling Policy** – Categorizes data (public, confidential, sensitive) and the rules for each.
- **Data Privacy Policy** – Ensures compliance with privacy laws (e.g., GDPR, CCPA, HIPAA if applicable).
- **Data Retention and Disposal Policy** – Defines how long records are kept, and secure destruction processes.
- **Confidentiality Policy** – Protects donor, client, and volunteer information.
- **Encryption Policy** – Requires encryption of sensitive data both at rest and in transit.
- **Access Control Policy** – Grants access on a least-privilege basis and reviews user rights regularly.

- **Third-Party Data Sharing Policy** – Outlines rules for sharing donor/member data with vendors or partners.

Cybersecurity & Risk Management Policies

- **Information Security Policy** – Establishes general principles for safeguarding systems and data.
- **Incident Response Policy** – Provides steps for reporting, managing, and mitigating security incidents.
- **Disaster Recovery and Business Continuity Policy** – Ensures that operations can resume after IT disruptions.
- **Backup & Recovery Policy** – Defines the frequency, storage, and testing of data backups.
- **Network Security Policy** – Covers firewalls, VPNs, wireless access, and intrusion detection.
- **Anti-Malware and Patch Management Policy** – Requires timely software updates and antivirus protections.
- **Phishing and Social Engineering Policy** – Includes awareness training and reporting procedures.

Governance & Compliance Policies

- **IT Governance Policy** – Clarifies roles and responsibilities for technology decisions.
- **Vendor Management Policy** – Ensures that IT vendors meet security and compliance standards.
- **Audit and Monitoring Policy** – Provides for periodic reviews of IT systems and data security.
- **Compliance Policy** – Ensures adherence to applicable nonprofit, tax-exempt, and data protection laws.
- **Training and Awareness Policy** – Requires ongoing cybersecurity and privacy training for staff and volunteers.

Program-related policies are essential for mitigating and risks tied directly to mission delivery. These policies define how services are designed, implemented, and evaluated to ensure effectiveness and accountability. Risk arises when programs fail to deliver intended outcomes, misuse resources, or expose beneficiaries to harm. Program policies should require needs assessments, evidence-based design, and the ongoing evaluation of outcomes. Safeguarding policies are especially critical for nonprofits working with vulnerable populations such as children, seniors, or individuals with disabilities. These include background checks for staff and volunteers, clear reporting procedures for suspected abuse, and strict boundaries to protect client safety. By embedding safeguards into program delivery, nonprofits reduce liability and reinforce trust with stakeholders.

Strategic planning policies also play a role in risk mitigation, as they help organizations anticipate and adapt to long-term challenges. Strategic risks include mission drift, funding volatility, and changes in the external environment such as economic downturns or political shifts. Policies that require periodic review of strategic plans, stakeholder input, and scenario analysis ensure that nonprofits remain adaptable and resilient. Risk assessments can be built into the strategic planning process, identifying potential threats to mission sustainability and outlining contingency plans. Diversifying revenue streams through policies on fundraising, grant-seeking, and earned income further mitigates financial risk by reducing reliance on a single funding source.

Board development and training policies support risk mitigation by ensuring that those charged with governance are prepared to fulfill their responsibilities. Policies requiring orientation for new board members, ongoing education about fiduciary duties, and periodic self-evaluations strengthen governance capacity. Succession planning policies prepare the organization for leadership transitions, reducing the risk of disruption when key leaders depart. When boards are equipped with knowledge and structures to guide decision-making, they can anticipate risks and take proactive measures to address them.

Finally, monitoring and evaluation policies create feedback loops that reinforce risk mitigation efforts. Nonprofits should establish procedures for regularly reviewing the effectiveness of their risk management policies and adapting them as circumstances evolve. Internal audits, risk management committees, and annual risk assessments provide structured mechanisms for identifying emerging threats and measuring progress. Embedding a culture of continuous improvement ensures that risk management remains dynamic rather than static.

In conclusion, nonprofit organizations face a wide array of risks that could threaten their operations, finances, reputation, and mission. To mitigate these risks, nonprofits must adopt comprehensive policies and procedures spanning governance, financial management, human resources, compliance, insurance, safety, data protection, program delivery, strategic planning, and board development. These policies not only reduce the likelihood of adverse events but also prepare the organization to respond effectively when challenges arise. By embedding risk mitigation into everyday practices and fostering a culture of accountability and resilience, nonprofits safeguard their ability to serve their communities and fulfill their missions in the face of uncertainty. In this way, risk management becomes not merely a protective measure but a strategic asset that strengthens trust, sustainability, and impact.

Summary

A small nonprofit with few resources may conclude that it cannot financially support the purchase of any insurance policies (or very few). If so, a reasonable approach is to purchase insurance that covers the highest-probability risks, along with a limited payout and high deductible; doing so at least provides some limited coverage in areas where the organization is mostly likely to suffer losses. Over time, and as the organization (hopefully) expands and becomes more financially secure, it can slowly improve its insurance coverage and opt for more favorable deductibles and payouts. In the meantime, the organization can roll out a reasonably complete suite of risk-reduction policies and procedures; doing so reduces the risk of loss, and can be done at low cost.

Chapter 9
Marketing Activities

Introduction

The marketing activities of a nonprofit are essential to how it is perceived by its donors, volunteers, and beneficiaries. When properly formulated, marketing can greatly enhance donations and the willingness of individuals to volunteer for a nonprofit. In this chapter, we discuss branding basics, media relations, donor communications, and many other marketing topics.

Branding Basics

Branding for a nonprofit is often misunderstood as little more than having a recognizable logo, a set of colors, or a catchy tagline. While these elements are part of a brand, they represent only the surface. Branding is the holistic process of shaping how an organization is perceived by its stakeholders: donors, volunteers, beneficiaries, employees, and the general public. For nonprofits, effective branding is not about selling products but about communicating mission, values, and impact in ways that inspire trust and engagement. A strong brand makes a nonprofit stand out in a crowded philanthropic landscape, strengthens donor relationships, and reinforces credibility. It also aligns internal culture with external messaging, ensuring consistency and authenticity in every interaction. Understanding the basics of nonprofit branding requires exploring what a brand is, why it matters, and how it can be built and maintained.

At its core, a brand is a promise. It communicates what people can expect when they interact with the nonprofit, whether by giving money, volunteering time, or receiving services. For example, a nonprofit focused on environmental protection must ensure that its messaging, imagery, and programs consistently reflect values of sustainability and stewardship. Inconsistencies between what an organization claims to stand for and what it actually does weaken its brand. This is particularly important for nonprofits, which depend heavily on trust. Donors want reassurance that their contributions are used effectively, beneficiaries want confidence in the quality of services, and volunteers want to feel their time has meaning. A coherent brand provides this assurance by presenting a unified identity.

The basics of nonprofit branding begin with defining the organization's mission, vision, and values. These statements serve as the foundation upon which all branding efforts rest. The mission explains why the nonprofit exists, the vision paints a picture of the future it seeks to create, and the values articulate the principles that guide its work. Together, they form the brand's essence, shaping how the organization tells its story and interacts with stakeholders. For instance, a nonprofit dedicated to literacy might emphasize inclusivity, empowerment, and opportunity as its values, and these principles would then inform everything from the tone of its communications to the design of its programs. Without clarity in mission, vision, and values, branding efforts risk becoming superficial or inconsistent.

Visual identity is another cornerstone of branding, though it is only one part of the whole. Logos, color schemes, typography, and imagery work together to create recognizable cues that differentiate the nonprofit. A strong visual identity reflects the organization's mission while appealing to its target audiences. For example, a children's charity might use bright colors and playful fonts to convey warmth and hope, while a human rights organization might opt for bold, serious designs that reflect urgency and strength. Visual identity must be applied consistently across all platforms – websites, brochures, social media, fundraising appeals, and even event signage. Consistency builds recognition, and recognition fosters trust.

Messaging forms the verbal counterpart to visual identity. Nonprofits must be able to articulate who they are, what they do, and why it matters in ways that resonate with different audiences. Messaging basics include developing an "elevator pitch" (a concise explanation of the mission that can be delivered in under a minute) as well as longer narratives that highlight stories of impact. Storytelling is especially powerful in nonprofit branding. Sharing personal accounts of individuals whose lives have been changed by the nonprofit's work creates emotional connections that statistics alone cannot. However, effective messaging also balances emotion with evidence, combining moving stories with measurable outcomes to demonstrate both heart and credibility.

Another basic element of nonprofit branding is audience understanding. Nonprofits must identify and segment their audiences – donors, beneficiaries, volunteers, policymakers, and the general public – because each group interacts with the brand differently. For donors, branding communicates impact and trustworthiness. For beneficiaries, it signals accessibility and relevance. For volunteers, it conveys community and shared values. Understanding these different perspectives allows nonprofits to tailor communications while maintaining a consistent core identity. Audience research through surveys, focus groups, or analytics helps nonprofits refine their branding strategies to ensure resonance.

Internal alignment is just as important as external presentation. Branding is not only about how the public perceives the nonprofit but also about how staff and volunteers understand and embody its mission. Employees and volunteers are brand ambassadors; their interactions with the public shape perceptions as much as logos or slogans do. Training staff to speak consistently about the mission, ensuring that internal policies reflect stated values, and fostering a positive organizational culture all contribute to brand integrity. If there is a disconnect between external messaging and internal reality (for example, if a nonprofit promotes inclusivity but fails to practice it internally), then the brand suffers.

Digital presence plays a growing role in nonprofit branding. Websites are often the first point of contact for potential supporters, and they must communicate the brand clearly and immediately. A strong nonprofit website highlights the mission, tells compelling stories, provides transparent information about finances and impact, and makes it easy for visitors to engage through donations, volunteering, or advocacy. Social media platforms extend the brand's reach, offering opportunities for storytelling, engagement, and community building. Each platform requires adapting the brand voice to fit the medium while maintaining consistency in tone and visual identity. For instance, Instagram may emphasize visuals and stories, while LinkedIn might focus on professional impact and partnerships.

Trust and transparency are fundamental to nonprofit branding. Unlike businesses, which deliver tangible products in exchange for money, nonprofits ask for resources with the promise of creating impact. Donors, therefore, need reassurance that their money is being used responsibly. Transparency in financial reporting, clarity in program outcomes, and honesty in communications all strengthen the brand. Sharing both successes and challenges builds credibility, showing that the nonprofit is committed to accountability. Many organizations publish annual reports or impact statements as part of their branding efforts, using them not only as compliance documents but also as tools to reinforce the brand story.

Another important branding basic is differentiation. The nonprofit sector is crowded, with multiple organizations often working in the same space. To attract supporters, a nonprofit must articulate what makes it unique. Differentiation may come from a particular approach, a geographic focus, a target population, or a history of innovation. For example, two nonprofits may both focus on hunger relief, but one might differentiate itself by emphasizing local partnerships with farmers, while the other highlights large-scale food distribution networks. Clarity in positioning allows the brand to stand out, ensuring that stakeholders understand why they should choose to engage with this organization over others.

Sustainability in branding means ensuring that efforts are not one-time campaigns but long-term commitments. A nonprofit's brand must evolve with changing times, donor expectations, and community needs while remaining anchored in its mission and values. This requires the periodic evaluation of branding strategies, including audience perception studies, message testing, and reviews of visual identity. Refreshing the brand may be necessary to stay relevant, but changes should always reinforce, rather than undermine, the core identity.

In conclusion, branding basics for a nonprofit extend far beyond logos or taglines. A strong brand begins with clarity of mission, vision, and values, and is expressed consistently through visual identity, messaging, and storytelling. It requires understanding diverse audiences, aligning internal culture with external communications, and leveraging digital platforms to extend reach. Transparency, trust, and differentiation form the bedrock of credibility, while consistency ensures recognition and loyalty. Branding is not a superficial exercise but a strategic tool that strengthens donor confidence, engages communities, and sustains mission-driven impact. When done effectively, branding transforms a nonprofit from simply being one of many in a crowded field into a trusted, distinctive, and influential voice for change.

Crafting the Nonprofit's Message

Crafting a nonprofit's message is one of the most important tasks an organization can undertake. A message is more than words on a website or a slogan on a brochure; it is the articulation of the organization's purpose, values, and impact in a way that resonates with audiences. A well-crafted message not only explains what the nonprofit does but also inspires people to act, whether by donating, volunteering, or spreading the word. In an environment where countless nonprofits compete for attention and resources, clarity and authenticity in messaging make the difference between being overlooked and being embraced.

At its core, a nonprofit's message must start with its mission. The mission statement captures the essence of why the organization exists and what it seeks to accomplish. But while mission statements are important, they often read as broad, formal declarations. A nonprofit's crafted message must translate this formal statement into language that is accessible, relatable, and emotionally engaging. The message should answer three essential questions: Who are we? What do we do? Why does it matter? If audiences cannot grasp these answers quickly and clearly, they are unlikely to engage further.

To craft a compelling message, a nonprofit must first understand its audiences. Unlike businesses that target customers, nonprofits must communicate with multiple groups: donors, volunteers, beneficiaries, policymakers, and the broader public. Each of these audiences has distinct motivations and interests. Donors want to know that their contributions will make a tangible impact. Volunteers want to feel that their time will be valued. Beneficiaries want reassurance that services are accessible and relevant. Policymakers may seek evidence of effectiveness and alignment with broader social goals. By segmenting audiences and tailoring messages to their needs while maintaining a consistent core identity, nonprofits can maximize the effectiveness of their communications.

Emotional resonance is another cornerstone of nonprofit messaging. Facts and statistics are important for credibility, but stories create connections. People are more likely to act when they feel emotionally moved by an issue. This is why storytelling is central to nonprofit communications. A message that introduces a single person's experience – a child gaining access to education, a family lifted out of poverty, or an endangered animal rescued – often has more impact than abstract descriptions of large-scale programs. Stories put a human face on the mission, making abstract problems tangible and solvable. Still, emotion must be balanced with evidence. Donors and other stakeholders want to know that the nonprofit's work produces measurable results, so effective messaging combines compelling stories with data that demonstrates scale and effectiveness.

Clarity and simplicity are vital in crafting a nonprofit's message. Many organizations fall into the trap of using technical jargon, policy-heavy language, or overly detailed descriptions of their programs. While these may have a place in grant applications or academic reports, they obscure the message for the general public. A nonprofit's message should be easily understood in a few sentences, free of acronyms and technical terms that alienate audiences. The "elevator pitch" concept (being able to explain the mission in under a minute) is a helpful guideline. A concise, clear message ensures that anyone associated with the nonprofit, from board members to volunteers, can communicate the mission consistently.

Consistency is another critical element. Nonprofits interact with audiences across multiple platforms: websites, newsletters, social media, events, and direct conversations. If the message differs from one platform to another, confusion results. A strong nonprofit ensures that its message is consistent in tone, content, and values across all channels. This does not mean repeating the same words verbatim but rather maintaining a coherent voice and emphasis. For example, a nonprofit focused on youth empowerment might consistently highlight themes of opportunity, hope, and potential, whether in a fundraising appeal, a press release, or a social media post.

Authenticity is equally essential. In the nonprofit sector, trust is the currency of engagement. Stakeholders must believe that the organization is genuine in its intentions and truthful in its claims. Exaggerated promises, sensationalized stories, or overly polished messaging that feels disconnected from reality can backfire. Instead, nonprofits should embrace authenticity by being transparent about challenges as well as successes. Sharing honest stories about struggles, setbacks, and learning experiences builds credibility. People respond to messages that feel real, and authenticity creates long-term trust that fosters sustained engagement.

In addition to being clear, emotional, consistent, and authentic, a nonprofit's message must also be actionable. It should not simply describe problems; it should invite audiences to be part of the solution. Every message should answer the unspoken question: What can I do to help? Calls to action can vary depending on the audience; donors may be asked to contribute, volunteers to sign up for shifts, policymakers to support legislation, or community members to share the message on social media. The action must feel accessible and meaningful. For example, a nonprofit tackling hunger might say: "For $25, you can provide a week's worth of meals for a family," offering a specific, tangible way for donors to engage.

Visuals play an important supporting role in crafting messages. Images, videos, and design elements reinforce the nonprofit's story and evoke emotions that words alone may not capture. A photograph of volunteers working in a community garden or a short video of a beneficiary sharing their story can make a message more memorable and impactful. However, visuals must be used ethically, respecting the dignity of beneficiaries and avoiding exploitative imagery. Ethical storytelling ensures that the nonprofit's message aligns with its values, showing beneficiaries as partners in change rather than passive recipients of aid.

Crafting a message also involves aligning internal culture with external communications. Staff and volunteers are ambassadors of the brand, and their interactions with the public shape perceptions as much as formal communications do. Training and orientation should include guidance on how to talk about the mission and impact, ensuring that everyone represents the organization consistently. When internal culture reflects the external message, authenticity is strengthened, and the nonprofit's credibility grows.

Over time, a nonprofit must revisit and refine its message to remain relevant. Social, political, and economic contexts change, and so do donor expectations and community needs. Periodic evaluations of messaging, through surveys, focus groups, or digital analytics, help nonprofits understand whether their message continues to resonate. Refreshing the message does not mean abandoning the core mission but rather adapting the way it is communicated. For example, an environmental nonprofit might shift from talking primarily about "conservation" to emphasizing "climate action" to reflect current discourse and engage new audiences. Flexibility ensures that the non-profit's message remains timely and effective without losing its essence.

Ultimately, crafting a nonprofit's message is about building relationships. It is not a one-way broadcast but an ongoing conversation with stakeholders. A message that inspires, informs, and invites participation fosters deeper engagement. It transforms donors into partners, volunteers into advocates, and beneficiaries into storytellers. The most successful nonprofits are those that craft messages that not only describe their work but also create a sense of shared purpose and belonging.

In conclusion, crafting a nonprofit's message requires clarity about mission, understanding of audiences, emotional resonance through storytelling, and the balance of authenticity with consistency. It demands actionable calls to engagement, supported by compelling visuals and aligned with internal culture. Above all, it requires ongoing reflection and adaptation to remain relevant in a changing world. When a nonprofit crafts its message effectively, it does more than communicate what it does – it inspires people to believe in its mission, to trust in its capacity, and to join in creating meaningful change. A strong message becomes the thread that ties together all aspects of the organization, weaving its identity, values, and impact into a narrative that compels action and sustains its mission for the long term.

Digital and Social Media Marketing

Digital and social media marketing have become essential tools for nonprofits seeking to raise awareness, engage supporters, and generate resources to sustain their missions. In the past, nonprofits relied heavily on in-person events, printed brochures, and direct mail campaigns to reach their audiences. While these traditional methods still hold value, the digital environment now dominates how people discover, evaluate, and engage with organizations. For nonprofits, digital and social media marketing is not simply about visibility; it is about building communities, telling compelling stories, and fostering long-term relationships with supporters in ways that are cost-effective, measurable, and scalable. Understanding how to leverage these tools is critical for nonprofits to remain relevant and impactful in an increasingly connected world.

At its core, digital marketing encompasses all online strategies used to reach and engage target audiences. This includes websites, email campaigns, search engine optimization, online advertising, content marketing, and social media platforms. For nonprofits, digital marketing provides opportunities to communicate mission, demonstrate impact, and invite participation at relatively low cost compared to traditional advertising. Social media, as a subset of digital marketing, emphasizes platforms such as Facebook, Instagram, LinkedIn, and YouTube. These platforms allow nonprofits to connect with audiences where they already spend their time, enabling real-time interaction and storytelling.

A strong digital presence begins with a nonprofit's website, which serves as the central hub of its marketing ecosystem. The website should communicate the mission clearly, highlight programs and impact, and provide easy ways for visitors to get involved, whether through donations, volunteering, or advocacy. Clear calls to action, mobile-friendly design, and user-friendly navigation are essential. Integrating blog posts, videos, and downloadable resources enhances engagement and improves search engine rankings, making the nonprofit more discoverable online. A well-designed website is not just an informational resource, it is a critical marketing and fundraising tool that reinforces the organization's credibility and brand identity.

Email marketing remains one of the most effective digital tools for nonprofits, offering a direct line of communication to supporters. Email campaigns can nurture relationships by providing regular updates, sharing impact stories, and offering exclusive opportunities for engagement. Segmentation (dividing recipients into groups based on donor history, volunteer status, or areas of interest) allows nonprofits to tailor messages for greater relevance and impact. For instance, lapsed donors might receive re-engagement messages, while long-time supporters might be invited to special events. Personalized and targeted communication builds stronger relationships and increases the likelihood of repeat giving.

Social media marketing extends the nonprofit's reach beyond its existing supporter base. Platforms such as Facebook and Instagram are particularly effective for storytelling through photos, videos, and live streams. TikTok and YouTube allow nonprofits to experiment with creative, short-form or long-form video content that engages younger demographics. LinkedIn is valuable for building professional networks, recruiting volunteers, and sharing thought leadership in specific fields. Each platform has its own culture and strengths, requiring nonprofits to adapt their content while maintaining a consistent brand voice. The immediacy of social media also enables nonprofits to respond quickly to events, join broader conversations, and mobilize support for urgent needs.

Storytelling is the heart of nonprofit social media marketing. Audiences connect more deeply with stories than with statistics, and social media provides the perfect space to share personal narratives of beneficiaries, volunteers, and staff. A nonprofit working on homelessness might post a video interview with a family that has transitioned to stable housing, accompanied by a caption explaining the donor's role in making it possible. This humanizes the mission and provides tangible evidence of impact. At the same time, data and metrics can complement these stories, offering proof of scale and effectiveness. Together, stories and data create a powerful message that appeals to both emotion and reason.

Engagement is another key aspect of digital and social media marketing. Unlike one-way communication through brochures or press releases, digital platforms allow for dialogue. Nonprofits can interact directly with supporters by responding to comments, acknowledging contributions, and participating in conversations. Engagement strategies might include interactive polls, live Q&A sessions with program staff, or challenges that encourage user-generated content. When supporters feel heard and valued, they are more likely to become advocates who share the nonprofit's message with their own networks. This peer-to-peer amplification expands reach far beyond what the nonprofit could achieve alone.

Digital and social media marketing also provide powerful fundraising opportunities. Online fundraising campaigns can be launched through dedicated platforms or integrated into social media. Features such as Facebook and Instagram fundraising tools allow individuals to create personal campaigns, such as birthday fundraisers, which leverage peer networks to attract donations. Crowdfunding platforms like Go-FundMe or GlobalGiving enable nonprofits to raise money for specific projects with clear goals and deadlines. Social media creates urgency and excitement by providing real-time updates, progress bars, and opportunities to celebrate milestones. These digital tools democratize philanthropy by allowing people to give small amounts easily and collectively generate significant resources.

Analytics and measurement are major advantages of digital and social media marketing compared to traditional approaches. Nonprofits can track website traffic, email open rates, social media engagement, and conversion rates to evaluate the effectiveness of campaigns. Tools such as Google Analytics, Facebook Insights, or email marketing dashboards provide data that helps organizations understand what content resonates, which audiences are most engaged, and how resources should be allocated. For example, if analytics reveal that Instagram posts featuring videos generate more donations than static images, the nonprofit can adjust its strategy accordingly. Data-driven decision-making ensures that limited marketing budgets are used effectively.

Despite the benefits, digital and social media marketing also present challenges for nonprofits. The digital space is crowded, and audiences are inundated with content daily. Standing out requires creativity, authenticity, and consistency. Nonprofits must also contend with the rapid pace of technological change, as platforms evolve and algorithms shift. What works today may not be effective tomorrow. Additionally, maintaining an active digital presence requires time, skill, and resources – commodities that many nonprofits lack. Small organizations, in particular, may struggle to dedicate staff to social media management or to invest in high-quality content creation. Partnerships with volunteers, pro bono professionals, or peer organizations can help fill these gaps.

Another challenge lies in balancing accessibility with professionalism. Nonprofits must ensure that their digital and social media content is inclusive and respectful while reflecting the organization's values. Using exploitative images of beneficiaries to provoke donations, for example, can damage trust and dignity. Ethical storytelling requires care in how individuals and communities are portrayed. Nonprofits must also ensure compliance with privacy regulations when sharing stories or collecting donor information online. Safeguarding data and respecting confidentiality are essential to maintaining trust.

To succeed in digital and social media marketing, nonprofits should integrate these tools into a broader communications strategy rather than treating them as standalone activities. Digital channels should reinforce and complement each other. For instance, a nonprofit might publish a detailed impact story on its website, share highlights on social media with a link back to the site, and then send a targeted email inviting donors to contribute to a related campaign. This integrated approach creates multiple touchpoints with supporters, increasing the likelihood of engagement.

In conclusion, digital and social media marketing are indispensable for modern nonprofits. They provide cost-effective ways to tell compelling stories, engage diverse audiences, mobilize resources, and measure impact. By building strong websites, leveraging email, mastering storytelling on social platforms, and using data to refine strategies, nonprofits can extend their reach and deepen their relationships with supporters. Challenges such as resource constraints, content saturation, and ethical considerations must be addressed with creativity, collaboration, and integrity. Ultimately, digital and social media marketing allow nonprofits not only to promote their work but also to create communities of supporters who share their vision and contribute to meaningful change. When used strategically, these tools transform nonprofits from organizations asking for help into movements inviting participation, strengthening their capacity to achieve lasting impact.

Media Relations

Nonprofit organizations depend heavily on public awareness and trust to achieve their missions. One of the most effective ways to build that awareness and credibility is through media relations and the strategic use of press releases. While fundraising campaigns, social media, and community outreach are important tools for engagement, relationships with the press provide nonprofits with access to broader audiences. Effective media relations help nonprofits amplify their stories, highlight their impact, and influence public opinion in ways that direct communications cannot accomplish alone. Press releases, meanwhile, serve as the primary vehicles for delivering newsworthy information to journalists and media outlets, creating opportunities for coverage that extends the organization's reach.

At its core, nonprofit media relations is about building mutually beneficial relationships between the organization and members of the press. Nonprofits have stories to tell – about their programs, beneficiaries, volunteers, or advocacy efforts – that can provide compelling content for media outlets. Journalists, in turn, are always seeking credible, relevant, and timely stories to share with their audiences. Establishing trust and credibility with the press ensures that a nonprofit becomes a reliable source of information when reporters are covering issues related to its mission. This requires consistency, responsiveness, and transparency. Nonprofits that respect journalists' deadlines, provide accurate information, and make themselves available for follow-up inquiries are more likely to be covered positively and regularly.

Developing a media relations strategy begins with identifying appropriate media outlets and journalists. Nonprofits must research which outlets align with their audience and which journalists cover topics relevant to their mission. For example, a health-related nonprofit might focus on health reporters at local newspapers, specialized trade publications, or national outlets covering public health. Building relationships with these journalists can involve introductory meetings, sharing background information about the nonprofit's work, and offering access to experts within the organization. Media relations is not only about promoting stories but also about becoming a trusted resource. By positioning leaders, staff, or board members as thought leaders and subject matter experts, nonprofits increase their chances of being quoted or featured in media stories, even beyond their own press releases.

Press releases are central tools within this broader media relations strategy. A press release is a concise, formal statement sent to media outlets to announce something newsworthy. For nonprofits, common uses include announcing major donations, launching new programs, releasing annual reports, hosting fundraising events, or responding to urgent community issues. The purpose of a press release is not simply to inform but to spark media interest in covering the story more broadly. To succeed, a press release must be clear, professional, and written in a format that aligns with journalistic standards. Journalists often work under tight deadlines and receive many releases daily, so clarity and brevity are essential.

A typical press release begins with a headline that captures attention and conveys the main point of the announcement. The opening paragraph should provide the essential information in straightforward language, often framed by the "five W's": who, what, when, where, and why. The body of the release then elaborates with supporting details, quotes from organizational leaders or stakeholders, and context that explains the significance of the news. Quotes add a human voice and emotional resonance, while factual details provide credibility. A boilerplate section at the end gives background about the nonprofit, including its mission, history, and contact information. Press releases should be no longer than one page when possible, ensuring that journalists can quickly determine the story's relevance.

Timing is another critical factor in press releases. Nonprofits should send releases early enough for media outlets to plan coverage, especially if announcing an upcoming event. Aligning press releases with broader news cycles can also increase impact. For example, a food bank announcing a new program might issue its release during National Hunger Awareness Month, when journalists are already covering related stories. Following up with journalists after distributing a release can help ensure that it is noticed and considered for coverage.

Digital tools have transformed the distribution and reach of press releases. While traditional methods involved faxing or mailing releases to newsrooms, nonprofits now use email, online newswires, and their own websites or social media channels to share announcements. Posting press releases on a nonprofit's website increases transparency and provides an accessible archive for media and the public. Sharing the release on social media platforms broadens its visibility, allowing supporters to engage directly with the announcement. Some nonprofits also maintain online press rooms, offering easy access to press releases, high-quality photos, logos, and background information, making it easier for journalists to cover stories.

Strong media relations extend beyond simply sending press releases. Nonprofits must also engage in proactive outreach, such as pitching story ideas tailored to specific journalists, offering interviews with organizational leaders, or providing access to program sites. When crises occur (such as scandals, accidents, or sudden leadership changes) having established media relationships is invaluable. Journalists who already trust the nonprofit are more likely to present balanced coverage, and the organization will have channels through which to share accurate information quickly. A crisis communication plan, including designated spokespeople and clear messaging, helps mitigate reputational risks while maintaining public trust.

Nonprofits also benefit from integrating media relations with broader marketing and advocacy strategies. Press coverage lends credibility to fundraising campaigns, demonstrating to donors that the organization is visible and respected. Media stories can highlight advocacy efforts, influencing policymakers and shaping public discourse around social issues. By amplifying nonprofit voices through earned media, press relations complement paid advertising and grassroots outreach, providing a multiplier effect for limited resources.

In conclusion, nonprofit media relations and press releases are powerful tools for advancing nonprofit goals. Media relations focus on building ongoing relationships with journalists and outlets, positioning the nonprofit as a trusted source of credible stories and expertise. Press releases serve as structured announcements that provide timely, newsworthy information in formats journalists can use. Together, they help nonprofits raise visibility, strengthen credibility, and connect with broader audiences than they could reach on their own. In a competitive and crowded nonprofit sector, the ability to craft compelling press releases and maintain strong media relationships can be the difference between obscurity and influence. For nonprofits committed to making an impact, media relations and press releases are not optional add-ons but central components of their communication and engagement strategies.

Measuring Marketing Effectiveness

Measuring marketing effectiveness is a crucial practice for nonprofit organizations. Unlike for-profit businesses, which can often track success directly through revenue growth or profit margins, nonprofits must evaluate marketing in terms of awareness, engagement, trust, and ultimately, support for their mission. Every dollar spent on marketing is carefully scrutinized, since stakeholders want to ensure that resources are being used responsibly and not wasted on ineffective campaigns. For nonprofits, measuring marketing effectiveness is not simply an administrative exercise; it is a way to prove accountability to donors, guide strategic decision-making, and maximize impact with limited resources.

At its core, marketing effectiveness for nonprofits is about determining whether marketing activities are producing the desired outcomes, such as increased donations, higher volunteer engagement, broader community awareness, or stronger advocacy support. To measure this effectively, nonprofits must begin with clear goals. Without defined objectives, it is impossible to determine success. Goals may include raising awareness of an issue, generating a specific amount of donations during a campaign, recruiting a certain number of volunteers, or building an email list to expand future outreach. Once goals are set, nonprofits can identify metrics that serve as indicators of progress toward those objectives.

One of the most common ways nonprofits measure marketing effectiveness is through fundraising outcomes. Since donations are essential to nonprofit survival, tracking how marketing activities influence giving is critical. Metrics might include the number of new donors acquired, donor retention rates, average donation size, and the total amount raised through specific campaigns. For example, if a nonprofit invests in a digital ad campaign, it should evaluate how many donations were generated directly from that campaign, and whether the cost of the campaign was justified by the revenue produced. Beyond immediate results, long-term donor engagement is another indicator of effectiveness, showing whether marketing efforts are cultivating sustained relationships rather than one-time contributions.

Awareness is another key area of measurement. Many nonprofit marketing activities are designed to raise visibility for the organization or highlight specific issues. Metrics for awareness can include media mentions, social media impressions, website traffic, and attendance at events. For example, a nonprofit focused on environmental issues might measure how many people viewed or shared its social media posts during Earth Day campaigns. While awareness is more difficult to link directly to donations or volunteer hours, it is nonetheless an important precursor to deeper engagement. Effective measurement in this area requires nonprofits to track both the reach and quality of exposure, ensuring that they are connecting with the right audiences rather than merely generating numbers.

Engagement metrics help nonprofits understand whether their marketing messages are resonating with audiences. On digital platforms, engagement is often measured through likes, shares, comments, email open rates, and click-through rates. High engagement indicates that supporters are not only seeing the message but also interacting with it. For example, an email newsletter with a high open rate and click-through rate suggests that the nonprofit is delivering content that interests recipients. Similarly, strong interaction on social media signals that the organization is fostering community and dialogue rather than simply broadcasting messages. Engagement can also be measured offline through participation in events, volunteer sign-ups, or attendance at advocacy rallies.

Volunteer recruitment and retention are additional measures of marketing effectiveness. Many nonprofits rely heavily on volunteers to deliver programs and support operations. Marketing campaigns that successfully attract and retain volunteers demonstrate effectiveness by expanding the organization's human resources. Tracking volunteer numbers, hours contributed, and retention rates provides insights into how marketing messages are inspiring people to take action. Moreover, volunteer engagement often correlates with financial support, as committed volunteers may eventually become donors. Measuring volunteer outcomes thus provides a fuller picture of marketing's role in advancing the mission.

Advocacy impact is another area where measurement is important for nonprofits engaged in social or political change. Marketing efforts may aim to influence policymakers, mobilize public opinion, or shape legislative outcomes. Metrics here can include petition signatures, policy endorsements, meetings with officials, or media coverage of advocacy campaigns. While more complex to measure than donations or event attendance, advocacy outcomes highlight the broader social influence of nonprofit marketing and demonstrate its effectiveness beyond financial contributions.

Cost-effectiveness is also a critical aspect of measurement. Nonprofits must evaluate whether the resources invested in marketing are justified by the outcomes. Cost per dollar raised, cost per new donor acquired, or cost per impression are common metrics that compare inputs to results. For example, if a direct mail campaign costs $10,000 but generates $50,000 in donations, the return on investment is strong. Conversely, if a campaign consumes significant resources without producing proportional outcomes, the nonprofit must reconsider its strategy. Evaluating cost-effectiveness ensures that marketing supports the mission efficiently, maximizing the value of limited resources.

Surveys and feedback mechanisms provide qualitative measures of marketing effectiveness. Asking donors, volunteers, and community members how they heard about the nonprofit, what motivated them to give or get involved, and how they perceive the organization offers valuable insights. This feedback helps nonprofits refine messaging, identify gaps in communication, and strengthen relationships. For instance, if surveys reveal that most new donors learned about the nonprofit through social media, the organization can allocate more resources to that channel. Qualitative feedback complements quantitative metrics, providing a fuller understanding of impact.

Finally, effective measurement requires nonprofits to use data consistently and strategically. Many organizations now employ customer relationship management systems or donor databases to track interactions across channels. These systems allow nonprofits to analyze donor journeys, monitor engagement trends, and evaluate campaign effectiveness over time. Regular reporting and analysis ensure that insights are not overlooked and that lessons from one campaign inform the next. Importantly, measurement should not be an afterthought but an integral part of the marketing process, beginning with goal-setting and continuing through post-campaign evaluation.

In conclusion, measuring marketing effectiveness for a nonprofit involves assessing whether marketing activities achieve intended outcomes such as increased donations, heightened awareness, greater engagement, volunteer growth, or advocacy impact. This requires clear goals, appropriate metrics, and consistent use of data. By evaluating both quantitative outcomes like fundraising totals and qualitative feedback like donor perceptions, nonprofits can refine their strategies and ensure accountability. Cost-effectiveness is particularly important, as nonprofits must demonstrate that limited resources are being used wisely. When measurement is done well, it becomes a tool not only for evaluation but also for learning and improvement. Ultimately, effective measurement empowers nonprofits to strengthen their marketing, build deeper relationships, and advance their mission with greater impact.

Newsletters and Donor Communications

Newsletters and donor communications are essential tools for nonprofits, providing a structured way to maintain connections with supporters, strengthen relationships, and cultivate ongoing engagement. While fundraising campaigns, events, and social media activity often receive more attention, consistent communication through newsletters ensures that donors and stakeholders are regularly reminded of the organization's mission, impact, and needs. In many ways, newsletters act as the narrative thread that ties a nonprofit's activities together, while donor communications more broadly encompass the strategic choices that determine how an organization interacts with its supporters on a daily, monthly, and annual basis.

At their core, newsletters are a vehicle for storytelling. Nonprofits exist to solve problems and create positive change, and newsletters allow them to share this story in an ongoing, serialized format. Whether monthly or quarterly, newsletters give nonprofits the opportunity to highlight recent achievements, showcase beneficiary success stories, provide updates on ongoing projects, and remind donors of the broader impact of their contributions. Unlike a fundraising appeal, which often has a direct ask, newsletters generally focus on building trust and rapport. The goal is to ensure that supporters remain emotionally connected to the cause, which in turn increases the likelihood that they will respond positively when a fundraising appeal is made. A well-crafted newsletter therefore becomes a crucial element in the cultivation process, transforming one-time donors into long-term partners.

Donor communications extend beyond newsletters and include emails, letters, phone calls, social media messages, stewardship events, and even personalized thank-you notes. What unites these varied forms of communication is their purpose: to deepen donor engagement and reinforce the sense that each donor is an integral part of the nonprofit's mission. Nonprofits that fail to communicate effectively risk alien-ating donors, leaving them uncertain about how their contributions are being used or whether they are making a difference. Conversely, organizations that consistently en-gage in thoughtful donor communications build loyalty, increase retention, and en-courage larger gifts over time. In this sense, newsletters represent one of the most visible elements of a larger donor communications strategy, but they cannot succeed in isolation.

The effectiveness of newsletters and donor communications lies largely in the ability of nonprofits to strike a balance between information and emotion. Donors want to see measurable results: how many children were fed, how many acres of forest were preserved, or how many families received legal aid. At the same time, they are motivated by emotional connection, which requires stories that humanize the statis-tics. A newsletter that only reports numbers may come across as sterile, while one that only relies on anecdotes may lack credibility. The best communications combine both approaches, presenting data in a way that supports narratives of transformation. For example, a food bank might include a story about a single mother who was able to provide meals for her children thanks to the program, alongside statistics showing how many thousands of families were served during the quarter.

Another important feature of newsletters is their role in transparency and account-ability. Donors increasingly expect nonprofits to demonstrate the responsible stew-ardship of funds, and newsletters offer a direct way to showcase how contributions are being used. Updates on budget goals, program milestones, and even challenges faced by the organization foster trust. When nonprofits acknowledge difficulties rather than only highlighting successes, they project authenticity, which donors value. This kind of open communication reduces skepticism and strengthens credibility. In turn, donors are more likely to continue their support, knowing that they are part of an organization that is honest about both victories and struggles.

The format and style of newsletters can vary widely depending on a nonprofit's size, audience, and resources. Some organizations rely on printed newsletters, espe-cially when their donor base includes older supporters who may prefer physical mail. Others use digital newsletters, delivered by email, which allow for lower costs and faster distribution. Many nonprofits now integrate multimedia content, such as videos, interactive graphics, or links to blog posts, to make newsletters more engaging. The choice of format is less important than consistency and alignment with donor prefer-ences. A small nonprofit with limited staff might focus on a simple monthly email update, while a large institution might produce a full digital magazine. In all cases, clarity, brevity, and relevance are critical. Donors are inundated with communications from many organizations, so newsletters that are concise, visually appealing, and directly tied to donor interests are more likely to be read.

Personalization is another essential aspect of donor communications. While newsletters often go out to a broad audience, individual communications (such as thank-you letters, year-end tax summaries, or invitations to donor events) should be tailored to the donor's level of involvement. Addressing donors by name, referencing their past support, and highlighting the specific programs they helped fund creates a sense of individual recognition. This personalization signals that the nonprofit values each donor as more than just a source of revenue. Advances in donor management software have made it easier for even small nonprofits to segment their audiences and customize communications accordingly, ensuring that major donors, monthly givers, and occasional contributors all receive messages that resonate with their level of commitment.

The timing and frequency of communications also play a critical role. A newsletter sent too frequently may overwhelm donors, while one sent too rarely may cause them to forget about the organization. Most nonprofits find success with monthly or quarterly newsletters, supplemented by periodic donor communications that are tied to campaigns or events. Key moments, such as the end of the fiscal year, holidays, or major program milestones, offer natural opportunities for targeted outreach. Importantly, nonprofits must avoid the mistake of only contacting donors when asking for money. Communications that express gratitude, celebrate successes, or simply update donors on progress ensure that donors feel engaged year-round, not just during fundraising drives.

Newsletters and donor communications also serve an important internal function. They require nonprofits to regularly reflect on their achievements, challenges, and goals. By curating stories, gathering data, and presenting a coherent narrative, staff and leadership gain a clearer understanding of the organization's progress and direction. This process can inform strategic planning and program development, creating a cycle in which communication supports both external engagement and internal growth. Moreover, consistent messaging across newsletters and donor communications strengthens the nonprofit's brand identity, ensuring that the organization is recognized and remembered for its unique mission and values.

In addition, newsletters and donor communications foster a sense of community. Donors are not only giving to an organization; they are joining a collective effort to achieve social good. By sharing stories of volunteers, highlighting partnerships, and featuring donor spotlights, nonprofits can cultivate a sense of belonging. This community-building aspect is especially powerful in an era when many people seek meaningful connections and want to be part of something larger than themselves. A well-designed newsletter that celebrates the collective achievements of donors, staff, and beneficiaries reinforces this sense of shared purpose.

Finally, newsletters and donor communications must be evaluated and adapted over time. Open rates, click-through rates, response rates, and donor feedback provide valuable insights into what is working and what is not. Nonprofits that analyze this data can refine their messaging, adjust the length or frequency of newsletters, and experiment with new formats to keep communications fresh. By treating donor communications as a dynamic process rather than a static task, nonprofits can continually strengthen their relationships with supporters and maximize the impact of their outreach efforts.

In sum, newsletters and donor communications are central to nonprofit sustainability. They function as tools of storytelling, transparency, personalization, and community-building, while also reinforcing accountability and supporting internal reflection. By consistently engaging donors with meaningful, relevant, and authentic communication, nonprofits not only increase donor retention and financial support but also cultivate a base of advocates who are emotionally invested in the mission. In a sector where trust and loyalty are as important as dollars raised, newsletters and donor communications remain indispensable instruments for advancing both relationships and results.

Brochures, Flyers, and Outreach Materials

Brochures, flyers, and outreach materials have long been cornerstones of nonprofit communication strategies, providing organizations with tangible and accessible tools to engage communities, educate stakeholders, and attract support. While digital communication dominates today's landscape, printed and visual outreach materials continue to play a critical role in conveying a nonprofit's mission and programs in a clear, portable, and memorable way. These materials serve as both informational and persuasive instruments, bridging the gap between awareness and action by helping individuals understand the organization's purpose and motivating them to get involved through volunteering, donating, or advocacy.

A nonprofit brochure is typically a multi-panel document that provides a more in-depth look at an organization, its services, and its impact. Unlike a flyer, which usually delivers a concise message tied to a specific event or campaign, brochures are designed for broader purposes and often serve as a comprehensive overview of the nonprofit. They introduce the organization's mission statement, outline the problems it seeks to solve, highlight programs and services, and provide testimonials or stories that illustrate impact. For many nonprofits, a brochure acts as a "leave-behind" piece following meetings with prospective donors, corporate partners, or community leaders. Its durability and informational depth make it an essential tool for cultivation, as it allows recipients to revisit the content later, reinforcing the message long after the initial encounter. When thoughtfully designed, a brochure also enhances an organization's credibility by presenting a polished, professional image that signals competence and trustworthiness.

Flyers, by contrast, are shorter, more focused materials often used to promote specific events, fundraising drives, or initiatives. They are less comprehensive but more immediate in their call to action. Nonprofits distribute flyers in community spaces, at events, or through direct mail to quickly capture attention and encourage participation. For example, a nonprofit hosting a food drive might produce flyers highlighting the date, location, and items needed, while an organization launching a fundraising gala might use flyers to build excitement and encourage ticket sales. Flyers are typically inexpensive to produce, making them accessible even for smaller organizations with limited budgets. Their visual design is usually bold and concise, relying on striking graphics and minimal text to quickly deliver key information. In many cases, flyers serve as the first point of contact between a nonprofit and the public, functioning as invitations to learn more and engage with the organization in other ways.

Beyond brochures and flyers, nonprofits rely on a variety of outreach materials, both print and digital, to extend their visibility and connect with diverse audiences. Outreach materials can include postcards, fact sheets, posters, banners, and informational packets distributed at events, health fairs, schools, or community centers. These materials often highlight specific programs, provide educational resources, or promote advocacy efforts. For instance, a public health nonprofit might design outreach packets with brochures, posters, and infographics about disease prevention, while an environmental organization might distribute fact sheets on recycling and conservation practices. In each case, outreach materials are intended to be shareable and easily understood, allowing nonprofits to spread their message widely and empower individuals to act on the information provided.

One of the enduring strengths of brochures, flyers, and outreach materials is their physical presence. While digital content can disappear quickly in the noise of email inboxes and social media feeds, tangible printed materials linger on desks, bulletin boards, and community walls. They serve as constant reminders of a nonprofit's mission and create opportunities for repeated exposure. This is particularly important for reaching demographics that may not be as digitally connected, such as older adults or communities with limited Internet access. In these contexts, printed outreach materials ensure inclusivity and widen the nonprofit's reach. Even in highly digital environments, physical materials can complement online efforts, providing reinforcement and credibility. For example, a donor might receive a flyer about a fundraising event and later see a follow-up email or social media post, with both touchpoints working together to strengthen engagement.

The design and messaging of brochures, flyers, and outreach materials are crucial to their effectiveness. Nonprofits must distill complex missions and programs into language that is clear, concise, and compelling. The visual elements (logos, color schemes, typography, and images) must align with the organization's branding and evoke the desired emotional response. A brochure featuring stories of children supported by a literacy program, paired with photographs of smiling students and clear calls to action, can leave a lasting impression on potential donors. Similarly, a flyer for a volunteer recruitment drive must highlight not only the logistics but also the personal rewards of participating. In this way, outreach materials do more than provide information; they inspire action by creating an emotional connection between the audience and the cause.

Another important consideration is distribution strategy. Outreach materials only have impact if they reach the right audiences in the right contexts. Nonprofits must identify where potential supporters are most likely to encounter these materials, whether it be local businesses, schools, houses of worship, community centers, or public events. Partnerships with other organizations can expand distribution, allowing nonprofits to place brochures or flyers in spaces frequented by their target demographics. For example, a mental health nonprofit might leave brochures at local clinics and libraries, while an arts nonprofit might distribute flyers at cultural festivals. Digital adaptations of these materials, such as downloadable PDFs or shareable graphics, can further extend their reach, blending traditional outreach with modern digital tools.

Finally, brochures, flyers, and outreach materials should be evaluated for effectiveness. Nonprofits can track attendance at events promoted by flyers, monitor increases in website traffic following the distribution of brochures, or gather feedback from community members about the clarity and appeal of outreach materials. By analyzing outcomes, organizations can refine their design, messaging, and distribution strategies to maximize impact. Even small adjustments, such as simplifying language or changing the placement of contact information, can significantly improve engagement.

In summary, brochures, flyers, and outreach materials remain vital communication tools for nonprofits, complementing digital channels and providing tangible connections to supporters and communities. Brochures offer comprehensive overviews that build credibility and provide lasting reference points. Flyers generate immediate attention and action for specific initiatives. Broader outreach materials extend the organization's presence into communities, educating and empowering individuals to get involved. Together, these tools enhance visibility, foster trust, and inspire support, ensuring that nonprofits can effectively communicate their mission and mobilize recipients.

Annual Reports and Impact Statements

Annual reports and impact statements are two of the most important communication tools used by nonprofits to demonstrate accountability, celebrate accomplishments, and strengthen relationships with donors, stakeholders, and the broader community. While they share common objectives in highlighting an organization's achievements, these tools differ in format, focus, and usage. Both, however, are central to building trust and credibility, and they serve as crucial instruments in translating the often complex work of nonprofits into compelling narratives that resonate with supporters and affirm the organization's value to society.

The annual report has long been considered a staple of nonprofit transparency and governance. Traditionally modeled after corporate financial reports, nonprofit annual reports have evolved beyond mere compilations of financial statements and program descriptions. Today, effective annual reports are carefully designed publications that blend financial accountability with storytelling. They provide a comprehensive overview of the organization's activities during the year, outlining strategic priorities, program highlights, fundraising performance, and financial position. For donors, board members, and regulators, the annual report serves as evidence that the organization is managing resources responsibly and pursuing its mission with measurable results. For the nonprofit itself, producing an annual report is a reflective exercise that forces staff and leadership to assess accomplishments, challenges, and goals.

The financial transparency offered by annual reports is particularly important in the nonprofit sector, where donor confidence directly influences sustainability. Supporters want assurance that their contributions are being used effectively and that the organization is stable and accountable. By including audited financial statements, revenue and expense breakdowns, and explanations of financial decisions, nonprofits reinforce credibility and answer questions before they arise. At the same time, annual reports must balance financial detail with accessibility. Most readers are not accountants, and too much technical language risks alienating the audience. Successful reports translate financial information into plain language and pair it with graphics, charts, and summaries that highlight the key takeaways without overwhelming the reader.

In addition to financial data, annual reports are opportunities for nonprofits to showcase their impact through stories and statistics. Nonprofits exist to create change, and an annual report must illustrate how that change has occurred over the past year. This often involves featuring case studies, personal testimonials, or profiles of individuals and communities served. These narratives humanize the numbers and help donors see the tangible results of their support. For instance, a housing nonprofit might pair statistics about how many homes were built or families housed with a personal story of one family's journey to stability. By weaving together metrics and human experiences, annual reports create a fuller picture of the organization's effectiveness and purpose.

Impact statements, while similar in purpose, are generally more concise and focused than annual reports. They are often produced as standalone documents or integrated into other communications, such as donor updates, grant applications, or newsletters. An impact statement distills the outcomes of a nonprofit's work into a short, powerful summary that communicates achievements in a way that is both accessible and persuasive. Rather than providing the full financial and operational overview of an annual report, an impact statement zeroes in on results and outcomes. It answers the question donors most often ask: what difference has my contribution made?

Where annual reports are typically lengthy, formal, and produced once a year, impact statements are versatile and can be used throughout the year. They might take the form of a one-page infographic, a brief digital publication, or a concise report highlighting the outcomes of a specific program. Their brevity makes them particularly effective in a fast-paced environment where stakeholders may not have time to read lengthy documents. Impact statements are also highly adaptable to different audiences. A corporate sponsor might receive an impact statement showing how their funding supported a specific initiative, while an individual donor might see one highlighting the broader community outcomes made possible by collective support. In both cases, the emphasis is on demonstrating value, reinforcing gratitude, and inspiring continued engagement.

One of the key strengths of impact statements lies in their focus on outcomes rather than outputs. While outputs refer to the immediate activities of a nonprofit (such as the number of workshops held or meals served), outcomes highlight the longer-term changes that result from those activities, such as improved literacy rates or reduced food insecurity. By focusing on outcomes, impact statements elevate the conversation from what the organization does to what it achieves. This distinction is critical for donors, who increasingly expect nonprofits to demonstrate not only activity but also effectiveness. Impact statements thus serve as strategic advocacy tools, positioning the nonprofit as a results-driven organization that creates meaningful, measurable change.

The design and tone of annual reports and impact statements also play a significant role in their effectiveness. Both must align with the nonprofit's brand identity and values, using consistent logos, colors, and messaging. A professional and visually appealing presentation conveys competence and respect for the audience. Storytelling techniques, such as featuring photographs of beneficiaries, quotes from stakeholders, or graphics that simplify complex data, enhance readability and emotional impact. The tone should balance pride in accomplishments with humility, acknowledging ongoing challenges and the continued need for donor support. By striking this balance, nonprofits demonstrate both confidence in their work and awareness of the larger context in which they operate.

Together, annual reports and impact statements form complementary elements of a nonprofit's communication strategy. The annual report provides the depth and transparency that builds trust, while impact statements provide the concise and targeted messaging that sustains donor engagement throughout the year. When used in combination, they reinforce each other: the annual report offers the comprehensive evidence of effectiveness, and the impact statement distills that evidence into digestible pieces for broader dissemination. Both tools help nonprofits cultivate relationships by keeping stakeholders informed, inspired, and invested in the mission.

Ultimately, the use of annual reports and impact statements reflects the nonprofit sector's broader commitment to accountability, transparency, and relationship-building. Nonprofits operate in an environment of high expectations, where trust is paramount and resources are scarce. These communication tools are not merely administrative requirements but opportunities to affirm values, demonstrate stewardship, and celebrate the collective achievements of staff, volunteers, donors, and beneficiaries. By investing in the thoughtful creation of annual reports and impact statements, nonprofits ensure that their stories are not only told but also remembered, strengthening the foundation for continued support and impact.

Leveraging Content for Credibility

Publications are one of the most effective ways for a nonprofit to build credibility, both with its existing stakeholders and with new audiences. Whether in the form of annual reports, newsletters, brochures, impact statements, or research papers, these documents serve as visible demonstrations of the organization's professionalism, expertise, and commitment to transparency. The way in which a nonprofit develops and shares its publications determines whether they are simply routine materials or powerful instruments of trust-building. By leveraging the content of these publications strategically, nonprofits can establish authority in their field, showcase accountability, and deepen engagement with supporters.

One of the most direct ways a nonprofit gains credibility through its publications is by presenting clear, verifiable information. Donors, grantors, and community partners want to see evidence that the organization is achieving its mission and stewarding resources responsibly. Publications that include accurate data on program outputs and outcomes, financial information, and long-term progress serve as proof of effectiveness. For example, an annual report that provides audited financial statements alongside statistics on program achievements demonstrates both fiscal responsibility and measurable impact. When readers can see that resources are being used efficiently and that real change is being made, confidence in the organization grows. Furthermore, presenting data in a transparent way, even when the results are mixed, can enhance credibility by showing honesty and a commitment to improvement rather than perfection.

Beyond numbers, publications offer nonprofits the opportunity to frame their work within compelling narratives. Storytelling is a powerful tool for building trust, as it connects abstract goals with the lived experiences of beneficiaries. When an organization shares stories of individuals whose lives have been transformed by its programs, it demonstrates not only impact but also empathy and authenticity. These stories humanize the data and make the nonprofit's mission tangible. For example, a literacy nonprofit that highlights the journey of an adult learner who achieved employment after completing its program provides a vivid example of success that resonates far more deeply than statistics alone. Publications that balance rigorous data with heartfelt stories strike the right chord between professionalism and relatability, reinforcing the idea that the nonprofit is both effective and compassionate.

Another way nonprofits build credibility through publications is by positioning themselves as thought leaders in their area of focus. White papers, research briefs, or issue-focused reports allow organizations to share their expertise with policymakers, academics, and the general public. By producing well-researched content that sheds light on emerging challenges or offers solutions to systemic problems, a nonprofit demonstrates its knowledge and influence. This thought leadership not only builds trust among donors and partners but also enhances the organization's reputation within its sector. For example, an environmental nonprofit that publishes an annual report on climate-related risks in local communities can become a go-to source for reliable information, strengthening its voice in advocacy and policymaking. Credibility is often linked to authority, and publications are one of the most direct ways to demonstrate that authority.

The style and quality of publications also contribute significantly to perceptions of credibility. Professional design, clear writing, and accessible formatting send signals about organizational competence. A well-organized report with consistent branding, visually engaging charts, and error-free text conveys seriousness and reliability. Conversely, poorly edited or cluttered materials can undermine even the most effective programs by creating doubts about the nonprofit's overall professionalism. High-quality publications suggest that the organization values its stakeholders enough to invest time and resources in communicating effectively with them. This attention to detail reflects positively on the nonprofit's broader operations, reinforcing confidence that the same level of care is applied to program delivery.

Publications can also build credibility by highlighting partnerships and collaborations. When nonprofits include mentions of alliances with government agencies, corporations, foundations, or other nonprofits, they demonstrate that their work is respected and supported by credible institutions. These endorsements, implicit or explicit, function as social proof that the nonprofit is trustworthy and effective. Similarly, featuring testimonials from donors, volunteers, or beneficiaries adds external validation that strengthens the organization's reputation. By carefully curating whose voices appear in its publications, a nonprofit can leverage credibility by association while also underscoring its role in larger collective efforts.

Transparency is a recurring theme in building credibility, and publications offer nonprofits an ideal space to practice it. While it may be tempting to highlight only successes, credibility is often enhanced when organizations also acknowledge challenges and limitations. When a nonprofit candidly discusses the obstacles it faced in implementing a program, explains what was learned, and outlines steps for improvement, it communicates honesty and resilience. Stakeholders are more likely to trust organizations that admit imperfections than those that present an unrealistically flawless picture. Publications that take this approach not only strengthen trust but also position the nonprofit as a learning organization committed to growth.

Consistency across publications further reinforces credibility. When newsletters, annual reports, brochures, and impact statements all communicate the same core values, mission, and tone, stakeholders perceive the nonprofit as coherent and dependable. Mixed messages or contradictions can create doubt, while consistent messaging across different formats builds recognition and reinforces trust. This consistency should extend not only to language but also to visual identity, ensuring that every publication aligns with the nonprofit's brand and communicates stability.

Finally, publications gain credibility when they are used as tools for ongoing dialogue rather than one-way communication. Nonprofits that invite feedback on their reports or use their publications to highlight questions for future exploration demonstrate that they value stakeholder input. This approach transforms publications into platforms for relationship-building rather than static documents. When supporters feel included in the conversation, they are more likely to trust the organization and continue their involvement.

In sum, nonprofits can leverage the content of their publications to gain credibility by combining transparent data with authentic stories, demonstrating thought leadership, ensuring professional quality, highlighting partnerships, embracing transparency about challenges, maintaining consistency, and fostering dialogue. Each publication becomes not just a piece of communication but a strategic asset that reinforces the nonprofit's reliability, competence, and integrity. Over time, this consistent demonstration of credibility builds trust, strengthens relationships, and ensures that the organization is recognized as both effective and trustworthy in advancing its mission.

Summary

This chapter has outlined a broad array of marketing activities that may be beneficial to a nonprofit. The problem is that there can be a substantial cost associated with these activities, such as the preparation of a glossy annual report, or a research paper. To make marketing cost-effective, the management team needs to prepare an annual plan that identifies which marketing activities will be pursued, what the associated costs will be, and the expected outcomes. At the end of the year, the team should review the outcomes of these activities, and decide whether the marketing investment should be changed – either in terms of the funds allocated to it or the types of marketing activities that will be pursued. There is no perfect mix of marketing activities; a nonprofit will probably have to continually adjust its marketing plan every year, and possibly by a substantial amount. If the organization is growing, then a further area of discussion is which additional marketing activities to pursue with the associated larger budget. This is an incremental decision, where each activity added is presumed to have the greatest possible impact in comparison to the other marketing actions that were not pursued. In short, the marketing plan is worthy of a great deal of discussion by the management team, given its outsized impact on the fortunes of the organization.

Chapter 10
Managing the Organization's Finances

Introduction

In order to adequately understand its finances, a nonprofit needs an adequate accounting system that is backed by a prudently-constructed set of controls. With this system in place, the organization is better able to manage its assets responsibly, and ensure that it is expending funds in a manner that will not result in any unexpected cash shortages. In this chapter, we discuss nonprofit accounting systems, the financial statements that nonprofits are expected to use, and the need for variance analyses and systems of controls to maintain tight control over the organization.

Accounting Systems for Nonprofits

Accounting systems for nonprofits are essential tools that allow organizations to manage their financial resources effectively, maintain transparency, and comply with legal and regulatory requirements. The unique operating environment of a nonprofit requires accounting systems that can handle complex reporting obligations, track restricted and unrestricted funds, and demonstrate accountability to donors, regulators, and the public. An effective accounting system is not just a mechanism for recording transactions; it is a framework that supports stewardship, strategic decision-making, and organizational sustainability.

One of the defining characteristics of nonprofit accounting systems is the emphasis on fund accounting. Unlike commercial enterprises that focus on profitability, nonprofits must segregate resources according to donor-imposed or legally mandated restrictions. Fund accounting divides financial resources into categories such as unrestricted funds, temporarily restricted funds, and permanently restricted funds. This segregation ensures that money designated for a specific purpose, such as scholarships, building projects, or research, is not used for unrelated activities. A robust accounting system for nonprofits must therefore have the ability to track multiple funds simultaneously, produce reports showing fund balances, and demonstrate compliance with donor requirements. This capability is critical for maintaining donor trust, as contributors want assurance that their gifts are used as intended.

The choice of accounting method also plays a crucial role in nonprofit systems. Most organizations use the accrual basis of accounting, which records revenues when earned and expenses when incurred, regardless of when cash changes hands. This approach provides a more accurate picture of financial position and performance over time. For example, a grant awarded in December but not received until January would still be recorded in the year it was awarded under accrual accounting. Some smaller nonprofits, however, may use cash basis accounting for simplicity, recording transactions only when money is received or paid. While the cash basis of accounting may be easier to manage, it is generally not acceptable for audited financial statements or for organizations receiving significant grant funding. Therefore, accounting systems must be flexible enough to support accrual accounting and, when necessary, convert cash records into accrual formats for reporting purposes.

Nonprofits also face unique reporting requirements that shape their accounting systems. In the United States, organizations must follow accounting standards established by the Financial Accounting Standards Board, specifically those outlined in Accounting Standards Codification Topic 958, which governs nonprofit entities. One of the key requirements under these standards is the presentation of a statement of financial position (similar to a balance sheet), a statement of activities (similar to an income statement), and a statement of cash flows. In addition, nonprofits must provide disclosures regarding liquidity, functional expenses, and the nature of donor restrictions. The requirement to report expenses by both function (program, management and general, and fundraising) and nature (salaries, supplies, depreciation, etc.) is particularly significant. This dual classification ensures that stakeholders can see how resources are allocated not only in terms of categories but also in terms of mission-related versus administrative activities. An accounting system designed for nonprofits must therefore facilitate this type of expense tracking and reporting.

Another core feature of nonprofit accounting systems is grant and contribution management. Many nonprofits rely heavily on grants from governments, foundations, and other institutions, each of which may come with specific reporting requirements. An effective system must be able to track the receipt of grant funds, allocate expenses to the correct grant, and produce detailed reports that demonstrate compliance with funding conditions. Similarly, donations from individuals and corporations often come with restrictions or earmarks. Accounting systems must track these donor-imposed restrictions and ensure that funds are released to unrestricted status only when the conditions are met. Failure to comply with donor requirements can damage reputations and jeopardize future funding, making meticulous tracking a critical component of nonprofit accounting.

Budgeting is another area where nonprofit accounting systems play a vital role. Nonprofits often operate with tight margins and must carefully plan how to allocate resources to maximize impact. A strong accounting system provides tools for creating, monitoring, and adjusting budgets in real time. By comparing actual results with budgeted amounts, organizations can identify variances, assess financial performance, and make timely adjustments. For instance, if a fundraising campaign falls short of expectations, the nonprofit may need to scale back certain activities or seek alternative funding sources. Budgetary control is essential not only for internal decision-making but also for demonstrating to donors and boards that the organization is managing its resources prudently.

Internal controls are another critical aspect of nonprofit accounting systems. Because nonprofits often rely on public trust, they are particularly vulnerable to reputational damage from fraud or financial mismanagement. Accounting systems must incorporate safeguards such as the segregation of duties, approval hierarchies, audit trails, and restricted access to sensitive data. These controls help prevent errors and deter fraudulent activity while also providing evidence of accountability in the event of an audit. For example, the system might require that no single employee can both authorize and record a payment, reducing the risk of unauthorized transactions. Strong internal controls are not only good practice but also often required by regulators, auditors, and major funders. We deal with controls in detail later in this chapter.

Technology has significantly transformed nonprofit accounting systems in recent years. Cloud-based platforms allow nonprofits to manage finances from anywhere, collaborate across departments, and integrate with other software such as donor management systems and payroll providers. These integrations streamline workflows by reducing duplicate data entry and ensuring consistency across systems. For instance, when a donor makes an online gift, the information can flow directly into both the donor database and the accounting system, automatically updating revenue accounts and donor records. Many modern accounting systems also include dashboards and reporting features that provide real-time insights into financial health, enabling managers to make informed decisions more quickly. This technological shift is especially beneficial for small and mid-sized nonprofits that may lack the staff capacity for manual bookkeeping.

Training and staffing also play a role in the effectiveness of nonprofit accounting systems. Even the most sophisticated software cannot substitute for staff who understand nonprofit accounting principles and compliance requirements. Nonprofits must invest in training bookkeepers, accountants, and managers to use their systems effectively and interpret the data they produce. The board of directors also has a fiduciary responsibility to understand financial reports, so systems should produce outputs that are comprehensible to non-accountants. An overly complex or poorly configured system can obscure critical information and lead to poor decision-making, so usability and training are key considerations.

The use of accounting systems in nonprofits also extends beyond compliance to strategic impact. Financial data can be used to evaluate program effectiveness, assess sustainability, and support long-term planning. For example, by analyzing cost per beneficiary, an organization can determine whether a program is efficient compared to alternatives. Similarly, examining trends in revenue sources can highlight risks of overreliance on a single donor or funding stream. Accounting systems that provide timely, accurate, and detailed information allow nonprofits to align their financial practices with their mission and make strategic choices that enhance their impact.

In addition to internal use, the information generated by nonprofit accounting systems is crucial for external stakeholders. Donors, grantmakers, and regulators rely on financial reports to evaluate the health and effectiveness of organizations. Watchdog groups and charity rating agencies often use financial data to assess efficiency and transparency. A nonprofit with reliable, well-documented accounting records is more likely to earn favorable ratings, which in turn can attract additional support. Thus, the credibility of a nonprofit is closely tied to the quality of its accounting system.

In conclusion, accounting systems for nonprofits are not simply tools for recording transactions. They are comprehensive frameworks that ensure compliance with regulations, safeguard donor trust, support internal decision-making, and communicate impact to external audiences. By incorporating fund accounting, grant tracking, expense classification, budgeting, internal controls, and technological innovations, these systems address the unique challenges of nonprofit financial management.

When implemented effectively, accounting systems empower nonprofits to manage their resources responsibly, demonstrate transparency, and pursue their missions with confidence. In an environment where accountability and trust are paramount, a well-designed accounting system is one of the most valuable assets a nonprofit can possess.

Nonprofit Financial Statements

Financial statements are at the heart of accountability and transparency for nonprofit organizations. They provide a structured means of communicating financial position, performance, and stewardship of resources to a wide range of stakeholders, including donors, grantmakers, regulators, board members, and the public. Unlike for-profit businesses, nonprofits are not judged by their profitability but by their ability to carry out a mission in a financially responsible manner. For this reason, nonprofit financial statements emphasize accountability, donor restrictions, and functional allocation of expenses rather than net income or shareholder returns. Understanding the unique nature of nonprofit financial statements is essential to appreciating how these organizations demonstrate credibility and manage their resources.

The primary financial statements used by nonprofits are the statement of financial position, the statement of activities, the statement of functional expenses, and the statement of cash flows. Together, these reports provide a comprehensive picture of a nonprofit's financial health, resource allocation, and operational effectiveness. Each has a distinct purpose, but they work together to fulfill the organization's reporting obligations under GAAP and to meet the expectations of stakeholders who demand both transparency and clarity.

The statement of financial position, which closely resembles the balance sheet used by for-profit entities, presents the assets, liabilities, and net assets of a nonprofit at a specific point in time. Assets represent resources controlled by the organization, including cash, receivables, investments, property, and equipment. Liabilities capture obligations such as accounts payable, accrued expenses, and loans payable. The difference between assets and liabilities is presented as net assets, which in the nonprofit sector take the place of owners' equity in a for-profit business. Unlike equity, net assets are not owned by individuals but represent resources available for mission-driven use. Importantly, nonprofit net assets are classified into two categories: net assets without donor restrictions and net assets with donor restrictions. This classification reflects the fact that some resources are freely available for general use, while others are subject to specific donor-imposed stipulations. For example, a restricted donation to build a new facility cannot be used to fund operational expenses. By presenting net assets in this way, the statement of financial position allows stakeholders to understand the flexibility and constraints on the organization's financial resources. A sample statement of financial position appears in the following exhibit.

Sample Statement of Financial Position

Archimedes Education
Statement of Financial Position
As of April 30, 20X1

ASSETS		LIABILITIES AND NET ASSETS	
Cash and cash equivalents	$25,000	Accounts payable	$12,000
Accounts and pledges receivable	63,000	Accrued expenses	5,000
Prepaid expenses	5,000	Grants payable	14,000
Investments	10,000	Deferred revenue	8,000
Fixed assets	180,000	Debt	10,000
		Net assets:	
		Without donor restrictions	114,000
		With donor restrictions	120,000
Total assets	$283,000	Total liabilities and net assets	$283,000

The statement of activities serves as the nonprofit equivalent of the income statement. It reports revenues, expenses, and changes in net assets over a period of time, showing how resources were generated and used. Revenues can include contributions, grants, membership dues, program service fees, investment income, and special events revenue. Expenses are categorized by function, with an emphasis on program services, management and general expenses, and fundraising. The distinction between these categories is critical because stakeholders want to see that the majority of resources are being directed toward mission-related activities rather than administrative overhead. The statement of activities also shows the change in net assets without donor restrictions and net assets with donor restrictions, highlighting how restricted funds were used or released when donor conditions were satisfied. This provides transparency to donors, who can verify that their contributions were applied as intended. The overall result is a narrative of financial performance that connects resources to mission execution, rather than to profit-making. A sample statement of activities appears in the following exhibit.

Sample Statement of Activities

Archimedes Education
Statement of Activities
For the month ended June 30, 20X1

	Without Donor Restrictions	With Donor Restrictions	Totals
Revenues, gains, and other support:			
Contributions	$48,000	$10,000	$58,000
Net unrealized and realized gains on long-term investments	2,000		2,000
Net assets released from restrictions	12,000	-$12,000	
Total revenues, gains, and other support	$62,000	-$2,000	$60,000
Expenses and losses:			
Program expenses	$29,000		$29,000
Management and administration expenses	11,000		11,000
Fundraising expenses	6,000		6,000
Total expenses	$46,000		$46,000
Change in net assets	$16,000	-$2,000	$14,000
+ Beginning net assets	32,000	12,000	44,000
= Ending net assets	$48,000	$10,000	$58,000

The statement of functional expenses is unique to nonprofit organizations and reflects the sector's emphasis on accountability for resource allocation. This statement provides a detailed breakdown of expenses by both function and natural classification. Functional classification refers to the purpose of the expense, such as program services, management and general, or fundraising. Natural classification refers to the type of expense, such as salaries, benefits, occupancy, office supplies, depreciation, or professional fees. By presenting expenses in a matrix format, the statement of functional expenses allows stakeholders to see, for example, how much of the nonprofit's payroll costs are attributable to program activities versus administrative functions. This transparency is essential because donors and regulators often evaluate nonprofits based on their efficiency, looking at the proportion of resources spent on direct mission delivery compared to overhead. While such ratios can sometimes oversimplify organizational effectiveness, the statement of functional expenses provides the raw data for these analyses and helps nonprofits tell a fuller story about how their expenses support the mission. A good way to view the statement of functional expenses is through one of the exhibits in the IRS Form 990; a sample layout appears in the following exhibit.

Form 990 Reporting Requirement for the Statement of Functional Expenses

Part IX Statement of Functional Expenses				
Section 501(c)(3) and 501(c)(4) organizations must complete all columns. All other organizations must complete column (A).				
Check if Schedule O contains a response or note to any line in this Part IX				
Do not include amounts reported on lines 6b, 7b, 8b, 9b, and 10b of Part VIII.	**(A)** Total expenses	**(B)** Program service expenses	**(C)** Management and general expenses	**(D)** Fundraising expenses
1 Grants and other assistance to domestic organizations and domestic governments. See Part IV, line 21				
2 Grants and other assistance to domestic individuals. See Part IV, line 22				
3 Grants and other assistance to foreign organizations, foreign governments, and foreign individuals. See Part IV, lines 15 and 16				
4 Benefits paid to or for members				
5 Compensation of current officers, directors, trustees, and key employees				
6 Compensation not included above to disqualified persons (as defined under section 4958(f)(1)) and persons described in section 4958(c)(3)(B) . .				
7 Other salaries and wages				
8 Pension plan accruals and contributions (include section 401(k) and 403(b) employer contributions)				
9 Other employee benefits				
10 Payroll taxes				
11 Fees for services (nonemployees):				
a Management				
b Legal				
c Accounting				
d Lobbying				
e Professional fundraising services. See Part IV, line 17				
f Investment management fees				
g Other. (If line 11g amount exceeds 10% of line 25, column (A), amount, list line 11g expenses on Schedule O.) .				
12 Advertising and promotion				
13 Office expenses				
14 Information technology				
15 Royalties				
16 Occupancy				
17 Travel				
18 Payments of travel or entertainment expenses for any federal, state, or local public officials				
19 Conferences, conventions, and meetings .				
20 Interest				
21 Payments to affiliates				
22 Depreciation, depletion, and amortization .				
23 Insurance				
24 Other expenses. Itemize expenses not covered above. (List miscellaneous expenses on line 24e. If line 24e amount exceeds 10% of line 25, column (A), amount, list line 24e expenses on Schedule O.)				
a				
b				
c				
d				
e All other expenses				
25 Total functional expenses. Add lines 1 through 24e				
26 Joint costs. Complete this line only if the organization reported in column (B) joint costs from a combined educational campaign and fundraising solicitation. Check here ☐ if following SOP 98-2 (ASC 958-720) . . .				

The statement of cash flows, much like its for-profit counterpart, tracks the movement of cash in and out of the organization over a specific period. It is divided into three categories: operating activities, investing activities, and financing activities.

Operating activities include cash received from contributions and grants, payments to employees and vendors, and other day-to-day financial flows. Investing activities capture transactions related to long-term assets, such as purchasing property or selling investments. Financing activities include cash flows related to borrowing or repayment of debt, as well as restricted contributions for capital projects. The statement of cash flows is critical because it highlights liquidity and the nonprofit's ability to meet its short-term obligations. Even if the statement of activities shows strong financial performance, a nonprofit with weak cash flow may face serious operational challenges. Donors and boards look to this statement for assurance that the organization has adequate liquidity to sustain its programs and manage unexpected financial pressures. A sample statement of cash flows appears in the following exhibit.

Sample Statement of Cash Flows

Newton Education
Statement of Cash Flows
For the year ended 12/31/20X1

Cash flows from operating activities		
Change in net assets		$3,000,000
Adjustments to reconcile change in net assets to net cash provided by operating activities:		
Depreciation and amortization	$125,000	
Provision for losses on pledges receivable	20,000	
Gain on sale of facility	-65,000	
		80,000
Increase in pledges receivable	-250,000	
Decrease in inventories	325,000	
Decrease in trade payables	-50,000	
		25,000
Cash generated from operations		3,105,000
Cash flows from investing activities		
Purchase of fixed assets	-500,000	
Proceeds from sale of equipment	35,000	
Net cash used in investing activities		-465,000
Cash flows from financing activities		
Proceeds from new mortgage	325,000	
Payment of mortgage	-45,000	
Net cash used in financing activities		280,000
Net increase in cash and cash equivalents		2,920,000
Cash and cash equivalents at beginning of period		2,080,000
Cash and cash equivalents at end of period		$5,000,000

Together, these four statements provide a comprehensive view of a nonprofit's financial condition. The statement of financial position captures resources and obligations at a given point. The statement of activities shows how those resources were used and whether the organization's net assets increased or decreased. The statement of functional expenses provides detailed accountability for spending, particularly with respect to mission-related activities. The statement of cash flows demonstrates how cash is being generated and used, shedding light on the organization's liquidity and financial flexibility. When taken as a whole, these statements not only meet accounting standards but also address the broader demand for transparency and stewardship in the nonprofit sector.

Beyond these core statements, nonprofits often provide supplementary disclosures in the notes to financial statements. These notes explain accounting policies, provide detail on restricted funds, outline commitments and contingencies, and disclose related-party transactions. For example, a nonprofit may explain how it allocates joint costs between fundraising and program activities, or it may provide detail on endowment funds subject to donor-imposed restrictions. Such disclosures add depth to the financial statements, helping stakeholders interpret the numbers accurately and understand the context behind them. Notes also provide an opportunity for nonprofits to demonstrate transparency about risks and challenges, reinforcing trust among donors and regulators.

The preparation and presentation of financial statements are not simply compliance exercises. They are strategic opportunities for nonprofits to demonstrate competence, accountability, and impact. Donors increasingly demand evidence that organizations are efficient and effective, and financial statements are central to this assessment. A nonprofit that presents clear, accurate, and transparent financial statements builds credibility and enhances its ability to attract future funding. Conversely, poorly prepared or opaque financial statements can undermine donor confidence and lead to reputational damage. For this reason, many nonprofits undergo external audits, even when not legally required, to provide assurance that their financial statements fairly present their financial condition in accordance with GAAP. An unqualified audit opinion signals to stakeholders that the nonprofit has strong financial management practices and can be trusted with donor resources.

Financial statements also play an important role in internal decision-making. Nonprofit boards and managers use these reports to evaluate performance, plan budgets, and assess financial risks. For instance, by reviewing the statement of activities, leadership can determine whether revenue sources are diversified or overly dependent on a single donor. The statement of financial position may reveal whether liquidity is sufficient to cover upcoming obligations, while the statement of functional expenses can highlight areas where cost efficiencies may be achieved. These insights help boards and executives make informed choices that support both mission fulfillment and financial sustainability.

In addition, financial statements are increasingly being integrated with measures of program outcomes and impact. While the statements themselves focus on financial data, many nonprofits pair them with annual reports or impact statements that connect dollars to results. For example, alongside financial data, an organization may highlight how many meals were served, how many students were educated, or how many acres of land were preserved. This integration of financial and programmatic reporting strengthens the connection between stewardship of funds and achievement of mission, providing a holistic picture of organizational performance.

In conclusion, the financial statements used by nonprofit organizations are indispensable tools for accountability, transparency, and decision-making. They reflect the unique priorities of the nonprofit sector by emphasizing donor restrictions, functional allocation of expenses, and stewardship of resources. Through these statements, nonprofits communicate their financial health to donors, regulators, and the public while also equipping boards and management with the information needed to guide the organization strategically. When combined with supplementary disclosures and program impact measures, financial statements become powerful narratives that reinforce trust, support fundraising, and ensure that nonprofits can continue to serve their communities effectively.

Budget Monitoring and Variance Analysis

Budget monitoring and variance analysis are critical practices for nonprofit organizations, ensuring that scarce resources are used effectively, donor expectations are met, and financial sustainability is preserved. Unlike for-profit businesses that rely on profit margins and equity capital, nonprofits must operate with a heightened sense of accountability, since they are entrusted with funds provided by donors, grantors, and the public. These stakeholders expect that resources will be directed toward mission-related activities and managed prudently. A nonprofit's ability to monitor its budget and analyze variances between planned and actual results is therefore not only a matter of financial control but also of credibility and trust. Effective budget monitoring and variance analysis allow nonprofits to remain adaptable in uncertain environments, manage risks, and make informed decisions that align resources with their mission.

The starting point for understanding the importance of budget monitoring lies in the nature of nonprofit funding. Nonprofits often receive a mix of revenue from sources such as contributions, government grants, membership dues, program service fees, and investment income. Many of these revenues are restricted by donors or grantors for specific purposes, while others are unrestricted and available for general use. Budgets help nonprofits allocate these funds strategically, ensuring that restricted money is used in compliance with donor intent and unrestricted resources are allocated to core operations. Monitoring the budget throughout the year is essential to verify that revenues are being received as expected, that expenses remain within approved limits, and that restricted funds are being applied correctly. Failure to do so could result in overspending, noncompliance with grant requirements, or the inability to sustain essential programs.

Variance analysis is the process of comparing actual financial results to the budgeted amounts and investigating the reasons for differences. Variances may be favorable, such as when fundraising revenue exceeds expectations, or unfavorable, such as when program expenses are higher than anticipated. Understanding why these variances occur is crucial for effective financial management. Some variances may be due to external factors outside of management's control, such as economic downturns or sudden increases in utility costs. Others may stem from internal issues, such as overly optimistic revenue projections, weak cost controls, or delays in implementing programs. By analyzing variances, nonprofits can distinguish between temporary fluctuations and systemic problems, enabling them to take corrective action before small issues escalate into serious financial challenges.

The practice of budget monitoring and variance analysis also supports informed decision-making by nonprofit leadership. Boards of directors and management teams rely on accurate financial information to assess whether the organization is on track to achieve its goals. For instance, if program expenses are trending significantly over budget, leadership may need to consider scaling back activities, seeking additional funding, or reallocating resources. If fundraising revenue is underperforming, the organization might adjust its development strategy or revise its spending plans. Regular monitoring ensures that these decisions are made proactively rather than reactively, reducing the risk of financial shortfalls. Variance analysis further enhances decision-making by providing insights into the underlying drivers of performance, allowing leaders to focus on strategic adjustments rather than superficial fixes.

Nonprofit organizations also face heightened expectations of accountability from donors, regulators, and watchdog groups. Budget monitoring and variance analysis are tools that allow nonprofits to demonstrate responsible stewardship of funds. For grant-funded programs, variance analysis ensures compliance with grant budgets and reporting requirements. Many grants require detailed financial reporting that reconciles budgeted amounts with actual expenditures. A failure to monitor budgets effectively can result in grant funds being withheld, clawed back, or denied in the future. For donors, variance analysis provides assurance that contributions are being used as intended. An organization that can explain how it managed variances, whether by cutting costs, adjusting timelines, or identifying new funding sources, projects transparency and professionalism. This, in turn, strengthens donor trust and supports long-term fundraising success.

Another critical aspect of budget monitoring is its role in risk management. Nonprofits operate in an environment of uncertainty, often facing fluctuating funding streams, changes in government policies, and shifting community needs. A carefully prepared budget provides a roadmap, but without continuous monitoring, the organization may veer off course without realizing it. Variance analysis functions as an early warning system, signaling when revenue targets are unlikely to be met or when expenses are trending higher than anticipated. For example, if actual membership dues are significantly below budget, this may indicate declining engagement that requires strategic intervention. If utility costs are consistently higher than expected, management might explore energy efficiency measures or renegotiate supplier contracts. By addressing these issues promptly, nonprofits reduce their exposure to financial shocks and maintain organizational resilience.

Budget monitoring also fosters a culture of accountability and performance management within nonprofits. Staff and managers who are responsible for budget lines are more likely to exercise care in spending when they know that their results will be compared against budgets and reviewed regularly. This discipline encourages careful planning, accurate forecasting, and prudent decision-making at all levels of the organization. Variance analysis further reinforces accountability by highlighting areas where managers are excelling or falling short. For instance, if a program manager consistently delivers results under budget without compromising quality, this may demonstrate strong financial stewardship. On the other hand, persistent unfavorable variances may point to the need for additional training, support, or process changes. In this way, budget monitoring and variance analysis contribute not only to financial control but also to organizational learning and improvement.

Technology has significantly enhanced the ability of nonprofits to conduct effective budget monitoring and variance analysis. Modern accounting systems provide real-time access to financial data, automated reporting, and dashboard visualizations that make it easier to track performance against budget. These systems allow organizations to drill down into variances to understand their root causes, such as specific expense categories or revenue streams. Cloud-based solutions also enable collaboration between accounting staff, program managers, and executive leadership, ensuring that everyone has access to the information needed to make timely decisions. By leveraging technology, nonprofits can move beyond static, retrospective budget reports to dynamic, forward-looking financial analysis that supports agility and strategic planning.

While budget monitoring and variance analysis are essential, nonprofits must approach them with care to avoid potential pitfalls. One challenge is the risk of focusing too narrowly on short-term variances at the expense of long-term strategy. For example, an organization that cuts program expenses simply to stay within budget may inadvertently compromise service quality or mission impact. Another challenge is the temptation to judge performance solely based on budget adherence, when some variances may reflect positive innovation or necessary adaptation to changing circumstances. Effective variance analysis requires context and judgment, recognizing when deviations are reasonable and even beneficial. Boards and managers must therefore strike a balance between enforcing financial discipline and allowing flexibility for mission-driven decisions.

The frequency and scope of budget monitoring depend on the size and complexity of the nonprofit, but regular review is essential for all organizations. Larger nonprofits with multiple programs and funding streams may monitor budgets monthly or even weekly, while smaller organizations may find quarterly reviews sufficient. Regardless of frequency, timely analysis is key. A variance identified months after it occurred is of limited value, whereas early detection allows for corrective action. In addition, budget monitoring should not be limited to accounting staff; program managers, executive directors, and board members all play roles in reviewing and interpreting variances. This collaborative approach ensures that financial insights are integrated with programmatic and strategic perspectives.

The importance of budget monitoring and variance analysis becomes even more apparent in times of financial uncertainty or crisis. During economic downturns, natural disasters, or pandemics, nonprofits may face sudden drops in revenue or spikes in demand for services. Without vigilant budget monitoring, these shocks can quickly destabilize operations. Variance analysis allows organizations to adapt by identifying areas where spending can be reduced, resources can be reallocated, or fundraising can be intensified. By maintaining discipline in financial oversight, nonprofits can navigate crises more effectively and continue serving their communities when they are needed most.

In conclusion, budget monitoring and variance analysis are indispensable practices for nonprofit organizations, serving as cornerstones of financial management, accountability, and strategic decision-making. By regularly comparing actual results with budgeted amounts, nonprofits can identify risks, understand performance drivers, and take corrective action in a timely manner. These practices demonstrate to donors, grantors, and regulators that resources are managed responsibly, reinforcing trust and credibility. They also foster a culture of accountability within the organization, where staff and managers take ownership of financial stewardship. Supported by modern technology and guided by thoughtful leadership, budget monitoring and variance analysis empower nonprofits to remain adaptable, resilient, and mission-focused in a complex and uncertain environment. Ultimately, these practices are not just financial tools but essential elements of organizational sustainability and impact.

Control Principles

There are a number of principles to keep in mind when constructing a system of controls for a nonprofit. These principles are frequently the difference between a robust control system and one that appears adequate on paper, but which never seems to work in practice. The principles are:

- *Separation of duties.* The separation of duties involves assigning different parts of a process to different people, so that collusion would be required for someone to commit fraud. For example, one person opens the mail and records a list of the checks received, while a different person records them in the accounting system and a third person deposits the checks. By separating these tasks, it is much more difficult for someone to (for example) remove a check from the incoming mail, record a receivables credit in the accounting system to cover his tracks, and cash the check into his own account. Unfortunately, there is a major downside to the separation of duties, which is that shifting tasks among multiple people interferes with the efficiency of a process. Consequently, only use this control principle at the minimum level needed to establish the desired level of control – too much of it is not cost-effective.
- *Process integration.* Controls should be so thoroughly intertwined with business transactions that it is impossible for employees *not* to perform them as part of their daily activities. This level of integration substantially reduces the incidence of errors and the risk of fraud. An example of minimal process integration that will likely result in frequent control problems is requiring employees to record this information by hand on a paper form.
- *Management support.* The management team must make it abundantly clear to employees that it thoroughly supports the system of controls. This does not mean that a general statement of ethics is included in the employee manual. Instead, it means that management takes the time to explain controls to

employees, is highly visible in investigating control breaches, and takes sufficient remedial action to make it clear to the entire staff that controls are to be taken seriously. Management also does not override its own controls, nor does it set performance standards that are so difficult to attain that employees would be forced to circumvent controls in order to meet the standards.

- *Responsibility.* No control system will work unless people are made responsible for them. This means that someone should be assigned responsibility for every control, and that they receive regular updates on the status of those controls. It would also be useful if the status of their controls are noted in their compensation reviews, and have a direct impact on changes in their pay.

- *Conscientious application.* Employees cannot simply treat controls in a perfunctory manner. Instead, there should be a culture that encourages the close examination of control breaches to determine what went wrong, and how the system can be adjusted to reduce the risk that the same issue will occur again. This level of conscientious behavior must be encouraged by the management team through constant reinforcement of the message that the system of controls is important. It also requires the availability of communication channels through which employees can anonymously report suspected improprieties.

- *Systems knowledge.* It is impossible to expect employees to conscientiously inspect controls unless they already know how systems operate. This calls for the ongoing training of employees to ensure that they thoroughly understand all aspects of the systems with which they are involved. This requires not only an initial training session for new employees, but also reminder sessions that are timed to coincide with any changes in processes and related controls, as well as thorough documentation of the systems. A good level of systems knowledge may call for the use of procedures, training materials, and a core group of trainers.

- *Error reporting.* It is impossible to know if a control is functioning properly unless there is a system in place for reporting control breaches. This may be a report generated by a computer system, but it may also call for open communication channels with employees, donors, and suppliers to solicit any errors that have been found. In this latter case, error reporting is strongly supported by a management group that is clearly interested in spotting errors and correcting them in a way that does not cast blame on those reporting the information. In addition, errors should be communicated all the way up through the organization to the audit committee and board of directors, who can enforce the establishment of enhanced controls.

- *Staffing.* There must be an adequate number of employees on hand to operate controls. Otherwise, there will be great pressure to avoid manual controls, since they take too much time to complete. This is actually a profitability issue, since a nonprofit experiencing losses is more likely to cut back on staffing, which in turn impacts the control system.

- *Outlier analysis.* Most businesses create control systems to deal with problems they have seen in the past, or which have been experienced elsewhere in the industry. They rarely create controls designed to mitigate outlier issues –

that is, problems that occur very infrequently. The sign of a great control system is one in which employees take the time to examine the control system from a high level, and in light of the current and future business environment, to see if there are any outlier events that present a risk of loss in sufficiently large amounts to warrant the addition of controls. This outlier analysis requires excellent knowledge of the industry and a perceptive view of the direction in which it is headed.

Of the principles just noted, management support is the most crucial. Without it, a system of controls is like a building with no supporting framework – the entire structure crashes to the ground if there is any pressure placed upon it at all. For example, the control system may appear to have proper separation of duties, but this makes no difference if the management team ignores these separations for transactions that it has an interest in ramming through the system.

The Proper Balance of Control Systems

A person who has been trained in control systems will likely want to install every possible control, and will then feel satisfied that he or she has saved the organization from an impending failure. Those on the receiving end of these controls have a different opinion of the situation, which is that controls slow down transactions, require more staff, and have the same general effect on a nonprofit as pouring sand into the gas tank of a car.

Because of these radically differing views of the utility of control systems, it is useful to adopt a set of controls that are based on the following points:

- *Risk – monetary*. If a control can prevent a large loss, such as one that could bankrupt a nonprofit, then it makes sense to install it, as long as the probability of the event is reasonably high. For example, having two people involved in every wire transfer transaction is a reasonable precaution, given the amount of funds that could be transferred out in a single wire transfer. Conversely, if a control can never save more than a few dollars (such as locking the office supply cabinet) it is entirely likely that the sheer annoyance caused by the control outweighs any possible savings to be achieved from it.
- *Risk – financial statements*. A nonprofit must understand its performance, and it can only do so with reliable financial statements. Consequently, controls over recordkeeping should be among the most comprehensive in an organization. However, this does not necessarily call for an oppressive amount of controls in those areas where the amounts involved are essentially immaterial to the financial statements.
- *Repetitiveness*. Only install comprehensive controls for those transactions that a nonprofit will engage in on a recurring basis. For example, if an organization sells excess assets to a foreign customer once a year and wants to hedge the outstanding receivable, a once-a-year transaction does not require an elaborate control system (unless the receivable is for a large amount – see the preceding point about risk). Thus, it behooves a nonprofit to concentrate on a

finely-tuned set of controls for the 20% of its processes that make up 80% of its business (the Pareto Principle). Of the remaining 80% of the nonprofit's processes, those items involving the most inherent risk should be the prime candidates for strong controls.

- *Offsetting controls.* It may be acceptable to have weak controls in one part of an operation, as long as there are offsetting controls elsewhere. For example, it may not be necessary to have someone sign checks, as long as all purchases are initiated with an authorizing purchase order. This concept can be used to great effect if there is a good business reason to keep one process running as smoothly as possible (i.e., without controls), with offsetting controls in a less noticeable part of the organization.

- *Cost.* The cost of controls must be balanced against the expected reduction in risk. This is not a simple calculation to make, for it can be quite difficult to estimate the reduction of risk that will be achieved by implementing a control. One approach to quantifying risk is to multiply the risk percentage by the exposure to the business, which is known as the *expected loss*. See the following example.

Conversely, it is easy enough to measure the labor cost and other factors required to implement and maintain a control, so there is a tendency for nonprofits to focus on the up-front cost of a control and downplay the savings that may or may not arise from having the control. The result tends to be a control level that is lower than it should be.

EXAMPLE

Archimedes Education operates a payroll system that pays employees on a semi-monthly basis. When there are a significant number of data errors in the payroll, Archimedes' payroll manager requires that the payroll be run again, at a cost of $5,000.

The payroll manager is considering the installation of an automated data validation software package that is expected to reduce the payroll data error rate from 8% to 1%, at a software rental cost of $250 per payroll. The cost–benefit analysis is:

- *No data validation.* There is an 8% chance of incurring a $5,000 payroll reprocessing cost, which is an expected loss of $400 ($5,000 exposure × 8% risk) per payroll.
- *Data validation.* There is a 1% chance of incurring a $5,000 payroll reprocessing cost, which is an expected loss of $50 ($5,000 exposure × 1% risk) per payroll. There is also a charge of $250 per payroll for the software rental cost.

Thus, there is a reduction of $350 in the expected loss if the control is implemented, against which there is a control cost of $250. This results in a net gain of $100 per payroll by using the control. Changes in the estimated probabilities can have a significant impact on the outcome of this analysis.

The resulting system should be one where some failures will still occur, but either in such small amounts that they do not place the organization at risk, or where the probability of occurrence is very low. It is difficult to maintain this balance between controls and operational effectiveness over time, seeing that a growing nonprofit is constantly in a state of flux, expanding some programs, curtailing others, and installing any number of new systems. It is the job of the accountant to watch the interaction of these processes with existing control systems, and know when it is an acceptable risk to pare back some controls, while introducing new ones elsewhere.

It is quite common to see a control system that lags behind the current state of its processes, usually due to inattention by the accountant. This means that some controls are so antiquated as to be essentially meaningless (while still annoying the staff), while new systems are devoid of controls, and will only see new ones when a system failure occurs.

In summary, there is a balance between the system of controls and the efficient operation of a nonprofit that is difficult to manage. A good accountant will understand the needs of employees to keep operations efficient, and so should be willing to subsist in some areas on control systems that may appear rather skimpy, as long as the tradeoff is between a notable improvement in efficiency and the risk of only modest losses that would have been prevented by controls.

Cash Controls

Cash receipts is an area in which a poorly-controlled nonprofit can lose a large amount of money, since cash is one of the more easily negotiable assets, and so is a continual target for theft. In addition, it is a high-volume application, so some data entry errors will arise occasionally that will require time-consuming investigation and correction.

In this section, we cover the controls that can be imposed on the core cash receipts activities. The list appears long, because different controls apply only to certain types of cash receipt, such as checks, cash, or credit cards.

1. Accept Cash

This section includes controls for three very different types of payment – checks sent to the organization, checks sent to a lockbox, and cash. After perusing these controls, it will be clear that the area most inundated with controls is the receipt of cash, which are needed to prevent theft. The controls are:

- *Open the mail and record cash receipts.* Someone not otherwise involved in the handling or recordation of cash receipts opens the mail, records all cash and checks received, and then forwards the cash receipts to the cashier. To strengthen this control, have two people jointly open the mail.
- *Endorse for deposit only.* The person opening the mail should also immediately endorse all checks received with a "For Deposit Only" stamp, preferably one that also lists the entity's bank account number. This makes it much more difficult for someone to extract a check and deposit it into some other account.
- *Direct payments to lockbox.* An excellent control is to set up a lockbox at a bank, and direct customers and donors to send their payments directly to the bank. This eliminates all risk of cash or checks being stolen from within the

nonprofit, and may also accelerate the recognition of cash in the nonprofit's bank account by a day or so.

- *Record cash in cash register.* The primary purpose of a cash register is as its name indicates – it registers the amount of cash received. Therefore, when there is any reasonable expectation for a large number of cash receipts, always have a cash register available for recording the transactions.

- *Record cash on pre-numbered receipts.* In situations where relatively small quantities of cash are anticipated, it may not be cost-effective to operate a cash register. If so, record cash received on pre-numbered receipts, and be sure to use the receipts consecutively. By doing so, the numbers on the receipts can be scanned to see if any receipts are missing. A missing receipt indicates that cash has not been recorded.

- *Give receipt to customer or donor.* If a customer or donor is paying with cash, have cashiers give them a copy of the receipt. If the cash is recorded in a cash register, the amount printed on the receipt will match the amount punched into the register. If the cash is recorded on pre-numbered receipts, the form should be a two-part form, so that the amount written on it by the clerk is identical for the versions kept by the customer and the nonprofit. Handing over a receipt is a reasonable control, since it means that the recipient might examine the receipt to see if the amount recorded matches what they paid.

- *Document fundraisers.* When a fund raising event is held, validate the amount of the winning bid with the person who placed the bid, to ensure that the amount of cash recorded matches the amount paid by the person. Also, have a second person reconcile the bid documentation and the deposit slip to ensure that all funds were received and that they were deposited correctly.

- *Document table sponsors.* When a table is sponsored at a fund raiser, payments for a table may be made at the event. If so, provide a sealable envelope at each table, in which sponsors can place their cash payments. Then have two people collect, open, and document the contents of the envelopes. Also, send a confirmation letter to each donor, so that donors will have a chance to complain if the amount is incorrect.

2. Record Cash

The recordation of cash within the accounting system is essentially the same for all types of payment, with the main difference being that the cashier should record the type of payment received when recording each payment. Thus, there should be a "cash," "check," or "credit card" flag in the software. This makes it easier to later track down the types of cash payments made. The controls for recording cash are:

- *Apply cash at once.* There are several reasons why the cashier should apply cash to programs or customer accounts as soon as the cash is received. First, it removes overdue accounts receivable from the aged receivables report, and therefore keeps the collection staff from wasting time on collection calls. Also, immediate cash application means that the cash will then be shifted off the premises and deposited, leaving little time for anyone to steal it.

> **Tip:** Encourage donors to include the name of the program to which they are donating on their check payments, so that these checks can be applied more easily.

- *Apply cash based on check copies.* This control can be applied in two situations. If a nonprofit is using a bank lockbox, the bank will either mail copies of all checks and remittance advices received to the organization, or it will make them available on a website as scanned images; in either case, the cashier uses these documents as the basis for cash applications. In the second situation, the cashier photocopies all checks, thereby allowing for the immediate deposit of the checks and a somewhat more leisurely application of the payments to outstanding receivables.
- *Record undocumented receipts in a clearing account.* One of the best ways to destroy accounts receivable record accuracy is to apply cash receipts to receivables even when there is no indication of the invoice numbers to which they should be applied. Instead, these receipts should always be recorded into a clearing account for further review.
- *Match documents.* The cashier should match the initial list of checks generated by the person opening the mail to the related cash receipts journal. This highlights cash that the cashier may not have applied to receivables, and will also spot any cash that was removed between the mailroom and the cashier's office.

3. Deposit Cash

The depositing of cash and checks is essentially the same, since they are routinely recorded under a single deposit slip and transported to the bank together. This means that their deposit-related controls are identical. However, if a nonprofit uses remote deposit capture to scan checks on-site and send an electronic file to the bank, there are different controls for those checks. The controls are noted below:

- *Deposit daily.* If checks or cash are left on-site overnight, there is an increased chance that they may be stolen. To mitigate this risk, always deposit cash and checks at the end of every business day.
- *Lock up cash during transport.* Store all cash in a locked container while transporting it to the bank for deposit. This is not a good control, since someone could steal the entire container. A better approach for transporting large amounts of cash is to hire an armored car company to transport the cash on behalf of the entity.
- *Match cash receipts journal to bank receipt.* When funds are deposited at the bank, the bank clerk hands over a receipt for the amount deposited. The person transporting the cash to the bank gives this receipt to the cashier, who compares it to the cash receipts journal. If the numbers do not match, it may mean that the person transporting the cash removed some cash prior to the deposit, though it may also mean that either the cashier or the bank incorrectly recorded the amount of cash.

Credit card payments do not involve the handling of cash, so their controls are quite different from the ones used for cash. Possible controls include:

- *Use a form to take down information.* If a nonprofit manually enters credit card information into an on-line site, there is a significant chance that the information it enters will be incorrect in some respect, and so will be rejected. To reduce this risk, use a standard form to take down the name, billing address, and credit card information associated with the card being used to pay an invoice, as well as the name and address to which a receipt should be sent, and the number of the invoice being paid. The form should also require a phone number for the person paying the invoice, in case someone needs to call them back to verify the information or ask for a different credit card number.

- *Reconcile credit card receipts to pledges and accounts receivable.* When cash appears on the bank statement from a credit card transaction, have a procedure to trace it back to cash applied to specific accounts receivable or pledges. Otherwise, there is a chance that the accountant will process a credit card but forget to also process the matching cash receipt against the related invoice or pledge.

> **Tip:** When entering credit card payments in the cash receipts system, always designate them as credit card payments. A report can then be created that shows only the credit card payments assigned to pledges receivable during the month. Compare the amounts on this report to the receipts appearing on the bank statement to ensure that all credit card payments were applied against open receivables.

Donated Merchandise Controls

It is quite common for a nonprofit entity to have poor or nonexistent controls over the merchandise donated to it. This can be a problem, especially when the merchandise in question includes consumer goods that can be readily sold off to third parties. For example, an employee could take items home for personal use, or sell them online, or give them away to friends and family.

The risk of merchandise loss can be mitigated to some extent by segregating duties. Specifically, one person should be responsible for receiving donated merchandise, while someone else is responsible for its disposition. Further, any merchandise to be retained for use or resale should be logged into an inventory database, after which periodic inventory counts can be conducted to verify whether these items are still on the premises. In addition, physical controls can be implemented to restrict access to the most valuable donated merchandise.

Fixed Asset Controls

In this section, we cover the controls that can be imposed on the various stages of the fixed asset life cycle. This life cycle encompasses the initial acquisition of assets, as well as their depreciation and disposal.

1. Fixed Asset Acquisition

The key focus of controls for the acquisition of key assets is to ensure that the non-profit needs the assets. This means that controls are designed to require an evaluation of how a proposed acquisition will fit into operations, and what kind of return on investment it will generate. A secondary set of controls is also needed to ensure that all acquisition transactions are forced to follow this review process. With these goals in mind, consider using the following controls:

- *Require an approval form.* There should be an approval form that requires an applicant to describe the asset, how it is to be used, and the return on investment that will be generated (if any). This standardizes the information about each fixed asset, and also provides a handy signature form for various approvals.

- *Require independent analysis of the approval form.* Someone who is skilled in asset analysis should review each submitted approval form. This analysis includes a verification that all supporting documents are attached to the form, that all assumptions are reasonable, and that the conclusions reached appear to be valid. The person conducting this analysis does not necessarily render an opinion on whether to acquire the asset, but should point out any flaws in the proposal. This person should *not* report to the person who submitted the proposal, since that would be a conflict of interest.

- *Require multi-level approvals for more expensive assets.* If an asset request is *really* expensive, impose a requirement for a number of approvals by people in positions of increasing levels of authority. Though clearly time-consuming, the intent is to make a number of people aware of the request, so that the organization as a whole will be absolutely sure of its position before allowing a purchase to proceed.

- *Focus more attention on rush requests.* Someone may try to avoid the usual review steps in order to obtain an asset right now on a rush basis. These are precisely the sorts of situations where it may make sense to impose a tighter review, since the rush nature of the purchase may be keeping people from due deliberation of the alternatives available. The exact nature of this control will vary under the circumstances, but the key point is to not eliminate *all* reviews and approvals just because someone says that an asset must be bought at once.

- *Impose a mandatory waiting period.* Though controversial, it may make sense to impose a waiting period before any asset is purchased, on the grounds that due deliberation may reveal that some assets are simply not needed, and so should not be bought. Taken to extremes, such a control can result in an excessively plodding organization, so use it with care.

- *Do not issue a purchase order without a signed approval form.* Train the staff to not order fixed assets unless the requestor has a signed approval form. Better yet, route all such purchase orders to a senior manager, such as the executive director, for approval.

- *Conduct milestone reviews.* For longer-term asset installations, there should be a series of milestone events at which the management team responsible for the project examines expenditures to date, progress on the project, and any issues relating to the remaining tasks to be completed. Though rare, the team may occasionally use the information obtained in this review to cancel the project entirely. A more common response is a variety of adjustments to improve the odds of successful completion within the cost budget.

The controls noted here will absolutely slow down the fixed asset acquisition process, and with good reason – part of their intent is to encourage more deliberation of why an asset is being acquired. Nonetheless, these controls will appear onerous to those people trying to obtain assets that are relatively inexpensive, so it is certainly acceptable to adopt a reduced set of controls for such assets, perhaps simply treating them as accounts payable that require a single approval signature on a purchase order.

Similarly, a more streamlined set of controls can be considered for assets that must be acquired at once. However, keep in mind that some managers intent on subverting the system of controls can characterize *everything* as a rush requirement, just to avoid the usual reviews and approvals. Consequently, if a reduced set of controls is adopted for such purchases, at least conduct an after-the-fact review of the circumstances of these purchases, to see if the reduced controls were actually justified.

2. Fixed Asset Depreciation

Depreciation calculation errors are extremely common, since there are opportunities to incorrectly enter the asset amount, useful life, salvage value, and depreciation method in whatever calculation spreadsheet or software is being used. Here are several controls that can mitigate this problem:

- *Conduct separate review of master file additions.* Have a second person review any records added to the fixed asset master file. This review should involve a comparison of the amounts paid to the amount listed in the master file, to ensure that the amount being depreciated is correct. Also, verify that the asset classification in which each asset is placed is the correct one, since this usually drives the depreciation method used and the useful life over which it will be depreciated. Further, verify that any salvage value used has been properly substantiated. Finally, verify that the recorded asset location is correct, so that anyone attempting to locate the asset in the future will be able to find it.
- *Audit depreciation calculations.* Periodically review a selection of the depreciation calculations, to see if an asset is being depreciated over the correct useful life, with the correct depreciation method, and with a verifiable salvage value. Errors will be more common if this information is being maintained on an electronic spreadsheet, given the greater risk of manual errors in this format.

3. Fixed Asset Disposal

There tends to be some amount of fixed asset "leakage" out of any organization, especially for smaller and more mobile assets, such as computers. In many cases, the resale value of these items near the end of their useful lives is so small that a nonprofit may very well be justified in giving them away to employees or simply dropping them into the scrap bin. However, there may be some residual value remaining in these assets, so consider using the following controls to recapture that value:

- *Conduct asset disposition reviews.* The goals of this review are to decide whether a nonprofit continues to need a fixed asset, and if not, how to obtain the highest price for it. If this control is not used, assets tend to remain on the premises long after they are no longer needed, and lose value during that time.
- *Require signed approval of asset dispositions.* Create a form that describes the asset to be disposed of, the method of disposition, and the cash to be received (if any). The person whose authorization is required could be a specialist in asset disposition, or perhaps the purchasing manager, who might have some knowledge of asset values. The point of this control is to require a last look by someone who might know of a better way to gain more value from a disposal.
- *Monitor cash receipts from asset sales.* Most fixed assets are sold for cash, and sometimes for large amounts of cash. Given the amount of funds involved, it can be quite a temptation for employees to find ways to either not record asset sales or falsify sale documents to record smaller sales, and then pocket the undocumented cash. This situation can be monitored by requiring that a bill of sale from the purchasing entity accompany the documentation for each asset sale. It is also useful to periodically audit asset sale transactions, if only to show the staff that these transactions are being monitored.
- *Send copy of disposal form to accounting.* If there is an asset disposal form that must be filled out prior to the disposal of a fixed asset, route a copy of it to the accounting department, so that the accounting staff can write off the asset and stop recording a periodic depreciation charge for it.

Hiring Controls

Nonprofits tend to be understaffed, and those people they can hire tend to be underpaid, due to funding constraints. When employees are overworked and underpaid, there is an increased risk that they will rationalize the need to steal from the organization, on the grounds that they deserve more income. Also, because there are so few people working within the typical nonprofit, it is not always possible to segregate duties to prevent theft. Instead, it is critical to implement hiring controls to spot problematic job applicants. This means checking references and examining criminal history records for all applicants before they are offered positions. Further, if someone will be hired into an accounting or finance-related position, then their credit report should also be examined. Someone with a low credit score is in more need of cash, and so will be more inclined to steal from the organization.

Payables Controls

Accounts payable is an area in which a poorly-controlled department can lose a large amount of money, as well as annoy those suppliers who are being paid late. In this section, we describe the control systems needed to remediate these issues.

1. Verify Obligation to Pay

The verification of obligation to pay can be accomplished through one of several possible controls. They are:

- *Invoice approval.* The person in a position to authorize payment signifies his or her approval of a supplier invoice. However, this is actually a relatively weak control if the approver only sees the supplier invoice, since there is no way to tell if the goods or services were received, or if the prices being charged were what the nonprofit originally agreed to. The approver may also want to know which general ledger account will be charged. Consequently, it is better to have the payables staff first assemble the supplier invoice, authorizing purchase order, and receiving documentation into a packet, then stamp the invoice with a signature block that includes the account number to be charged, and *then* have the approver review it. This approach gives reviewers a *very* complete set of information to work with.

> **Tip:** If invoices are sent out for approvals prior to being entered in the payable system, maintain a log of the invoices that are out for approval, and cross them off when they are eventually returned. This makes it easier to determine which invoices have *not* been returned.

- *Purchase order approval.* The purchasing department issues a purchase order for every purchase made. By doing so, the purchasing staff is, in essence, approving all expenditures before they have been made, which may prevent some expenditures from ever occurring. Since this control entails a certain amount of work by the purchasing staff, they will likely ask employees to request items on a formal purchase requisition form.

> **Tip:** In practice, it will be inordinately expensive to enforce the use of purchase orders for everything. Instead, this control is more enforceable for larger purchases, with an automatic exemption for all purchases below a minimum dollar amount.

- *Manual duplicate payment search.* A computerized payables system conducts an automatic search for duplicate invoice numbers. This is a much more difficult endeavor in an entirely manual accounting system. In this case, the payables clerk can search through the vendor file and unpaid invoices file to see if an invoice just received from a supplier has already been paid. In many situations, the volume of incoming supplier invoices makes this so difficult that the payables staff abandons any attempt to identify duplicate invoices, and simply accepts that it will occasionally pay for such items.

2. Data Entry

There are several ways to ensure that all supplier invoices have been entered in the accounts payable system, though these controls have varying degrees of success. The controls are:

- *Record after approval.* This control forces the accounts payable staff to verify the approval of every invoice before entering it into the system.

Tip: This control can be an expensive one, since some invoices will inevitably not be approved in time to be paid by their due dates. To avoid late penalties, use automatic approvals of smaller and recurring invoices, and have several alternate approvers available if the primary approvers are not available.

- *Record prior to approval.* This control places greater priority on paying suppliers than it does on obtaining authorizations to pay, since every invoice received is recorded in the payables system at once. This control works best where purchase orders have already been used to authorize a purchase.

Tip: When recording supplier invoices in advance, consider using *negative approvals*. This means that approvers receive a copy of each invoice, but only contact the payables staff if they *do not* approve an invoice. This largely eliminates the amount of feedback that the payables staff can expect from authorizers.

- *Adopt an invoice numbering guideline.* Perhaps the largest problem in the area of payables data entry is duplicate payments. This would not appear to be a problem, since most companies use accounting software that automatically detects duplicate invoices and prevents duplicate payments. However, there can be inconsistency in how invoice numbers are recorded. For example, should invoice number 0000078234 be recorded with the leading zeros or without them? If the same invoice is presented to the payables staff twice, and it is recorded as 0000078234 one time and 78234 the next time, the system will not flag them as being duplicate invoices. The same problem arises with dashes in an invoice number; an invoice number of 1234-999 could be recorded as 1234-999 or as 1234999.

  A simple control over the duplicate invoice problem is a one-page description of how invoice numbers are to be recorded, which is to be posted prominently next to the computer of every accounts payable data entry person for easy reference. A sample statement follows.

Invoice Number Policy

Leading zeros: Always delete all leading zeros from an invoice number.

For example: Record 0000078234 as 78234

Dashes: Always delete all dashes from an invoice number.

For example: Record 1234-999 as 1234999

No invoice number: Enter the invoice date as a six-digit number.

For example: Enter an invoice dated July 9, 2025 as 070925

---

3. Payment

The bulk of the controls noted below pertain to payment by check, since that is still the predominant form of payment. Several controls near the bottom of the list are targeted at electronic payments. The controls are:

- *Split check printing and signing.* One person should prepare checks, and a different person should sign them. By doing so, there is a cross-check on the issuance of cash.
- *Store all checks in a locked location.* Unused check stock should *always* be stored in a locked location. Otherwise, checks can be stolen and fraudulently filled out and cashed. This means that any signature plates or stamps should also be stored in a locked location.

> **Tip:** If there is a signature stamp or plate, store it in a different locked location from the check stock, and keep the keys to the two locations in different spots. Ideally, different people should be responsible for the check stock and the signature plate. This makes it more difficult for someone to obtain both and generate valid-looking check payments.

- *Secure check-printing equipment.* Some printers are only used for check printing. If so, keep them in a locked location so that no one can print checks and have the integrated signature plate automatically sign the checks.
- *Track the sequence of check numbers used.* Maintain a log in which are listed the range of check numbers used during a check run. This is useful for determining if any checks in storage might be missing. This log should not be kept with the stored checks, since someone could steal the log at the same time they steal checks.
- *Require manual check signing.* A nonprofit can require that all checks be signed. This is actually a relatively weak control, since few check signers delve into why checks are being issued, and rarely question the amounts paid. If an organization chooses to use a signature plate or stamp instead, it is much

174

more important to have a strong purchase order system; the purchasing staff becomes the de facto approvers of invoices by issuing purchase orders earlier in the payables process flow.

Tip: If a nonprofit requires manual check signing, do everything possible to strengthen the control. This means assembling a voucher package for each check that the check signer can review, and having a payables person sit with the check signer to answer questions during signing sessions.

- *Require an additional check signer.* If the amount of a check exceeds a certain amount, require a second check signer. This control supposedly gives multiple senior-level people the chance to stop making a payment. In reality, it is more likely to only introduce another step into the payment process without really strengthening the control environment.
- *Stamp invoices "paid".* In a purely manual payables environment, there is a risk of paying an invoice more than once, so a reasonable control is to stamp each paid invoice, or even perforate it with a "paid" stamp. This control is less necessary (if at all) in a computerized system, which automatically tracks which invoices have been paid.

Tip: If the choice is made to not use a "paid" stamp in a computerized environment, be sure to install a consistent procedure for assigning an invoice number to those invoices that are not numbered. Otherwise, the copies of the same invoice could be assigned different invoice numbers and then paid.

- *Lock up undistributed checks.* If a nonprofit does not distribute checks at once, they should be stored in a locked location. Otherwise, there is a risk of theft, with the person stealing the checks modifying them sufficiently to cash them.
- *Use positive pay.* Positive pay is a program under which a nonprofit sends a file containing its check payment information to its bank; if a check is presented for payment and it is not on the list of checks issued by the organization, the bank rejects it. This can eliminate check fraud, though there is some question of whether it is more beneficial to the bank (which could be liable for accepting fraudulent checks) or the nonprofit.

Tip: It is easy to forget to notify the bank of check payments, especially manual checks that are created outside of the normal check printing process. Therefore, have an iron-clad bank notification system in place before enacting positive pay. It may help to run positive pay on a test basis for a few months to see how many check notifications were not made, and what caused them.

- *Initiate banking transactions from a dedicated computer.* It is possible for someone to use keystroke logging software to detect the user identification and password information that a business uses to authorize direct deposit and wire transfer information. To reduce the risk, set up a separate computer that is only used to initiate transactions with the bank. This reduces the risk that keystroke logging software might be inadvertently downloaded onto the machine from an e-mail or other transaction.

- *Pay from a separate account.* There is a risk that someone could use an ACH debit transaction to move funds out of a nonprofit's bank account. To reduce this risk, only shift sufficient funds into a checking account to cover the amount of outstanding checks, ACH payments, and wire transfers that have not yet cleared the bank. Also, arrange with the bank to block all ACH debit transactions.
- *Password-protect the direct deposit file.* Some nonprofits accumulate bank account information for their supplier payments in a computer file, while others may access it online in their bank's systems. In either case, the file should be password protected to prevent tampering with the accounts. Also, the password should be changed regularly, and certainly after anyone with access to the file has left the organization.
- *Different person verifies or approves wire transfers.* When a nonprofit authorizes a wire transfer, one person issues the instructions to the bank, and a different person verifies or approves the transaction.

> **Tip:** If a different person is to verify or approve each wire transfer, set up the e-mail address of the verifying person in the confirmation contact list in the bank's records, so that notifications are automatically sent to that person.

> **Tip:** Direct deposit and wire transfer payments are frequently made outside of the accounts payable system, which means that someone has to manually record these payments in the payables system. If they forget to do so, there is a risk that these items will be paid again, or paid by check. Consequently, be sure to set up a default payment type for each supplier in the vendor master file, and stick to that payment type. Treat any request for a different type of payment as a policy violation, which requires extra approvals.

Payroll Controls

Payroll requires the assembly and marshaling of a great deal of timekeeping information, which presents the risk of many errors when it is converted into the payroll database. It is also an area in which fraud can be rife. Both circumstances require the creation of a robust system of controls, which are described in this section.

1. Collect Time Information

Controls are needed over time collection to ensure that all timesheets have been collected, and that the amounts reported are valid. These controls are:

- *Install automated timekeeping.* Install computerized time clocks. These clocks have a number of built-in controls, such as only allowing employees to clock in or out for their designated shifts, not allowing overtime without a supervisory override, and (for biometric clocks) eliminating the risk of buddy punching. Buddy punching occurs when a third party clocks an employee in and out of a timekeeping system, even though the employee is not working. Also, any exception reports generated by these clocks should be sent to supervisors for review.

- *Match timesheets to employee list.* There is a risk that an employee will not turn in a timesheet in a timely manner, and so will not be paid. To avoid this problem, print a list of active employees at the beginning of payroll processing, and check off the names on the list when their timesheets are received.

- *Verify hours worked.* Have supervisors approve hours worked by their employees, to prevent the employees from charging more time than they actually worked.

- *Verify overtime worked.* Even if supervisors are not required to approve the hours worked by employees, at least have supervisors approve overtime hours worked. There is a pay premium associated with these hours, so the cost to the nonprofit is higher, and is a temptation for employees to claim them.

> **Tip:** An additional control to consider is to track overtime hours by employee on a trend line. This may highlight those employees who persistently record very small amounts of overtime on a continuing basis, on the theory that a supervisor will approve these small amounts without much investigation.

2. Data Entry

It is quite easy to make mistakes when manually entering timekeeping information into a payroll system, and when setting up electronic payment information. Also, ensure that changes to employee deductions and pay rates have been authorized. The related controls are:

- *Verify aggregation calculations.* If payroll is being manually calculated, have a second person verify the aggregation of hours worked. A second person is more likely to conduct a careful examination than the person who originated the calculations.

- *Match entered totals to timesheets.* If there has been a history of errors in entering timekeeping information into the payroll software, consider adding a control to match the entered totals to the aggregated totals listed on employee timesheets. If automated timekeeping systems are in use, this information will be entered automatically, and no control is needed.

- *Require change authorizations.* Only allow a change to an employee's marital status, withholding allowances, or deductions if the employee has submitted a written and signed request for the nonprofit to do so. Otherwise, there is no proof that the employee wanted a change to be made. The same control applies for any pay rate changes requested by a manager.

- *Require pre-noting.* Pre-noting is used to conduct a trial test of a direct deposit transaction. Though this feature delays the start of direct deposits by one payroll, it is quite useful for spotting incorrect bank numbers and account codes. It is especially important when employees are allowed to alter their direct deposit information with a self-service system, since they are more likely than the payroll staff to input incorrect information. In particular, they may use information from their bank account deposit slips, rather than their checks; deposit slips do not necessarily contain the correct bank and account number information.

3. Calculate Gross and Net Pay

If payroll is being calculated manually, there is a risk that taxes will be incorrectly calculated, and that taxes and deductions may be incorrectly applied to gross pay. There are fewer concerns when payroll software is used, though the following payroll register controls should still be employed. The controls are:

- *Review calculations.* If payroll calculations are being conducted manually, have a second person verify the payroll calculations, tracing back to the summary totals to be paid to each employee, and checking taxes, deductions, and net pay calculations.
- *Review preliminary payroll register.* In a computerized system, the first evidence that the payroll clerk may have made a mistake will appear on the preliminary payroll register. A major control is to engage in as many iterations of this report as necessary, printing the register, looking for mistakes, correcting the mistakes, printing a replacement register, and so on.
- *Manager approves final payroll register.* Once all time information has been entered in the payroll system and wages and related deductions have been calculated, print a final payroll register that summarizes this information, and have a manager review and approve it.

4. Payment

The bulk of the controls noted below pertain to payment by check, since that is still a predominant form of payment. Several controls near the bottom of the list are targeted at cash payments. Many payment controls are necessary for checks, because there are risks of fraud and errors in multiple places during their storage, printing, and distribution. The controls are:

- *Use a separate bank account.* Pay employees from a separate checking account, and fund it only in the amount of the checks paid out. Doing so prevents someone from fraudulently increasing the amount on an existing paycheck or creating an entirely new one, since the funds in the account will not be sufficient to pay for the altered check.
- *Split check printing and signing.* One person should prepare checks, and a different person should sign them. By doing so, there is a cross-check on the issuance of cash.

- *Store all checks in a locked location.* Unused check stock should *always* be stored in a locked location. Otherwise, checks can be stolen and fraudulently filled out and cashed. This means that any signature plates or stamps should also be stored in a locked location.
- *Secure check-printing equipment.* Some printers are only used for check printing. If so, keep them in a locked location so that no one can print checks and have the integrated signature plate automatically sign the checks.
- *Track the sequence of check numbers used.* Maintain a log in which are listed the range of check numbers used during a check run. This is useful for determining if any checks in storage might be missing. This log should not be kept with the stored checks, since someone could steal the log at the same time they steal checks.
- *Match check total to calculations.* If paychecks are being manually created, have a second person compare the amount on the checks to the net pay amounts indicated in the payroll register. The person who writes the checks is less likely to be thorough in matching these amounts.

> **Tip:** A common mistake is to cut a manual check for the gross pay amount, rather than the net pay amount listed on the payroll register. To keep this from happening, use a highlighter to mark the net pay amounts on the register prior to writing checks.

- *Sign checks.* In a smaller nonprofit where there are few employees, it may make sense to avoid a signature plate or stamp, in favor of manual check signing. Doing so increases the odds that the check signer may spot an issue. A further control here is to require two check signers for really large payments, just to introduce an additional reviewer.
- *Hand checks to employees.* Where possible, hand checks directly to employees. Doing so prevents a type of fraud where a payroll clerk creates a check for a ghost employee and pockets the check. A ghost employee is a fake employee record to which payments are fraudulently made. It could be an entirely fabricated person, or else a former employee whose record still indicates that he or she is an active employee. If this is too inefficient a control, consider distributing checks manually on an occasional basis.
- *Lock up undistributed checks.* If a nonprofit does not distribute checks at once, they should be stored in a locked location. Otherwise, there is a risk of theft, with the person stealing the checks modifying them sufficiently to cash them.

5. Remit Taxes

A nonprofit is liable for remitting the correct amount of withheld, matching, and other payroll taxes to various government entities, so be sure to use the following control to avoid late payment penalties:

- *Verify tax remittances.* The penalties associated with a late or missing tax remittance are severe, so have someone independently verify the amount of tax to remit, verify that the funds were actually sent to the government, and that the organization received a receipt in exchange.

> **Tip:** Outsourcing payroll processing eliminates the tax remittance problem, since the supplier is now responsible for it.

Summary

Many nonprofits have skimpy systems of control, and sometimes pay for it when cash or other assets are stolen or misused. To highlight the issue, we paid a great deal of attention to the controls concept in this chapter. By routinely reviewing existing controls and evaluating the risks associate with any holes in the control system, the board of directors and managers can have an informed discussion about the risks they are willing to accept, and those that need to be mitigated by adding more controls. Ideally, this will result in the imposition of more controls, though probably not the full suite of controls that a large for-profit enterprise would be able to install.

Chapter 11
Working with Lawyers and Accountants

Introduction

The typical nonprofit is staffed by individuals who specialize in its mission – such as conservation advocacy, social work, or medical services. What they are usually *not* staffed with is lawyers and accountants, who can provide support in several critical areas. Instead, nonprofits commonly work with outside professionals to obtain legal and accounting assistance. In this chapter, we discuss the circumstances under which outside attorneys and accountants will probably be needed, as well as how to minimize their cost.

When to Consult Legal and Accounting Professionals

Nonprofit organizations operate within a complex environment that involves compliance with laws, stewardship of donor funds, and the pursuit of a mission that must remain aligned with public expectations. Unlike for-profit entities, nonprofits cannot rely solely on the profit motive to measure success; they must balance financial sustainability with accountability and ethical responsibility. In this context, there are many situations where consulting legal and accounting professionals is not just beneficial but necessary. These professionals provide expertise that ensures nonprofits remain compliant, transparent, and financially healthy, while also enabling them to make informed strategic choices. Understanding when to seek this guidance is crucial for safeguarding the organization's credibility and sustainability.

One of the earliest points at which a nonprofit should consult professionals is during the formation stage. Establishing a nonprofit requires drafting bylaws, creating articles of incorporation, and filing with the appropriate state and federal agencies to obtain tax-exempt status. Legal professionals can guide founders through the process of structuring the organization, ensuring that governance documents meet regulatory requirements and reflect best practices. At the same time, accounting professionals can help establish the initial chart of accounts, determine appropriate fiscal year reporting, and design systems for tracking restricted and unrestricted funds. Mistakes at this early stage, such as poorly written bylaws or inadequate accounting structures, can create long-term compliance issues or hinder the organization's ability to manage grants and contributions effectively.

Once a nonprofit is operational, one of the most common circumstances requiring legal and accounting expertise is compliance with tax-exempt regulations. In the United States, for example, organizations with 501(c)(3) status must adhere to strict rules about political activity, lobbying, and the use of funds. Legal counsel is essential for interpreting these rules and ensuring that advocacy or fundraising campaigns do not inadvertently jeopardize a nonprofit's tax-exempt status. Accounting professionals play an equally important role by preparing and filing Form 990, the annual informational return required by the IRS, which must be completed accurately and often becomes a public document that is scrutinized by donors and watchdog groups. A misstep in compliance can result in penalties, reputational damage, or even revocation of tax-exempt status, making professional guidance indispensable.

Nonprofits should also consult legal and accounting experts when entering into contracts, partnerships, or significant financial transactions. Legal professionals review contracts with vendors, grant agreements with funders, and memoranda of understanding with partner organizations to ensure that the nonprofit's interests are protected. They can identify clauses that may expose the nonprofit to excessive liability or financial risk. Accounting professionals assist in evaluating the financial implications of these agreements, such as how to recognize revenue from multi-year grants or account for lease agreements. Their input ensures that the nonprofit not only complies with accounting standards but also maintains accurate records that reflect the true financial position of the organization.

Another critical moment for seeking professional guidance arises when a nonprofit receives grant funding, especially from government sources. These grants often come with complex compliance requirements, such as cost allocation rules, documentation standards, and reporting deadlines. Accounting professionals are vital in setting up systems to track expenses and revenues that are tied to specific grants, ensuring that funds are used in accordance with the grant agreement. Legal counsel may also be needed to interpret the terms of the grant, clarify the organization's obligations, and advise on the consequences of noncompliance. Any failure to manage grants properly can result in repayment demands, loss of funding, and reputational harm.

Employment matters are another area where nonprofits benefit from legal expertise. Like any employer, nonprofits must comply with labor laws governing hiring, wages, benefits, and workplace safety. Legal professionals can draft employment agreements, advise on employee classification (exempt vs. nonexempt), and help resolve disputes or claims of discrimination. When layoffs, disciplinary actions, or terminations are necessary, consulting legal counsel minimizes the risk of lawsuits or regulatory violations. Accounting professionals contribute by ensuring that payroll systems comply with tax withholding requirements and that benefits are accounted for properly in financial statements. Together, legal and accounting experts provide a comprehensive framework for managing human resources responsibly.

Nonprofits should also consult professionals during times of organizational change or crisis. For example, mergers with other nonprofits, major program expansions, or the launch of a subsidiary organization introduce new legal and financial complexities. Legal counsel is critical in negotiating merger agreements, drafting governance structures for joint ventures, and ensuring compliance with state nonprofit corporation laws. Accounting professionals help analyze whether the organization can financially sustain new initiatives and assist in integrating financial systems after a merger. In times of crisis, such as allegations of fraud, financial mismanagement, or board disputes, professional guidance can be the difference between resolution and long-term damage. Legal professionals advise on investigations and potential liabilities, while accountants may perform forensic analysis to uncover irregularities.

Fundraising activities can also trigger the need for professional consultation. Many states require nonprofits to register before soliciting donations, and legal professionals can ensure compliance with these regulations. When planning major fundraising campaigns or events, attorneys may review contracts with event planners or advise on legal considerations surrounding raffles and lotteries. Accounting professionals, meanwhile, help determine how to record different types of contributions, such as pledges, in-kind donations, or restricted gifts. Their guidance ensures that donor funds are recognized and reported properly, building donor trust and avoiding compliance issues.

Finally, nonprofits should consult legal and accounting professionals in preparation for external audits or reviews. Many funders, regulators, and state governments require nonprofits of a certain size to undergo annual audits. Accountants play the central role in preparing the organization's financial records, ensuring that they comply with Generally Accepted Accounting Principles (GAAP) and are ready for examination. Legal counsel may also be consulted to address findings in management letters, advise on auditor independence, or interpret the implications of audit results for governance and compliance. These consultations not only ensure a smoother audit process, but also strengthen the nonprofit's credibility with stakeholders.

In conclusion, the need for legal and accounting professionals arises throughout a nonprofit's lifecycle, from formation to daily operations to periods of growth and crisis. Legal professionals ensure compliance with laws, reduce liability risks, and safeguard the nonprofit's governance and contracts. Accounting professionals provide the financial expertise needed to manage donor funds, comply with grant requirements, prepare accurate statements, and file tax returns. By knowing when to seek professional advice, nonprofits protect themselves from costly mistakes, maintain public trust, and enhance their ability to achieve their mission. Ultimately, the investment in professional consultation is not merely an administrative expense but a strategic necessity that underpins accountability, transparency, and long-term sustainability.

Common Legal Issues for Nonprofits

Nonprofit organizations play a vital role in society by addressing unmet needs, supporting vulnerable populations, and advancing social, educational, cultural, or religious missions. Yet, like all entities, nonprofits must operate within a legal framework that brings with it a wide range of compliance requirements and risks. Because nonprofits are entrusted with public and donor funds, the law places particular emphasis on transparency, accountability, and stewardship. The failure to recognize and address legal issues can undermine a nonprofit's credibility, jeopardize its tax-exempt status, or expose it to lawsuits and penalties. Common legal issues for nonprofits span areas such as governance, tax compliance, employment law, fundraising regulations, contracts, intellectual property, and liability. Each of these areas poses challenges that require careful attention and, in many cases, professional guidance to manage effectively.

One of the most significant legal issues for nonprofits involves maintaining tax-exempt status. In the United States, nonprofits often seek 501(c)(3) designation under the Internal Revenue Code, which allows them to operate as charitable organizations exempt from federal income tax and permits donors to deduct contributions. To qualify, nonprofits must demonstrate that they serve a recognized charitable purpose, and they must continue to comply with operational requirements to retain their exemption. Common pitfalls include engaging in prohibited political activity, exceeding permissible lobbying limits, or allowing earnings to benefit private individuals (known as private inurement). Additionally, nonprofits must file annual informational returns such as the Form 990, which disclose financial and governance practices. Failure to file these forms for three consecutive years results in automatic revocation of a nonprofit's tax-exempt status, a potentially devastating consequence. The need to stay in compliance with tax-exempt requirements is thus a central and ongoing legal issue for all nonprofits.

Closely related to tax compliance is the issue of unrelated business income. Nonprofits may generate revenue from activities unrelated to their exempt purpose, but such income may be subject to unrelated business income tax (UBIT). For example, a museum that runs a café or gift shop may need to report this revenue separately. The line between related and unrelated activities can be complex, and misclassification risks both penalties and the perception of mission drift. Navigating UBIT rules is a legal issue that requires careful attention, as excessive unrelated business income could even threaten an organization's tax-exempt status.

Governance issues also loom large for nonprofits. Boards of directors are legally responsible for ensuring that the organization operates in compliance with its mission and with applicable laws. Directors owe fiduciary duties of care, loyalty, and obedience. The duty of care requires board members to make informed decisions, the duty of loyalty requires them to act in the organization's best interest rather than for personal gain, and the duty of obedience requires adherence to the nonprofit's mission and governing documents. Legal problems often arise when boards fail to exercise proper oversight or when conflicts of interest are not adequately managed. For example, if a board member profits personally from a contract awarded by the nonprofit without proper disclosure and approval, the organization could face claims of self-dealing. Many states require nonprofits to adopt conflict-of-interest policies and maintain documentation of board decisions to ensure compliance with fiduciary duties.

Employment law represents another area of frequent legal challenges. Like for-profit employers, nonprofits must comply with federal and state labor laws, including those governing minimum wages, overtime, workplace safety, and anti-discrimination protections. Misclassifying employees as independent contractors is a common error that can result in fines and back pay obligations. Similarly, misclassifying employees as exempt from overtime when they should be nonexempt exposes nonprofits to liability under the Fair Labor Standards Act. Nonprofits that rely heavily on volunteers must also be cautious: while volunteers are generally not considered employees, compensating them improperly or assigning them duties that resemble employment could create legal risks. In addition, nonprofits must address workplace harassment, wrongful termination claims, and compliance with benefit and retirement plan regulations. Employment law issues can be particularly challenging for nonprofits with limited human resources staff or expertise.

Fundraising is central to nonprofit sustainability, but it carries its own legal requirements. Many states mandate charitable solicitation registration before nonprofits can raise funds. A failure to register can result in fines and reputational harm. Specific fundraising activities, such as raffles, lotteries, or bingo games, may be classified as gambling and subject to strict regulation. Solicitation of donations through professional fundraisers also brings legal obligations, including the disclosure of fundraising costs and compliance with truth-in-advertising laws. Donor intent adds another dimension: nonprofits are legally required to honor any restrictions placed on donations, such as gifts designated for scholarships or capital projects. Misusing restricted funds is a breach of fiduciary duty that can lead to lawsuits, regulatory intervention, and donor distrust. Proper legal oversight of fundraising activities is therefore critical to avoiding significant risks.

Contractual obligations are another common source of legal challenges. Nonprofits enter into contracts with vendors, service providers, landlords, and funders. These agreements may cover everything from renting office space to securing grants. Legal issues arise when contracts are poorly drafted, lack clarity about deliverables or responsibilities, or contain unfavorable terms. For example, a grant agreement might require specific performance metrics or the repayment of funds if conditions are not met. Without legal review, nonprofits may inadvertently accept terms that expose them to liability or financial risk. Similarly, disputes with contractors or service providers can escalate into litigation if contracts are vague or unenforceable. Regular consultation with legal counsel to draft and review contracts is therefore essential to protect the organization's interests.

Intellectual property represents another area of concern, particularly for nonprofits engaged in publishing, education, or cultural activities. Protecting the organization's name, logo, and other branding through trademarks is critical to preventing misuse by others. Nonprofits that produce educational materials, software, or creative works must consider copyright protection, both to secure their rights and to avoid infringing on others. For instance, using copyrighted music or images without permission in promotional materials could expose a nonprofit to infringement claims. In today's digital environment, where content is widely shared online, intellectual property issues have become increasingly complex. Nonprofits must develop policies to safeguard their own intellectual property and ensure that they respect the rights of others.

Liability issues also represent ongoing legal risks for nonprofits. Because they serve the public, nonprofits may face lawsuits for personal injury, negligence, or malpractice. For example, a nonprofit operating a shelter may face liability if a client is harmed on its premises, while a nonprofit offering counseling services could face malpractice claims. Directors and officers may also be personally sued for alleged mismanagement or breaches of fiduciary duty. Insurance, such as general liability and directors' and officers' coverage, helps mitigate these risks, but legal counsel is essential in structuring programs and policies to minimize exposure. Risk management practices, including waivers for participants, safety protocols, and board training, further reduce liability risks.

Regulatory compliance extends beyond tax and fundraising rules. Nonprofits may be subject to state nonprofit corporation laws, licensing requirements for certain services, and federal regulations governing areas such as health care, education, or environmental protection. For example, a nonprofit providing child care must comply with licensing and safety regulations, while one conducting medical research must adhere to human subject protections. Failure to comply with sector-specific laws can result in penalties, loss of funding, or suspension of operations. Staying abreast of applicable regulations is a continual legal challenge that requires vigilance and often professional guidance.

Finally, transparency and public accountability create their own legal pressures. Nonprofits are expected to disclose financial information, governance policies, and program outcomes to the public. Laws requiring disclosure of Form 990 or equivalent reports reflect this expectation. Legal issues can arise if disclosures are incomplete, misleading, or inconsistent with actual practices. In the era of online watchdogs and charity rating organizations, nonprofits that fail to demonstrate transparency may face reputational damage that is as harmful as legal penalties.

In conclusion, nonprofits face a wide range of common legal issues that extend across governance, tax compliance, employment law, fundraising, contracts, intellectual property, liability, and regulatory oversight. These challenges stem from the unique position nonprofits occupy as mission-driven organizations that rely on public trust and donor support. Addressing these legal issues effectively requires proactive policies, strong governance, and regular consultation with legal and accounting professionals. Nonprofits that understand and manage their legal obligations not only protect themselves from penalties and lawsuits but also strengthen their credibility and capacity to serve their missions. In a sector where trust is paramount, attention to legal compliance is not optional but an essential component of sustainability.

Tax Filings and Compliance Issues

Tax filings and compliance are among the most important responsibilities for nonprofit organizations. While nonprofits are generally exempt from federal income tax, that exemption does not relieve them of all tax obligations. Instead, they must navigate a complex system of federal, state, and sometimes local rules that govern how they file, report, and disclose their financial activities. Compliance with these requirements is not only a legal necessity but also critical for maintaining public trust, donor confidence, and eligibility for grants. Nonprofits that neglect their tax filings risk losing their tax-exempt status, facing penalties, or damaging their reputations. Understanding the tax filings and compliance issues required of U.S. nonprofit entities is therefore essential for boards, executives, and financial managers.

The first major compliance issue for a nonprofit begins at formation. To qualify for tax-exempt status under Section 501(c)(3) of the Internal Revenue Code (or other sections for different types of nonprofits, such as 501(c)(4) for social welfare organizations or 501(c)(6) for trade associations), an organization must apply to the Internal Revenue Service (IRS) using Form 1023 or the shorter Form 1023-EZ. This application requires detailed information about the nonprofit's mission, governance, financial structure, and planned activities. Approval by the IRS grants federal tax-exempt status, allowing the organization to avoid federal income tax on mission-related activities and enabling donors to deduct contributions in the case of 501(c)(3) entities. However, this status is conditional upon ongoing compliance with both federal and state requirements.

Once tax-exempt status is obtained, nonprofits must file annual information returns with the IRS. The primary filing is Form 990, which serves as a comprehensive report on the nonprofit's financial activities, governance practices, and mission-related accomplishments. Form 990 comes in several versions, depending on the size of the organization. Larger nonprofits with gross receipts of $200,000 or more, or total assets of $500,000 or more, must file the full Form 990. Medium-sized organizations with gross receipts less than $200,000 and total assets less than $500,000 may file Form 990-EZ, a shorter version. Small nonprofits with gross receipts normally less than $50,000 can file Form 990-N, also called the e-Postcard, which is an electronic notice providing minimal information. Regardless of the version, filing is mandatory, and failure to file for three consecutive years results in automatic revocation of tax-exempt status. This rule has led to the revocation of thousands of nonprofits each year, underscoring the seriousness of compliance.

Form 990 is not just a tax filing; it is also a public document. Nonprofits must make their Form 990 available for public inspection, and it is routinely posted on websites. As a result, the form is an important tool for transparency, allowing donors, journalists, and watchdog organizations to evaluate how nonprofits manage resources. Beyond financial information, the form requires disclosures about governance policies, the compensation of key employees, and the organization's mission and accomplishments. Nonprofits must therefore approach Form 990 as both a compliance document and a communication tool that reflects their professionalism and accountability.

Nonprofits must also comply with employment tax obligations. Like other employers, nonprofits must withhold federal income tax, Social Security, and Medicare from employee wages and remit them to the IRS. They must file quarterly employment tax returns on Form 941 and annual wage reports on Form W-2. Failure to meet employment tax obligations can result in severe penalties, including personal liability for responsible officers under the Trust Fund Recovery Penalty. Nonprofits must also consider whether they are subject to federal unemployment tax (FUTA), though many 501(c)(3) organizations are exempt from FUTA and instead may participate in state unemployment programs.

State-level compliance is another critical area. Most states require nonprofits to register with the state charity official, often the attorney general or secretary of state, before soliciting donations. Annual renewals are typically required, with filings that may include financial statements, copies of the Form 990, and disclosures about fundraising activities. A failure to comply with state registration requirements can lead to fines, revocation of the ability to solicit donations, and reputational damage. Nonprofits must also comply with state tax filings, which vary by jurisdiction. While most states follow federal recognition of tax-exempt status, some require separate applications or annual filings to maintain exemption from state income or sales taxes. For example, nonprofits may need to apply for exemption from state sales tax to avoid paying tax on purchases or to ensure that sales of goods and services are not taxable.

International activities add another layer of complexity. Nonprofits operating abroad or making grants to foreign organizations must comply with IRS rules to ensure that funds are used for charitable purposes. This may involve exercising expenditure responsibility or making equivalency determinations to confirm that foreign grantees are the equivalent of U.S. public charities. Reporting of foreign financial accounts may be required under the Foreign Account Tax Compliance Act (FATCA). These rules aim to prevent the diversion of charitable funds to non-charitable purposes, including terrorism financing, and carry significant penalties for noncompliance.

Lobbying and political activity also raise compliance issues. While 501(c)(3) organizations may engage in limited lobbying to influence legislation, excessive lobbying can jeopardize tax-exempt status. Nonprofits may elect to measure lobbying expenditures under Section 501(h), which provides clearer thresholds. Political campaign activity, by contrast, is strictly prohibited for 501(c)(3) organizations; they cannot endorse candidates or contribute to campaigns. Violations of these rules can result in excise taxes or loss of exemption. Other types of nonprofits, such as 501(c)(4) social welfare organizations, have more flexibility in political activity but face other reporting obligations. Legal counsel is often necessary to navigate these boundaries safely.

In conclusion, U.S. nonprofit entities face a wide array of tax filings and compliance issues that begin with obtaining and maintaining tax-exempt status and extend to annual reporting, employment taxes, state registrations, fundraising activities, and international operations. The cornerstone of compliance is the annual Form 990, which provides both regulatory oversight and public transparency. Additional obligations, such as Form 941 for employment taxes, reflect the multifaceted nature of nonprofit finance. State-level requirements add further complexity, requiring careful coordination. Nonprofits that approach these obligations with diligence not only avoid penalties but also build trust with stakeholders, strengthen governance, and secure the resources needed to advance their missions. Compliance, in this sense, is not a burden but a vital tool for accountability and long-term success.

Preparing for an Audit

Preparing for an audit is one of the most important financial management responsibilities for a nonprofit organization. An external audit, conducted by an independent certified public accountant, provides assurance to donors, regulators, and the public that the organization's financial statements are accurate and that internal controls are functioning effectively. While not all nonprofits are required by law to undergo an audit, many funders, foundations, and state governments mandate one once the organization reaches a certain size or receives government grants. Even when not required, some nonprofits pursue audits voluntarily as a way to demonstrate transparency and strengthen credibility. Preparing for an audit is not simply a matter of turning over records to the auditors. It is a structured process that involves careful planning, organization, and communication.

The first step in preparing for an audit is for the nonprofit to ensure that its financial records are complete, accurate, and up to date. Auditors will review financial statements prepared in accordance with GAAP, so the organization must confirm that transactions have been recorded correctly. This includes reconciling all bank accounts, ensuring that receivables and payables are accurately recorded, updating fixed asset schedules, and properly classifying expenses by both function and nature. The statement of financial position, statement of activities, statement of functional expenses, and statement of cash flows should all be finalized and internally reviewed before the audit begins. Nonprofits that use fund accounting must also confirm that restricted and unrestricted net assets are accurately tracked, since auditors will look closely at compliance with donor restrictions.

In addition to financial statements, auditors will request a wide range of supporting documentation. Preparing for an audit involves gathering this documentation in advance and organizing it for easy access. Common items include bank statements, invoices, payroll records, grant agreements, donor letters, board minutes, and contracts. The organization should prepare schedules that summarize this information, such as lists of outstanding receivables, grant activity by funder, and fixed asset additions and disposals. By compiling these schedules proactively, the nonprofit reduces the likelihood of delays during the audit. Many organizations create a "prepared by client" (PBC) list based on the auditor's request, ensuring that all required documents are ready at the start of fieldwork.

Internal controls are another area that auditors will examine closely, and preparing for an audit involves reviewing and strengthening these controls. Nonprofits should ensure that policies and procedures for authorization, segregation of duties, and documentation are in place and being followed. For example, the organization should be able to demonstrate that no single person has control over all aspects of a financial transaction, such as authorization, recording, and custody of funds. If weaknesses exist, management should take steps to correct them and document any improvements made. Auditors will also look at board oversight, so nonprofits should prepare to provide board minutes showing that financial statements, budgets, and audit reports have been reviewed and approved by the board or its finance or audit committee.

Grant compliance is a particularly important part of audit preparation for nonprofits that receive government or foundation funding. Auditors may test whether grant funds were spent in accordance with restrictions, whether required reports were filed on time, and whether cost allocation methods are reasonable. Preparing for this aspect of the audit requires maintaining detailed records of grant expenditures, time and effort reports for staff funded by grants, and documentation supporting cost allocations. Nonprofits subject to a Single Audit under federal regulations[1] must be especially diligent in preparing, since the auditor will assess compliance with federal requirements across multiple programs.

Communication with auditors is also a critical part of preparation. Early in the process, the nonprofit should meet with the audit firm to discuss the timeline, scope, and expectations for the audit. This meeting helps clarify what documents will be

---

[1] A single audit is a comprehensive audit required of organizations that spend $750,000 or more in federal funds during a fiscal year. It combines both a financial audit of the organization's overall financial statements and a compliance audit of how federal awards are managed.

requested, when fieldwork will occur, and how findings will be communicated. By establishing clear lines of communication, the organization can reduce misunderstandings and ensure that the audit proceeds efficiently. Nonprofits should also assign an internal audit coordinator, often the finance director or controller, to serve as the primary point of contact for auditors and to oversee the preparation of requested materials.

Staff preparation is another important element. Employees involved in finance, operations, and program delivery should be informed about the audit process and their potential roles in providing information or answering questions. Training staff on proper documentation practices, such as retaining receipts or maintaining time records, ensures that evidence is available when auditors request it. Program staff may be asked to explain how activities align with grant requirements, while finance staff must be ready to discuss accounting policies and procedures. A culture of accountability and cooperation helps audits proceed smoothly and reduces stress for staff.

Nonprofits should also prepare for the management letter that auditors typically issue at the conclusion of the audit. This letter highlights internal control weaknesses or areas where improvements are needed. Preparing for an audit involves anticipating these findings by conducting an internal review of policies and procedures. For instance, management may conduct a self-assessment to identify areas of risk or hire an outside consultant to perform a pre-audit review. Addressing issues before the audit not only improves operations but also demonstrates to auditors and stakeholders that the nonprofit is proactive in strengthening financial management.

Another important aspect of preparation is the role of the board of directors. The board, and particularly its finance or audit committee, has fiduciary responsibility for overseeing the audit process. Preparing for an audit means ensuring that board members understand their role, are familiar with the audit plan, and are prepared to review the results. The audit committee should meet with auditors independently of management to ensure open communication and objectivity. Strong board involvement signals to stakeholders that the nonprofit takes accountability seriously.

Finally, nonprofits should view audit preparation not as a one-time event but as part of an ongoing process of maintaining financial health. Good preparation begins long before auditors arrive, through consistent recordkeeping, strong internal controls, and regular financial reporting. Nonprofits that embed audit readiness into their daily operations experience less disruption when audit season arrives. By adopting best practices year-round, such as timely reconciliations, periodic internal reviews, and board oversight, organizations reduce the burden of preparation and demonstrate professionalism to funders and regulators.

In conclusion, preparing for an audit requires a comprehensive approach that includes accurate financial statements, organized documentation, strong internal controls, grant compliance, effective communication, staff readiness, and active board involvement. The process goes beyond compliance; it reflects a nonprofit's commitment to transparency, accountability, and stewardship of resources. A well-prepared audit not only satisfies legal or funder requirements but also strengthens donor confidence, improves financial practices, and enhances the organization's reputation. For nonprofits that depend on public trust, preparing thoroughly for an audit is not simply an administrative task but a strategic investment in their mission and long-term sustainability.

Cost Management for Professional Services

Cost management for professional services is an essential aspect of nonprofit financial stewardship. Unlike for-profit entities, nonprofits are mission-driven and must balance service delivery with fiscal responsibility. Professional services, such as legal counsel, accounting, auditing, IT consulting, marketing, and strategic planning, are often indispensable to ensure compliance, efficiency, and sustainability. At the same time, these services can be costly, and nonprofits often operate with limited budgets. Effective cost management ensures that the organization benefits from professional expertise while safeguarding donor funds and maintaining accountability.

One of the first steps in managing the costs of professional services is determining which services are essential and how they align with the nonprofit's mission. Not every service can or should be outsourced, and nonprofits must distinguish between functions that are core to mission delivery and those that require specialized expertise. For example, hiring auditors to conduct an external audit is often required by funders or regulators, making it non-negotiable. Similarly, legal services may be critical for issues such as contract negotiation, tax compliance, or employment disputes. On the other hand, functions such as marketing design or IT troubleshooting may be more discretionary, depending on the organization's priorities. By carefully evaluating which professional services are mission-critical, nonprofits can allocate resources more effectively and avoid unnecessary expenditures.

Another key aspect of cost management is budgeting and forecasting. Nonprofits should anticipate the need for professional services during their annual budget process and allocate funds accordingly. For example, if the organization expects to undergo an external audit, it should budget for auditor fees, potential consulting support, and any associated costs. Forecasting also allows nonprofits to plan for irregular but predictable expenses, such as legal fees for contract reviews or IT consulting for software upgrades. By incorporating these costs into the budget, nonprofits avoid unplanned expenditures that could disrupt program funding or create financial strain.

Competitive bidding and vendor selection also play an important role in controlling costs. Nonprofits should not automatically accept the first proposal for professional services but should instead request bids or proposals from multiple vendors. This process allows the organization to compare fees, evaluate the scope of services, and assess vendor qualifications. While the lowest bid is not always the best choice, competitive bidding ensures transparency and can result in more favorable terms. Additionally, building long-term relationships with trusted vendors can sometimes lead to discounted rates or added value, such as free training sessions or pro bono hours. Careful vetting and selection also reduce the risk of engaging vendors whose services may not meet the organization's needs, which could result in wasted funds.

Nonprofits can also explore cost-sharing and pro bono opportunities to reduce expenses. Collaborative arrangements with other organizations may allow nonprofits to share professional services, such as a joint IT consultant or shared legal retainer.

Professional service providers sometimes offer reduced rates for nonprofits or contribute pro bono work as part of their corporate social responsibility efforts. For instance, law firms may provide free legal advice to nonprofits, or accounting firms may offer discounted audit services to charitable organizations. Nonprofits should actively seek out such opportunities and cultivate relationships with providers who are committed to supporting mission-driven work.

Monitoring and evaluating service contracts is another critical component of cost management. Once professional services are engaged, nonprofits must ensure that they receive value for money. This involves setting clear expectations in contracts regarding deliverables, timelines, and costs, as well as monitoring performance to confirm that services are delivered as agreed. Regular evaluations help identify whether services are effective, whether the scope of work is appropriate, and whether costs remain within budget. If issues arise, nonprofits must be prepared to renegotiate contracts, adjust the scope of services, or seek alternative providers. Transparent oversight not only controls costs but also strengthens accountability to donors and stakeholders.

Internally, nonprofits should maximize their own capacity to reduce reliance on costly external services. Training staff to handle routine tasks such as basic bookkeeping, website updates, or grant compliance monitoring can reduce the need for frequent professional intervention. While professional expertise will always be necessary for complex issues, building staff skills helps nonprofits reserve professional service costs for higher-level needs. Volunteer expertise can also play a valuable role; many professionals are willing to donate time and skills to nonprofits, particularly in areas like legal advice, communications, or IT support. By leveraging staff and volunteers strategically, nonprofits can stretch limited resources further.

Finally, cost management for professional services must be guided by a long-term perspective. Cutting costs indiscriminately may save money in the short term but could create greater risks or expenses later. For example, failing to invest in proper legal review of contracts might lead to costly disputes, while neglecting IT security consulting could expose the organization to data breaches. Effective cost management therefore requires balancing prudence with investment in quality services that protect the nonprofit's mission, reputation, and sustainability.

In conclusion, cost management for professional services is a vital responsibility for nonprofits seeking to maximize mission impact while maintaining financial integrity. By prioritizing essential services, budgeting effectively, engaging in competitive bidding, pursuing pro bono opportunities, monitoring contracts, and leveraging internal capacity, nonprofits can obtain the expertise they need without overspending. Ultimately, thoughtful management of professional service costs ensures that donor funds are used responsibly, compliance is maintained, and the organization remains positioned to achieve its mission effectively and sustainably.

Summary

The cost of lawyers and accountants, as well as other outside advisors, can be prohibitively high, though this cost depends on the nature of the nonprofit and the unique risks to which it is subjected. Some organizations are so small and operate within such low-technology and risk-free environments that these costs may be relatively low. Conversely, other nonprofits will need extensive participation by outside advisors, possibly resulting in outside services being one of their most expensive cost areas. In the latter case, these costs may be so high that they threaten the ability of a nonprofit to operate in a cost-effective manner; if so, the only logical response may be an alteration of the organization's mission and/or structure, in order to reduce these costs to a more viable level.

Chapter 12
Measuring Success and Impact

Introduction

A nonprofit is unlikely to succeed over the long term unless it can report to its stakeholders that it is having a meaningful impact in its targeted program areas. In this chapter, we discuss the difference between impact and outputs, and discuss the need for various types of key performance indicators, while also highlighting the need for impact reporting in dealings with those who provide funding to the organization.

Defining Impact and Outputs

For nonprofit organizations, one of the most important yet challenging tasks is demonstrating the results of their work. Donors, funders, beneficiaries, and the public want to know not only that resources are being used responsibly, but also that programs are making a real difference. In this context, the distinction between outputs and impact is critical. While outputs describe the immediate, tangible products of an organization's activities, impact refers to the broader, long-term changes those activities bring about. Understanding and communicating the difference between the two allows nonprofits to more effectively measure performance, make strategic decisions, and build credibility with stakeholders.

Understanding Outputs

Outputs are the direct and quantifiable results of a nonprofit's activities. They capture what the organization produces or delivers, typically expressed in numerical terms. Examples include the number of meals served by a food pantry, the number of students attending after-school tutoring sessions, or the number of workshops conducted by a health education nonprofit. Outputs are important, because they demonstrate that the organization is active, delivering services, and using its resources to fulfill its mission.

Outputs are usually easier to track and report than impact. Nonprofits can rely on attendance sheets, service logs, or distribution counts to measure them. For example, a literacy nonprofit might report that it distributed 5,000 books in a year and enrolled 300 children in tutoring programs. These numbers are straightforward and can be quickly communicated in reports to funders and the public.

However, while outputs show what was done, they do not necessarily capture whether those activities made a meaningful difference. A nonprofit can distribute thousands of books without necessarily improving literacy rates, or it can conduct dozens of workshops without changing participants' behaviors. Outputs are therefore best understood as indicators of activity, not necessarily effectiveness.

Defining Impact

Impact goes beyond counting activities to measure the actual difference those activities make in people's lives or in the broader community. It is the long-term, transformative change that results from a nonprofit's work. Impact is often expressed in terms of improved outcomes, such as higher literacy levels, reduced rates of homelessness, improved community health, or greater economic self-sufficiency.

Unlike outputs, impact is harder to measure because it involves tracking changes over time and isolating the nonprofit's contribution from other factors. For example, a health clinic may want to demonstrate impact by showing a reduction in diabetes rates in its service area. Yet those changes may also be influenced by other clinics, public health campaigns, or broader societal shifts. Impact evaluation often requires surveys, longitudinal studies[2], and sophisticated data analysis to demonstrate that outcomes can be attributed to the nonprofit's efforts.

Impact is also qualitative as much as quantitative. Beyond numbers, it captures the human stories of transformation, such as a student who becomes the first in her family to graduate from college because of a mentoring program, or a family that moves from homelessness to stable housing thanks to supportive services. These stories personalize the data and help stakeholders understand the deeper significance of the nonprofit's work.

The Relationship Between Outputs and Impact

Outputs and impact are not opposites but rather parts of a continuum. Outputs are necessary to achieve impact; they are the building blocks that make longer-term change possible. A nonprofit must deliver services before it can expect to see outcomes. For instance, a workforce development program must conduct training workshops (outputs) before participants can secure stable jobs (impact).

The challenge for nonprofits lies in demonstrating how outputs connect to impact. This requires articulating a theory of change or logic model that explains how specific activities lead to measurable short-term outcomes and ultimately long-term impact. For example, a youth development organization might describe its theory of change as follows: providing after-school tutoring (output) improves students' grades (short-term outcome), which leads to higher graduation rates (intermediate outcome), ultimately resulting in greater economic opportunity for participants (long-term impact). This kind of framework helps stakeholders see how outputs are steps along the path to deeper impact.

---

[2] A longitudinal study is a type of research design in which data is collected from the same subjects repeatedly over a long period of time. Instead of taking a single snapshot, it tracks changes and developments across months, years, or even decades. This method is commonly used in fields like medicine, psychology, education, and social sciences to observe trends, identify cause-and-effect relationships, and study long-term outcomes.

Why the Distinction Matters

Differentiating between outputs and impact is critical for accountability, fundraising, and strategic planning. Donors and grantmakers increasingly demand evidence of impact rather than just activity. While they may appreciate that a nonprofit served 10,000 meals, they want to know whether those meals improved nutrition, reduced hunger, or enhanced quality of life. By focusing solely on outputs, nonprofits risk appearing busy without proving effectiveness. By measuring and communicating impact, nonprofits can demonstrate that they are achieving real, lasting change.

For internal management, distinguishing outputs from impact helps nonprofits allocate resources more effectively. An organization that only tracks outputs might believe it is succeeding because it delivers many services, even if those services are not producing meaningful outcomes. By examining impact, nonprofits can assess which programs are truly effective and make adjustments accordingly. This focus supports continuous improvement, ensuring that resources are invested in activities that deliver measurable results.

From a governance perspective, boards of directors also benefit from understanding impact versus outputs. Boards have fiduciary and strategic responsibilities to ensure that the nonprofit fulfills its mission. If they only receive reports on outputs, they may not fully understand whether the organization is creating real change. Impact-focused reporting enables boards to make better strategic decisions, align activities with mission, and hold management accountable for outcomes.

Challenges in Measuring Impact

While important, measuring impact is often more difficult than tracking outputs. One challenge is attribution: proving that observed changes are the result of the nonprofit's work and not external factors. For instance, an education nonprofit may see improved test scores among its students, but other influences, such as parental support or school policies, may also play a role. Nonprofits must use careful evaluation methods to establish their contribution to observed outcomes.

Another challenge is resources. Impact evaluation often requires significant time, money, and expertise. Smaller nonprofits may lack the capacity to conduct surveys, collect longitudinal data, or hire external evaluators. They may be limited to anecdotal evidence or proxy measures that approximate impact without fully capturing it.

There is also a risk of focusing too narrowly on easily measurable outcomes, potentially neglecting important but less tangible aspects of impact. For example, a community arts program may foster creativity, social cohesion, and civic engagement; impacts that are meaningful but difficult to quantify. Nonprofits must balance the demand for measurable impact with recognition of the qualitative dimensions of their work.

Best Practices for Linking Outputs to Impact

To address these challenges, nonprofits can adopt several best practices. First, they should develop a clear theory of change that articulates how outputs are expected to lead to outcomes and impact. This provides a roadmap for evaluation and communication. Second, nonprofits should invest in systems to collect both quantitative and qualitative data, balancing numerical indicators with personal stories. Third, they should engage stakeholders, including beneficiaries, in defining what impact means, ensuring that evaluation captures the changes that matter most to the community. Finally, nonprofits should be transparent about both successes and challenges, acknowledging the complexity of measuring impact and showing a commitment to learning and improvement.

Conclusion

For nonprofits, defining and distinguishing between outputs and impact is essential for demonstrating accountability, guiding strategy, and sustaining donor trust. Outputs capture the immediate products of organizational activity, while impact reflects the deeper, long-term changes those activities bring about. Both are important, but it is impact that ultimately defines whether a nonprofit is fulfilling its mission. By connecting outputs to impact through careful planning, evaluation, and communication, nonprofits can show not only that they are busy but that they are truly making a difference. In a sector where trust and results are paramount, clarity about impact versus outputs is not merely a technical distinction but a cornerstone of mission-driven effectiveness.

Program Evaluation Methods

Program evaluation is one of the most important tools available to nonprofit organizations. It allows them to assess whether programs are effective, efficient, and aligned with the mission, while also providing critical evidence for funders, donors, and community stakeholders. Evaluation not only demonstrates accountability but also fosters learning and continuous improvement. Nonprofits generally use two broad categories of evaluation methods: quantitative and qualitative. Each provides unique insights, and when used together, they offer a comprehensive understanding of program performance. Exploring both approaches helps nonprofits appreciate their strengths, limitations, and the ways in which they can be integrated to tell a fuller story about impact.

Quantitative Program Evaluation

Quantitative evaluation involves collecting numerical data and applying statistical methods to analyze outcomes. Its primary strength lies in its ability to measure and compare results in a way that appears objective and generalizable. Funders, regulators, and policymakers often value quantitative data because it can provide evidence of scale, efficiency, and measurable outcomes.

A common quantitative approach in nonprofits is outcome measurement. This method involves identifying key performance indicators (KPIs)[3] that reflect program

---

[3] A key performance indicator is a measurable value that indicates how effectively an organization is achieving a specific objective. KPIs are tied to strategic goals and are used to track progress, guide decision-making, and evaluate performance over time.

goals and systematically tracking them over time. For example, a job-training nonprofit might measure the number of participants who complete training, the percentage who secure employment within six months, and their average wages. These metrics allow the organization to quantify its success in helping participants achieve economic stability.

Another quantitative method is pre- and post-testing, often used in educational or health programs. Participants are given a baseline test before the program begins and the same or similar test afterward to measure changes in knowledge, skills, or behaviors. A health nonprofit, for instance, might measure participants' knowledge of nutrition before and after a workshop series to evaluate learning outcomes.

More rigorous quantitative approaches include experimental and quasi-experimental designs. Experimental designs, such as randomized controlled trials, involve assigning participants randomly to treatment and control groups to isolate the program's effect. Quasi-experimental designs, such as matched comparison groups, attempt to approximate this rigor when randomization is not feasible. These methods allow nonprofits to assess causality (whether the program itself, rather than outside factors, led to observed changes). For example, a literacy nonprofit might compare the reading levels of children who participated in its tutoring program with those of a similar group who did not.

Quantitative methods also enable large-scale data analysis. Nonprofits can use administrative records, surveys, or publicly available data to assess patterns and outcomes across broad populations. Statistical techniques such as regression analysis can help identify relationships between variables, such as whether participation in a youth program is associated with higher graduation rates after controlling for demographic factors.

The strength of quantitative evaluation is its ability to provide clear, comparable, and often persuasive evidence of outcomes. Numbers carry weight with funders and policymakers, and they make it possible to track trends over time. However, quantitative methods also have limitations. They may oversimplify complex social problems, overlook the experiences of individuals, or fail to explain *why* outcomes occurred. For example, a statistic showing that 70% of participants secured jobs does not explain the barriers faced by the 30% who did not. Quantitative evaluation alone can risk reducing people's experiences to numbers, missing the nuances that shape program effectiveness.

Qualitative Program Evaluation

Qualitative evaluation complements quantitative methods by focusing on experiences, perceptions, and context. Rather than asking "how many," qualitative evaluation asks "how" and "why." It explores the meaning behind program outcomes, providing rich detail about how participants experience services and how programs influence lives in ways not easily measured by numbers.

Common qualitative methods include interviews, focus groups, observations, and case studies. Semi-structured interviews with participants allow evaluators to capture personal narratives about how programs affected them. For instance, a participant in a housing program might share how stable housing improved not only her physical health but also her children's school performance. Focus groups provide an opportunity for multiple participants to share and discuss experiences collectively, revealing common themes and differences. Observations of program delivery can uncover how services are implemented in practice, highlighting strengths or areas for improvement. Case studies provide in-depth exploration of particular participants, programs, or contexts, offering detailed illustrations of impact.

Qualitative evaluation is particularly useful for understanding participant perspectives. It gives voice to beneficiaries, empowering them to share their experiences and inform program design. For example, a nonprofit providing services to immigrants might use interviews to understand cultural or linguistic barriers that hinder program participation. Such insights can inform program adjustments that make services more accessible and effective.

Another strength of qualitative methods is their ability to capture unintended outcomes. While quantitative evaluations usually focus on predetermined indicators, qualitative evaluations can uncover changes that were not anticipated. For instance, a youth leadership program might discover that participants not only developed leadership skills but also reported improved family relationships; a benefit that would not have been captured through standard quantitative measures.

Qualitative methods also illuminate the context in which programs operate. They help explain why a program succeeded in one community but struggled in another, or why certain participants benefited more than others. By revealing the "story behind the numbers," qualitative evaluation deepens understanding of how programs interact with broader social, cultural, and institutional factors.

Despite these strengths, qualitative methods also have limitations. They can be time-consuming, resource-intensive, and subject to bias in data collection and interpretation. Findings are often less generalizable than quantitative results, since they may be based on small samples. Funders may view qualitative evidence as less rigorous because it is not expressed in numbers. Nonetheless, when conducted systematically, qualitative evaluation provides essential insights that numbers alone cannot capture.

Integrating Quantitative and Qualitative Methods

While quantitative and qualitative evaluations have distinct strengths, the most effective nonprofit evaluations often combine the two in a mixed-methods approach. This integration allows organizations to measure outcomes broadly while also understanding the deeper context and meaning behind those outcomes.

For example, a health education nonprofit might use pre- and post-tests to measure changes in participants' knowledge about disease prevention (quantitative) while also conducting focus groups to learn how participants applied this knowledge in their daily lives (qualitative). The quantitative data show the scale of knowledge gains, while the qualitative data reveal barriers to behavior change and highlight success stories. Together, these findings provide a fuller picture of the program's effectiveness.

Mixed-methods evaluation also enhances credibility. Numbers can demonstrate accountability and scale, while stories provide relatability and emotional resonance.

Donors and funders often find that a combination of statistics and personal narratives is most persuasive. For instance, reporting that "85% of participants secured stable housing, and one participant described how the program allowed her children to feel safe for the first time in years" combines the strengths of both approaches.

Integration also supports learning and improvement. Quantitative findings may reveal patterns, such as certain groups benefiting less from a program, while qualitative methods can explore why those disparities exist. Conversely, qualitative findings may suggest new outcomes to measure quantitatively in future evaluations. By using both approaches, nonprofits can refine their programs based on evidence that is both broad and deep.

Strategic Considerations

When choosing evaluation methods, nonprofits must consider their resources, capacity, and the expectations of stakeholders. Quantitative evaluations often require robust data systems, staff training, and sometimes external evaluators, which may be costly. Qualitative evaluations require skilled facilitators, time for data collection and analysis, and sensitivity to participant privacy and consent. Nonprofits must balance rigor with feasibility, ensuring that evaluation adds value without overwhelming staff or detracting from service delivery.

Nonprofits should also consider the purpose of the evaluation. If the goal is to demonstrate accountability to funders, quantitative measures of outcomes may be most appropriate. If the goal is to improve program design or understand participant experiences, qualitative methods may be more useful. Ideally, nonprofits design evaluations with multiple purposes in mind, aligning them with both accountability and learning goals.

Ethical considerations are paramount in both approaches. Nonprofits must respect participant confidentiality, obtain informed consent, and avoid exploiting participants' stories. Evaluations should be designed and conducted in ways that empower participants and reflect their voices, rather than treating them as mere data points.

Conclusion

Program evaluation is essential for nonprofits striving to demonstrate accountability, improve performance, and achieve meaningful impact. Quantitative methods provide the numbers that funders and policymakers often demand, showing scale and measurable outcomes. Qualitative methods provide the depth and context that numbers alone cannot capture, revealing participant experiences, unintended outcomes, and the broader meaning of change. While each has strengths and limitations, integrating both approaches allows nonprofits to present a comprehensive picture of program effectiveness.

By combining quantitative rigor with qualitative richness, nonprofits can measure not only what they do but also what difference they make. This dual perspective strengthens credibility, supports continuous improvement, and ensures that programs remain responsive to the communities they serve. Ultimately, the thoughtful use of both quantitative and qualitative program evaluation methods enables nonprofits to demonstrate not just activity but true impact – fulfilling their mission and building lasting trust with stakeholders.

Key Performance Indicators for Nonprofits

Key performance indicators are measurable values that indicate how effectively an organization is achieving its objectives. For nonprofits, KPIs are particularly important because they provide a structured way to assess mission-driven performance, ensure accountability to donors and funders, and guide decision-making. Unlike for-profit organizations, which often focus primarily on financial profit, nonprofits must balance financial health with mission impact, community engagement, and operational sustainability. KPIs allow nonprofits to track progress in these areas, identify strengths and weaknesses, and make data-driven adjustments. A thoughtful KPI framework reflects both quantitative and qualitative measures, aligning activities with strategic goals and demonstrating the value of the organization's work to stakeholders.

The Importance of KPIs in the Nonprofit Sector

Nonprofits operate in an environment where resources are scarce and scrutiny is high. Donors, grantmakers, regulators, and beneficiaries all want to know whether the organization is effective and whether their contributions are being used responsibly. KPIs provide a way to answer these questions in a clear, measurable manner. They help nonprofits move beyond anecdotal success stories to provide evidence of results. At the same time, KPIs guide internal management by showing whether programs are meeting objectives, whether fundraising efforts are sustainable, and whether the organization is financially stable.

By tracking KPIs consistently, nonprofits can benchmark performance over time and against peer organizations. This not only supports transparency but also helps attract new funding by demonstrating accountability. In addition, KPIs support strategic planning, allowing leadership to set realistic goals, monitor progress, and adjust strategies as needed.

Categories of Nonprofit KPIs

Nonprofit KPIs can be grouped into several broad categories: program effectiveness, financial health, fundraising performance, operational efficiency, and stakeholder engagement. Within each category, specific indicators vary depending on the mission and size of the organization. However, the following areas represent common and widely accepted measures of nonprofit success.

Program Effectiveness KPIs

At the heart of nonprofit work is the delivery of programs and services that advance the mission. Program effectiveness KPIs measure how well those programs achieve their intended outcomes.

One important KPI is the number of beneficiaries served. This simple measure indicates the reach of the nonprofit's programs, such as the number of students tutored, meals distributed, or patients treated. While not a measure of impact in itself, it demonstrates activity levels and scope.

Another critical KPI is outcome achievement. This measures whether programs are achieving desired results, such as improved literacy rates, increased employment among program participants, or reduced rates of homelessness. Tracking outcomes requires the careful definition of success and often involves pre- and post-program assessments or surveys.

The cost per beneficiary is also a useful indicator of program efficiency. It shows how much the organization spends on average to serve each individual or household. This measure can highlight whether resources are being used efficiently and can help identify areas where costs can be reduced without compromising quality.

Finally, satisfaction ratings from beneficiaries provide valuable qualitative insights into program effectiveness. Surveys or interviews can capture whether participants feel that services met their needs, which is an important complement to quantitative measures.

Financial Health KPIs

While nonprofits do not exist to generate profit, financial sustainability is essential to their survival and ability to deliver impact. Financial health KPIs track liquidity, stability, and efficiency.

Operating surplus or deficit is a basic KPI showing whether the nonprofit's revenues exceed expenses in a given year. A consistent surplus indicates financial stability, while repeated deficits may signal the need for corrective action.

Liquidity ratios, such as the current ratio (current assets divided by current liabilities), indicate whether the nonprofit has enough short-term assets to cover obligations. Adequate liquidity ensures the organization can continue operations during cash flow fluctuations.

Another important KPI is months of operating reserves. This measures how long the organization could continue operating if all income ceased, based on current reserves. Funders often view strong reserves as a sign of prudent financial management.

Expense allocation ratios also provide insights. The program expense ratio, which shows the percentage of total expenses spent on program activities, is a widely scrutinized KPI. Donors generally prefer to see a high proportion of expenses going toward mission delivery rather than administration or fundraising. However, nonprofits must balance this ratio with the recognition that overhead investments are necessary for long-term effectiveness.

Fundraising Performance KPIs

Fundraising is the lifeblood of many nonprofits, and KPIs in this area measure how effectively organizations raise and manage contributions.

The donor acquisition rate measures the percentage increase in new donors over a given period. This indicator highlights whether fundraising efforts are attracting fresh support.

The donor retention rate is equally important, as retaining existing donors is often more cost-effective than acquiring new ones. A high retention rate suggests strong donor relationships and satisfaction with the organization's work.

The average gift size provides insights into donor giving behavior, helping nonprofits evaluate whether strategies are encouraging larger contributions. Related to this, lifetime donor value calculates the total expected contributions from a donor over their relationship with the nonprofit, guiding long-term fundraising strategies.

Fundraising efficiency is a widely used KPI that measures the cost of raising a dollar. It is calculated by dividing total fundraising expenses by total contributions. While efficiency should not be the sole measure of fundraising success, it provides useful insight into the return on investment of fundraising campaigns.

Operational Efficiency KPIs

Operational efficiency KPIs focus on how well the nonprofit uses its resources to deliver services. They often overlap with financial and program measures but emphasize processes and productivity.

The staff-to-beneficiary ratio is one such measure, showing how many staff members are needed to serve a given number of participants. This ratio can indicate whether staffing levels are appropriate or whether resources might be stretched too thin.

The volunteer utilization rate measures the extent to which volunteers are engaged in program delivery. High volunteer engagement often reduces costs and strengthens community ties, making this an important KPI for many nonprofits.

The administrative cost ratio, which shows the percentage of total expenses spent on general and administrative functions, is another common measure. While excessive administrative costs can raise concerns, too low a ratio may indicate underinvestment in essential infrastructure.

Process efficiency metrics, such as average time to deliver a service or complete an intake, provide operational insights that support continuous improvement.

Stakeholder Engagement KPIs

Nonprofits rely not only on beneficiaries and donors but also on a broader network of stakeholders, including volunteers, staff, community members, and partners. KPIs in this area measure engagement and satisfaction.

The volunteer retention rate shows whether volunteers are returning, which can be a proxy for satisfaction and alignment with the mission.

The staff turnover rate provides insights into organizational culture and stability. High turnover can be costly and disruptive, while low turnover often reflects effective management and employee engagement.

Community awareness or brand recognition can also be measured, often through surveys or social media metrics, to assess whether the nonprofit is effectively communicating its mission and attracting support.

Engagement on digital platforms (such as website traffic, email open rates, and social media interactions) is increasingly relevant for nonprofits in building awareness and mobilizing support.

Challenges in Using KPIs

While KPIs are powerful tools, nonprofits must use them carefully to avoid pitfalls. One challenge is overemphasis on easily measurable indicators, such as outputs, at the expense of harder-to-measure impacts. For example, counting the number of workshops delivered is easier than assessing whether those workshops changed behaviors. Nonprofits must therefore balance efficiency with meaningful outcomes.

Another challenge is context. KPIs should be interpreted in light of the organization's mission, size, and community needs. For instance, a high program expense ratio may be desirable, but not if it comes at the cost of underinvestment in fundraising or infrastructure. Similarly, donor retention rates may vary significantly depending on the type of nonprofit and the typical donor base.

Nonprofits also face resource limitations. Collecting and analyzing data requires staff time, systems, and expertise, which may strain budgets. Choosing a manageable set of KPIs that align with strategic priorities is often more effective than attempting to track too many indicators.

Conclusion

Key performance indicators are essential tools for nonprofits seeking to demonstrate accountability, improve performance, and advance their missions. By tracking KPIs in areas such as program effectiveness, financial health, fundraising performance, operational efficiency, and stakeholder engagement, nonprofits can assess whether they are achieving their goals and using resources responsibly. KPIs provide evidence for funders and donors, support internal decision-making, and highlight areas for improvement.

The most effective use of KPIs balances quantitative measures of efficiency and scale with qualitative insights into impact and experience. Nonprofits must choose KPIs carefully, ensuring they reflect mission priorities and are feasible to track. When used thoughtfully, KPIs not only strengthen transparency but also support learning and continuous improvement. Ultimately, they allow nonprofits to tell a more compelling story of how resources translate into meaningful outcomes, building trust and sustaining support for their mission.

Reporting Results to Stakeholders

Reporting results to nonprofit stakeholders is one of the most important responsibilities for any nonprofit; they are entrusted with resources that come from donors, grantmakers, volunteers, and the broader community, all of whom want assurance that their contributions are being used effectively. Unlike businesses, which can often point to profit as the measure of success, nonprofits must demonstrate accountability in other ways, chiefly by showing how their activities translate into meaningful social impact.

Reporting is not simply a compliance exercise but an essential means of building trust, sustaining relationships, and reinforcing credibility.

The importance of reporting results begins with the principle of accountability. Donors want to know that their financial contributions are producing tangible benefits, whether that means children receiving education, families moving into safe housing, or communities gaining access to health care. Foundations and government agencies that award grants often require detailed reporting on both finances and outcomes as a condition of funding. Volunteers want reassurance that their time is being put to good use, while beneficiaries want to see how programs are improving lives. Reporting fulfills all of these expectations by providing a clear window into the organization's work and results. Without regular, accurate, and transparent reporting, nonprofits risk losing credibility and, ultimately, the support that sustains their operations.

Effective reporting is not only about accountability but also about engagement. When nonprofits communicate their results in compelling ways, they deepen relationships with their stakeholders. Donors who see the difference their gifts make are more likely to give again and at higher levels. Volunteers who understand the broader outcomes of their service feel more connected to the mission and more motivated to continue. Beneficiaries who see their experiences reflected in organizational reports feel valued and empowered. Reporting thus serves both as a record of performance and as a tool for strengthening bonds within the community of support that surrounds the nonprofit.

A key challenge in reporting results is determining what to communicate and how. Outputs, such as the number of meals served or the number of clients counseled, are relatively easy to count and present. They demonstrate activity levels and organizational reach. Yet outputs alone rarely satisfy stakeholders who want to know about deeper outcomes. Impact is ultimately what matters most: did those meals reduce food insecurity? Did counseling sessions improve mental health outcomes? Did afterschool programs increase graduation rates? Nonprofits must therefore strike a balance between reporting outputs, which are clear and straightforward, and reporting outcomes, which capture the real difference programs make in people's lives. This requires thoughtful measurement and, in many cases, blending quantitative data with qualitative evidence such as stories, testimonials, and case studies.

Different stakeholder groups have distinct expectations for reporting, which means nonprofits must tailor their communications to their audiences. Donors are typically interested in knowing that their contributions are being used wisely and that they are having a measurable impact. They may want both statistics and stories that show the human face of change. Grantmakers often require more formal, detailed reports that account for how every dollar of grant funding was used and what outcomes were achieved. Volunteers want to see their contributions of time acknowledged and to understand how their work fits into the broader mission. Beneficiaries, in turn, want information that demonstrates respect for their role in the nonprofit's success and assurances that the organization is responsive to their needs. Regulators and watchdog organizations focus heavily on compliance and transparency, particularly regarding finances, governance, and adherence to tax-exempt requirements. Finally, the broader public and community want evidence that the nonprofit is credible and is addressing important issues effectively.

Because of this diversity of audiences, nonprofits use multiple formats and methods to report results. Annual reports remain a cornerstone, serving as comprehensive documents that provide a snapshot of the year's activities, finances, and accomplishments. These reports are often published both in print and online, and increasingly they incorporate infographics, photographs, and personal stories to bring data to life. Grant reports are more technical and tailored to funder requirements, providing detailed program data and financial statements. Newsletters and email updates serve as ongoing reporting tools, offering stakeholders timely information about current activities and outcomes. Social media and websites allow for continuous reporting in accessible and engaging formats, while community meetings and public presentations provide interactive opportunities for stakeholders to learn about and discuss results directly with leadership.

Effective reporting requires not just the right formats but also the right qualities. Reports must be accurate, reflecting reliable data collected through sound methods. They must be transparent, acknowledging both successes and challenges. Stakeholders are increasingly wary of overly polished reports that highlight only positive outcomes while ignoring difficulties. Acknowledging shortcomings demonstrates honesty and a commitment to improvement, qualities that strengthen rather than weaken trust. Reports must also be clear, avoiding jargon or technical language that might confuse or alienate readers. Most importantly, reports should be mission-centered, framing results in terms of how they advance the organization's core purpose.

Despite its importance, reporting results presents real challenges for nonprofits. Many organizations lack the resources to conduct rigorous program evaluations, relying instead on simple output measures that may not capture true impact. Data collection can be costly and time-consuming, stretching already limited staff capacity. Small nonprofits in particular may find it difficult to balance the need for comprehensive reporting with the demands of program delivery. There are also ethical challenges, especially when reporting involves sensitive beneficiary data. Protecting confidentiality while still conveying meaningful results requires careful attention and sensitivity. Finally, there is the challenge of managing funder expectations, since some donors or grantmakers may prioritize certain metrics that do not fully align with the nonprofit's understanding of its impact.

Nevertheless, investing in thoughtful reporting pays significant dividends. When nonprofits communicate results effectively, they demonstrate stewardship, reinforce their credibility, and build long-term sustainability. Reporting can inspire donors to increase their support, encourage volunteers to deepen their involvement, and reassure beneficiaries that the organization is committed to positive change. It also strengthens internal accountability, giving boards and staff the information they need to make informed decisions and improve programs. Reporting is therefore not simply an administrative task but a strategic function at the heart of nonprofit effectiveness.

In conclusion, reporting results to nonprofit stakeholders is about far more than compliance or meeting minimum obligations. It is an act of accountability, transparency, and engagement that reinforces the bond of trust between the organization and those who support it. Effective reporting balances quantitative measures with qualitative stories, tailoring communication to the diverse needs of donors, funders, volunteers, beneficiaries, regulators, and the community. While challenges exist, particularly in terms of resources and data collection, nonprofits that invest in clear, accurate, and mission-driven reporting position themselves for long-term credibility and success. Ultimately, reporting results is not just about documenting what an organization has done but about affirming the value of its mission and inspiring continued support for its work.

Using Impact Data to Secure Funding

For nonprofit organizations, securing funding is both a constant challenge and a critical necessity. Donors, foundations, corporations, and government agencies are increasingly selective about where they allocate resources, favoring organizations that can demonstrate measurable results. In this environment, impact data has emerged as one of the most powerful tools a nonprofit can use to attract and sustain funding. Impact data goes beyond counting activities or outputs; it provides evidence that a nonprofit's programs produce meaningful, measurable change in the lives of individuals and communities. By collecting, analyzing, and communicating impact data effectively, nonprofits can distinguish themselves in a crowded funding landscape, build trust with stakeholders, and secure the financial support needed to advance their mission.

The first way impact data helps secure funding is by demonstrating accountability. Donors want assurance that their contributions are being used responsibly and effectively. A nonprofit that can show concrete results provides funders with tangible evidence that their money is making a difference. This is particularly important for institutional funders such as foundations or government agencies, which often require rigorous reporting to justify grants. By presenting impact data, nonprofits demonstrate that they are not only active but also effective, aligning with funders' expectations for transparency and accountability.

Impact data also strengthens a nonprofit's credibility. In a funding environment where many organizations are competing for limited resources, data-driven evidence distinguishes one nonprofit from another. Funders are more likely to invest in organizations that can show results rather than simply promise them. For example, a health nonprofit applying for a grant to expand services will have a stronger case if it can demonstrate through data that its existing programs have reduced disease incidence by a measurable percentage. Numbers lend weight to narratives, transforming anecdotal claims into verified outcomes. This credibility reassures funders that the nonprofit is capable of managing resources and delivering on its commitments.

Beyond accountability and credibility, impact data allows nonprofits to align with funders' priorities. Most donors and grantmakers have specific objectives, such as reducing poverty, improving education, or enhancing public health. By collecting and analyzing impact data, nonprofits can demonstrate how their outcomes align with these objectives. For instance, a nonprofit focused on early childhood education can highlight data showing how its programs improve kindergarten readiness, directly addressing funders' concerns about long-term educational attainment. Tailoring impact data to funder priorities creates a compelling case that the nonprofit is not only effective but also relevant to the funder's mission.

Impact data also provides a basis for compelling storytelling. While numbers are important, they are often most persuasive when paired with human narratives that illustrate the meaning behind the data. A nonprofit can, for example, report that 85 percent of participants in a job-training program secured employment within six months, but this becomes more powerful when accompanied by the story of an individual participant who overcame barriers and achieved stability for her family. In this way, impact data enhances storytelling by providing context and scale, while stories bring the data to life. The combination of data and narrative is particularly effective in donor communications, grant applications, and fundraising campaigns, creating an emotional and rational appeal simultaneously.

Another important role of impact data is in demonstrating efficiency and return on investment. Funders want to know not only that programs are effective but also that they are efficient in using resources. By tracking metrics such as cost per beneficiary or cost per successful outcome, nonprofits can show that they are delivering value for money. For instance, a nonprofit may demonstrate that every $500 invested in its job-training program results in a participant obtaining stable employment. Such data helps funders see their contributions as investments with measurable returns, making them more likely to support the organization.

Impact data also enables nonprofits to build long-term relationships with funders. Providing ongoing, reliable data about program outcomes fosters trust and demonstrates consistency over time. A donor who sees that a nonprofit has consistently met or exceeded its goals for several years is more likely to continue funding and even increase its support. Similarly, institutional funders often renew or expand grants for organizations that can demonstrate sustained impact. By embedding impact data into regular reporting and communications, nonprofits position themselves as reliable partners capable of delivering long-term change.

In addition to attracting external funding, impact data can strengthen internal decision-making, which in turn enhances funding prospects. Funders are often impressed by organizations that use data not only for reporting but also for continuous improvement. When nonprofits can show that they analyze their results, identify areas for improvement, and adapt programs accordingly, they demonstrate a commitment to learning and accountability. For example, a youth development organization might show that its initial mentoring model produced moderate results but that, after adjusting based on impact data, outcomes improved significantly. This willingness to learn and adapt reassures funders that their investments will be used effectively and strategically.

Technology has expanded the possibilities for collecting and using impact data in funding efforts. Nonprofits now have access to tools such as data dashboards, customer relationship management systems, and survey platforms that allow them to track outcomes in real time and present results visually. Interactive dashboards that show trends in program outcomes or infographics that highlight key achievements make data more accessible and persuasive to funders. In addition, nonprofits can use data visualization to simplify complex information, ensuring that funders understand and appreciate the organization's impact quickly and clearly.

While impact data is a powerful asset, nonprofits must also navigate challenges in using it to secure funding. Collecting high-quality data requires resources, staff training, and sometimes external expertise. Smaller nonprofits may struggle to implement comprehensive evaluation systems. There is also the challenge of balancing funder demands with mission priorities; some funders may request data on outcomes that do not fully align with the nonprofit's understanding of its impact. In these cases, nonprofits must carefully communicate the value of their chosen metrics while also meeting funder requirements. Additionally, overemphasis on quantifiable data risks overlooking qualitative dimensions of impact, such as empowerment or social cohesion, which are harder to measure but equally important.

To overcome these challenges, nonprofits should develop a clear evaluation strategy that identifies key outcomes aligned with their mission, invests in data collection and analysis systems, and trains staff to use data effectively. Collaborating with external evaluators or academic partners can also enhance credibility and rigor. Importantly, nonprofits should integrate impact data into their organizational culture, making it a central part of decision-making, communication, and fundraising rather than a one-time exercise.

In conclusion, impact data is one of the most powerful tools nonprofits can use to secure funding. It provides evidence of accountability, builds credibility, aligns with funder priorities, enhances storytelling, demonstrates efficiency, and fosters long-term relationships. By collecting, analyzing, and communicating impact data effectively, nonprofits can distinguish themselves in a competitive funding environment and reassure donors that their resources are making a meaningful difference. While challenges exist in collecting and using impact data, nonprofits that invest in building strong evaluation systems and embedding data into their organizational culture position themselves for greater sustainability and success. Ultimately, impact data is not just a fundraising tool but a reflection of the nonprofit's mission, values, and commitment to creating lasting change.

Summary

A startup nonprofit will likely have few resources, making it difficult to use the evaluation methods described in this chapter. When this is the case, start with as much reporting as the organization can support at the current time, which usually means the assemblage of metrics that are relatively easy to collect. In addition, outline the types of additional information that stakeholders would like to see, and especially those that might support increases in funding – along with the monetary cost and staff time needed to produce this information. Over time, the management team can evaluate the nonprofit's ability to generate the additional reporting, and hopefully expand into more comprehensive measurements of the organization's success and impact.

Chapter 13
Scaling the Nonprofit

Introduction

Expanding programs and services is one of the most critical stages in the growth of a nonprofit organization. Done thoughtfully, it allows nonprofits to deepen their impact, reach new populations, and build long-term sustainability. Yet expansion also presents challenges, requiring careful planning, financial stability, and a strong commitment to mission alignment. This chapter explores the strategies, risks, and best practices that guide nonprofits in scaling their services responsibly and effectively.

Expanding Programs and Services

Expanding programs and services is a major milestone in the life of any nonprofit organization. Growth allows nonprofits to increase their reach, broaden their impact, and better fulfill their missions. Yet expansion is not a simple matter of scaling up existing operations; it requires strategic planning, careful resource allocation, and the ability to balance opportunity with sustainability. Nonprofits must consider not only how to grow but also whether they are ready to grow, ensuring that expansion strengthens rather than undermines their long-term effectiveness. Understanding the drivers, challenges, and strategies for program and service expansion is therefore essential for any organization seeking to serve more people or address unmet needs more comprehensively.

The first step in expansion is recognizing the demand for growth. Nonprofits often consider expanding programs when they see unmet needs in the community, when current services are oversubscribed, or when stakeholders encourage broader initiatives. For example, a food pantry that consistently turns people away due to limited capacity might explore expanding distribution sites or extending service hours. Similarly, a tutoring program with long waiting lists may decide to recruit additional volunteers and open new program locations. Stakeholder input, including feedback from beneficiaries, donors, and community partners, often plays a critical role in identifying when and how expansion should occur. By listening closely to the community, nonprofits can ensure that their growth responds to genuine needs rather than internal ambition alone.

Once a need is identified, nonprofits must assess their readiness for expansion. This involves evaluating organizational capacity, including financial stability, staff expertise, governance, and infrastructure. Expanding programs requires additional funding, and organizations must determine whether they can secure reliable revenue streams to support growth. It is not enough to rely on one-time grants or temporary surges in donations; sustainable funding is essential to avoid the risk of launching new programs that cannot be maintained. Staffing is another key consideration. Nonprofits must assess whether current staff can take on additional responsibilities or whether new hires are required. Infrastructure, such as office space, technology systems, and program facilities, must also be scaled appropriately. Without adequate capacity, expansion can strain existing resources, compromise quality, and ultimately harm the organization's reputation.

Strategic planning provides the roadmap for expansion. Nonprofits should develop a clear plan that outlines the goals of expansion, the specific programs or services to be scaled, and the methods for doing so. The plan should articulate the intended outcomes of growth, identifying both short-term objectives and long-term impact. For example, a health clinic expanding into new neighborhoods might set specific targets for patient visits within the first year, while also aiming to improve community health indicators over the next five years. The plan should also include detailed budgets, timelines, and staffing requirements, ensuring that expansion is pursued systematically rather than haphazardly. Engaging the board of directors in this planning process is essential, as they provide oversight, accountability, and strategic perspective.

Securing funding is perhaps the most critical step in expansion. Nonprofits can pursue multiple avenues to finance growth, including grants, individual donations, corporate sponsorships, and earned income strategies. Demonstrating impact through data is particularly important when seeking funding for expansion, as funders want evidence that the organization can deliver measurable results at a larger scale. Capital campaigns may be used to raise funds for infrastructure projects, while recurring donation programs can provide ongoing support for expanded services. Building long-term relationships with funders is especially important, as expansion often requires sustained financial commitments. Nonprofits that can show strong past performance, transparent reporting, and a clear plan for growth are best positioned to attract the necessary support.

Partnerships also play an important role in program expansion. Collaborating with other nonprofits, government agencies, schools, or businesses can help organizations extend their reach without shouldering the entire burden of growth. For instance, a literacy nonprofit might partner with public libraries to open new tutoring sites, while a health-focused nonprofit could work with local hospitals to expand screening services. Partnerships can provide access to new resources, facilities, and expertise, while also fostering a sense of shared responsibility within the community. By leveraging collaborative networks, nonprofits can achieve greater impact with fewer resources.

Innovation is another driver of expansion. Nonprofits can expand not only by increasing the scale of existing programs but also by introducing new services that address evolving needs. For example, a workforce development nonprofit that originally focused on job placement might expand into digital literacy training to meet the demands of a changing economy. Innovation often arises from ongoing evaluation and feedback, as nonprofits identify gaps in services or opportunities to improve outcomes. By remaining flexible and responsive, organizations can expand in ways that remain relevant to their communities.

As nonprofits expand, maintaining program quality becomes a central concern. Growth can stretch resources thin, increasing the risk of diluted impact or inconsistent service delivery. To prevent this, nonprofits must invest in strong systems for monitoring and evaluation. Establishing clear performance indicators and collecting reliable data allows organizations to assess whether expanded programs are meeting expectations. Continuous feedback loops enable staff to make timely adjustments, ensuring that quality remains high. Staff training and professional development are also essential, as expansion often introduces new challenges and responsibilities. By prioritizing quality control, nonprofits can scale responsibly and preserve the integrity of their mission.

Communication plays an important role in expansion efforts. Stakeholders must understand why expansion is occurring, how it will benefit the community, and what role they can play in supporting it. Clear, consistent communication builds trust and mobilizes resources. For donors, communication should emphasize the measurable impact of expanded programs, demonstrating that their support will create meaningful change. For beneficiaries, communication ensures that expanded services are accessible and responsive to their needs. Internally, clear communication among staff and volunteers ensures that everyone is aligned with the organization's growth strategy and prepared to implement it effectively.

Nonprofits must also be mindful of risk management during expansion. Growth introduces new uncertainties, from financial risks to reputational challenges. Conducting risk assessments helps organizations anticipate potential obstacles and develop contingency plans. For example, a nonprofit planning to expand into new geographic areas must consider risks related to unfamiliar regulatory environments, cultural differences, or competition with existing service providers. By proactively addressing these risks, nonprofits can expand more confidently and sustainably.

Technology can support expansion in multiple ways. Digital platforms allow nonprofits to deliver services more widely and efficiently, reducing barriers related to geography or resources. Online learning tools, telehealth platforms, and virtual support groups are examples of how technology can extend program reach. Technology also facilitates data collection and reporting, which are essential for managing expanded programs and demonstrating impact to funders. Investing in the right technology infrastructure can therefore amplify the benefits of expansion and ensure that growth is manageable.

Finally, expansion must remain mission-driven. Nonprofits should resist the temptation to grow simply for the sake of growth or in response to funder pressures that do not align with their core purpose. Mission drift occurs when organizations expand into areas that dilute their focus, leading to inefficiency and loss of credibility. By keeping the mission at the center of decision-making, nonprofits ensure that expansion strengthens rather than undermines their identity and effectiveness. Growth should always be a means to deepen mission impact, not an end in itself.

In conclusion, expanding programs and services is a complex but rewarding process for nonprofits. It begins with recognizing community needs and assessing organizational readiness, followed by careful strategic planning, funding development, and partnership building. Innovation, evaluation, and communication are essential to ensure that growth is both effective and sustainable. Risks must be managed, technology must be leveraged, and the mission must remain central at every stage. When pursued thoughtfully, expansion allows nonprofits to reach more people, address unmet needs, and enhance their long-term impact. By balancing ambition with responsibility, non-profits can grow in ways that honor their mission and strengthen the communities they serve.

Building Strategic Partnerships and Alliances

Building strategic partnerships and alliances is one of the most effective ways for a nonprofit organization to expand its reach, enhance its impact, and ensure sustainability. Unlike transactional relationships, strategic partnerships are built on shared values, mutual benefit, and a commitment to long-term collaboration. These alliances can take many forms; partnerships with other nonprofits, collaborations with government agencies, relationships with corporations, or networks with community organizations. When designed and managed well, partnerships allow nonprofits to leverage resources, share expertise, reduce duplication of efforts, and tackle complex problems that no single organization can address alone. Developing and maintaining such alliances requires planning, careful management, and a focus on trust and transparency.

The starting point for building strategic partnerships is clarity about the non-profit's mission, vision, and strategic goals. An organization must first understand what it is trying to achieve in order to identify partners that can help advance those objectives. For instance, a nonprofit dedicated to improving community health may find natural allies in hospitals, public health agencies, and fitness organizations. By articulating its priorities clearly, the nonprofit can approach potential partners with a compelling case for collaboration and demonstrate how the alliance will further the shared goal of improving health outcomes. Without a clear sense of direction, part-nerships risk becoming unfocused or diverting resources away from core mission activities.

Identifying the right partners is another critical step. Strategic alliances work best when the partners' missions, values, and goals are aligned, even if their strengths and resources differ. A youth development nonprofit, for example, may partner with a local business that provides internships, a school district that contributes facilities, and another nonprofit that offers mental health services. Together, they can create a holis-tic support system for young people. The key is to ensure that the collaboration is rooted in a common purpose, rather than driven solely by financial convenience or short-term opportunities. Aligning values at the outset reduces the likelihood of con-flict and builds a strong foundation for trust.

Once potential partners are identified, nonprofits must invest in relationship-building. Strategic alliances are based on trust, mutual respect, and open communica-tion, which take time to cultivate. Nonprofits should engage potential partners in con-versations that go beyond immediate needs to explore long-term visions and shared commitments. This may involve informal meetings, joint planning sessions, or pilot projects to test the feasibility of working together. By demonstrating reliability, com-petence, and a willingness to listen, nonprofits can establish credibility and lay the groundwork for durable partnerships. Trust-building is especially important when working with organizations from different sectors, such as businesses or government agencies, where cultures and expectations may differ significantly.

Formalizing partnerships through agreements is an important step in ensuring clarity and accountability. Memoranda of understanding, contracts, or partnership agreements should outline the roles, responsibilities, and expectations of each party. These documents clarify how resources will be shared, how decisions will be made, and how outcomes will be measured. For example, a nonprofit partnering with a university on a research project should establish clear terms regarding data ownership, publication rights, and the responsibilities of each partner. While written agreements cannot guarantee perfect collaboration, they provide a framework for resolving disputes and maintaining accountability.

Resource sharing is often a central element of nonprofit alliances. Partners may contribute different assets, such as funding, expertise, facilities, or networks. For example, a nonprofit may provide community connections, while a corporate partner contributes financial support and volunteers. Government agencies may offer access to data or policy expertise, while other nonprofits bring specialized programmatic skills. By pooling resources, partnerships can achieve outcomes that would be impossible for any single organization. For instance, addressing homelessness requires not only shelters but also healthcare services, job training, and housing support, which can only be delivered effectively through a coordinated alliance.

Collaboration also allows nonprofits to increase their advocacy power. When organizations join forces, they amplify their voices and strengthen their influence on public policy. A coalition of environmental nonprofits, for example, may be far more effective in lobbying for legislative changes than any one group working alone. By aligning messaging, coordinating campaigns, and presenting a united front, alliances can draw greater attention to critical issues and persuade policymakers more effectively. Strategic partnerships thus expand not only the resources but also the influence of nonprofits in shaping the environments in which they work.

Innovation is another major benefit of strategic alliances. By working with partners that bring diverse perspectives and skills, nonprofits can develop creative solutions to complex challenges. Cross-sector collaborations, in particular, often spark new ideas. For example, a technology company partnering with a literacy nonprofit might develop an innovative app to support children's reading at home. Such innovations may not emerge within the silo of a single organization but flourish when knowledge and resources are combined. Partnerships encourage nonprofits to think beyond their traditional approaches and embrace experimentation, which can significantly enhance their effectiveness.

Effective partnerships, however, do not come without challenges. Differences in organizational culture, priorities, or communication styles can create friction. Power imbalances may arise when one partner controls most of the resources, potentially leading to unequal decision-making. To address these challenges, nonprofits must emphasize transparency and equity from the outset. Establishing regular communication channels, joint governance structures, and clear mechanisms for conflict resolution helps maintain balance and trust. It is also important to set realistic expectations. Not every partnership will deliver immediate or dramatic results, and managing expectations ensures that alliances remain sustainable over time.

Evaluation and accountability are critical to maintaining strong partnerships. Non-profits should develop shared metrics and evaluation systems to track progress toward goals. Regular reviews of outcomes help ensure that each partner is fulfilling its commitments and that the alliance is achieving its intended impact. Transparent reporting also reinforces trust among partners and demonstrates to external stakeholders, such as donors and funders, that the collaboration is producing measurable benefits. For example, a coalition addressing childhood obesity might track indicators such as reduced obesity rates, improved access to healthy foods, and increased physical activity, reporting results to both partners and the public.

In addition to tracking results, celebrating successes is vital to sustaining partnerships. Acknowledging the contributions of all partners reinforces the value of collaboration and fosters goodwill. Public recognition, joint press releases, and shared celebrations of milestones can highlight the achievements of the alliance and inspire continued commitment. Celebrating successes also provides an opportunity to showcase impact to funders and the broader community, potentially attracting additional support for the partnership.

Technology has become an increasingly valuable tool for managing alliances. Online collaboration platforms, data-sharing systems, and virtual meeting tools make it easier for partners to coordinate activities and share information. Technology also enhances transparency by providing real-time access to data and progress reports. For example, an alliance focused on disaster relief might use shared digital dashboards to track resource distribution and service delivery across multiple organizations. Investing in appropriate technological infrastructure strengthens the efficiency and accountability of partnerships, particularly when multiple stakeholders are involved.

Ultimately, building strategic partnerships and alliances requires a mindset shift. Nonprofits must move beyond viewing other organizations solely as competitors for funding and instead recognize the potential for collaboration to multiply impact. This shift requires humility, openness to learning, and a willingness to share credit. At the same time, nonprofits must remain vigilant about mission alignment, ensuring that partnerships do not lead to mission drift or compromised core values. Strategic alliances should always serve as a means of advancing the mission more effectively, not as an end in themselves.

In conclusion, building strategic partnerships and alliances is both an opportunity and a necessity for nonprofits in today's interconnected world. By identifying aligned partners, investing in relationship-building, formalizing agreements, sharing resources, and evaluating outcomes, nonprofits can create powerful collaborations that amplify their impact. Partnerships enhance credibility, expand influence, and foster innovation, enabling nonprofits to tackle complex challenges more effectively. While challenges such as cultural differences and power imbalances must be managed carefully, the benefits of collaboration far outweigh the risks. At their best, strategic alliances allow nonprofits to achieve what no single organization could accomplish alone, bringing communities closer to lasting, transformative change.

Revenue Diversification Strategies

Revenue diversification is one of the most critical strategies for nonprofit sustainability. Nonprofits, unlike businesses, cannot rely primarily on profits from goods or services sold in the marketplace. Instead, they must piece together revenue from multiple streams to sustain operations, fund programs, and achieve their missions. Overreliance on a single funding source, whether government grants, foundation support, or a major donor, can place an organization in a precarious position. Economic downturns, political changes, or shifts in donor priorities can disrupt that funding source and jeopardize the organization's future. Revenue diversification spreads risk across multiple streams, enhances financial stability, and allows nonprofits to adapt to changing environments. At the same time, diversification must be pursued thoughtfully, with attention to mission alignment, resource capacity, and long-term sustainability.

One of the most common revenue sources for nonprofits is foundation and government grants. These can provide significant funding for programs, capacity building, and infrastructure. However, grants are often time-limited and come with specific restrictions on how funds may be used. A nonprofit that relies heavily on grants risks financial instability once the grant period ends. To diversify effectively, organizations should pursue grants strategically while simultaneously developing other revenue streams. For example, they might use grant funds to pilot innovative programs, which can then be sustained through earned income, donations, or fee-for-service models once the initial funding ends. By approaching grants as a catalyst rather than a lifeline, nonprofits avoid dependence while still leveraging this important revenue source.

Individual donations are another cornerstone of nonprofit revenue. Cultivating a broad base of donors provides not only financial support but also community engagement and advocacy. Individual giving can range from small recurring contributions to major gifts, and each type of donor requires different cultivation strategies. Revenue diversification in this area involves building systems that support all levels of giving. For instance, nonprofits may establish monthly giving programs that provide steady, predictable income while also investing in major gift strategies for high-capacity donors. Special events and campaigns can attract new supporters and encourage giving from existing donors. Importantly, expanding the donor base reduces reliance on a handful of large contributors, minimizing the risk of financial disruption if one major donor withdraws support.

Corporate partnerships also offer valuable opportunities for revenue diversification. Businesses may contribute through sponsorships, cause marketing campaigns, employee giving programs, or direct grants. These partnerships can provide not only funding but also visibility and credibility for the nonprofit. For example, a nonprofit focused on environmental sustainability might partner with a company committed to reducing its carbon footprint, aligning their missions for mutual benefit. However, nonprofits must carefully vet corporate partners to avoid reputational risks and ensure that partnerships are consistent with organizational values. When pursued thoughtfully, corporate support can provide a significant and stable revenue stream while opening doors to new audiences and resources.

Earned income strategies represent an increasingly important avenue for diversification. Many nonprofits generate revenue through the sale of products, services, or intellectual property related to their mission. For example, a museum may charge admission fees or run a gift shop, a training nonprofit may offer paid workshops, or a theater group may sell tickets to performances. Some nonprofits develop social enterprises, businesses that generate income while furthering mission goals. These might include thrift stores operated by community organizations or cafes providing job training for individuals facing barriers to employment. Earned income not only provides financial sustainability but also reinforces mission impact when designed thoughtfully. The challenge is ensuring that such ventures are financially viable and do not divert attention or resources away from core programs.

Membership models are another revenue diversification strategy. Nonprofits such as advocacy organizations, professional associations, or cultural institutions often offer memberships in exchange for benefits like newsletters, discounts, or exclusive access to events. Membership dues provide predictable annual revenue and foster a sense of belonging among supporters. They also create a base of engaged individuals who can be mobilized for advocacy, volunteerism, or additional giving. While membership revenue may not be sufficient to sustain an organization alone, it can be an important component of a diversified funding portfolio.

Planned giving programs add another dimension to revenue diversification. Encouraging donors to include the nonprofit in their wills or estate plans creates long-term stability by building a pipeline of future gifts. While planned gifts may not provide immediate revenue, they represent a powerful strategy for securing the organization's financial future. Nonprofits that invest in cultivating planned gifts demonstrate to donors that they are committed to long-term impact and sustainability. Planned giving also deepens donor relationships, as it often involves meaningful conversations about legacy and values.

Fee-for-service models, particularly relevant for nonprofits providing direct services, also contribute to diversification. For instance, a counseling center might charge clients on a sliding scale, or a workforce development program might contract with businesses to provide training. Government agencies may also pay nonprofits to deliver services through contracts. While fee-for-service models can provide reliable revenue, they require careful management to balance accessibility with sustainability. Nonprofits must ensure that charging fees does not exclude low-income beneficiaries or conflict with their mission. Nonetheless, for many organizations, fee-based services represent a sustainable and mission-aligned revenue stream.

Special events such as galas, auctions, and benefit concerts are another revenue source, though they are often resource-intensive. Events can generate significant income while also raising visibility and engaging donors. However, nonprofits should avoid overreliance on events, as the costs of planning and execution can sometimes outweigh the benefits. Incorporating events as part of a broader fundraising strategy, rather than as the centerpiece, helps ensure that they contribute meaningfully to revenue diversification without draining resources.

Investment income and endowments provide yet another diversification strategy. Nonprofits with substantial reserves can invest funds to generate interest or dividends, providing long-term financial stability. Establishing an endowment ensures that income continues to flow even in challenging times, supporting programs or operations in perpetuity. While building an endowment requires significant fundraising capacity, even small investment funds can contribute to diversification by creating passive income streams. Proper governance and financial management are essential to ensure that investments align with nonprofit values and fiduciary responsibilities.

Technology and digital platforms have opened new avenues for diversification as well. Online fundraising campaigns, crowdfunding platforms, and peer-to-peer giving models allow nonprofits to reach broader audiences and diversify donor pools. Social media campaigns can attract younger donors, while virtual events reduce overhead and expand reach. By embracing digital strategies, nonprofits can tap into new markets and revenue sources while building resilience in an increasingly digital world.

While diversification offers many benefits, it is not without challenges. Pursuing too many revenue streams without adequate capacity can spread an organization too thin, reducing effectiveness. Nonprofits must prioritize strategies that align with their mission, strengths, and resources. They must also balance diversification with focus, ensuring that revenue activities do not distract from program delivery. Strategic planning is therefore essential, allowing nonprofits to evaluate opportunities, assess risks, and make deliberate choices about which revenue streams to pursue.

Ultimately, revenue diversification is not just about financial survival but about advancing mission impact. By spreading risk across multiple funding sources, nonprofits reduce vulnerability and increase resilience. Diversification also strengthens credibility with donors and funders, who view financially stable organizations as better positioned to deliver lasting change. Moreover, diversified revenue allows nonprofits to innovate, invest in infrastructure, and take on long-term initiatives that might otherwise be too risky.

In conclusion, revenue diversification is a cornerstone of nonprofit sustainability, requiring a blend of traditional and innovative strategies. Grants, individual giving, corporate partnerships, earned income, memberships, planned giving, fee-for-service models, events, investments, and digital fundraising all play roles in a diversified portfolio. By approaching diversification strategically, aligning revenue streams with mission, building capacity, and investing in long-term relationships, nonprofits can reduce risk, enhance stability, and position themselves for growth. The ultimate goal is not simply to survive financially but to ensure that resources are available to fulfill the mission and make a lasting impact on the communities they serve.

Long-Term Planning and Leadership Succession

Long-term planning and leadership succession are essential practices for the sustainability of nonprofit organizations. Unlike for-profit businesses, nonprofits are not judged by profit margins alone but by their ability to remain mission-driven while navigating complex funding environments, community needs, and stakeholder expectations. To ensure continuity and resilience, nonprofits must look beyond day-to-day operations and build frameworks for long-term growth and leadership stability. The health of an organization depends not only on visionary leadership but also on its ability to plan for inevitable transitions, especially at the executive and board levels. Effective long-term planning coupled with thoughtful succession planning ensures that a nonprofit can endure leadership changes without losing momentum, focus, or credibility.

Long-term planning is the process by which nonprofits establish goals, anticipate challenges, and allocate resources to ensure future success. At its core, long-term planning is about envisioning the future while remaining rooted in the mission. It requires assessing internal strengths and weaknesses as well as external opportunities and threats. For instance, a nonprofit serving low-income families might anticipate demographic changes, shifts in public policy, or new funding priorities that will affect demand for services. By forecasting such trends, the organization can proactively adapt its programs and budgets rather than reacting to crises. Long-term planning typically involves developing a strategic plan, often covering a three-to-five-year horizon, that sets priorities, defines measurable outcomes, and outlines strategies to achieve them.

The strategic plan serves as a roadmap, guiding decision-making at all levels of the organization. It helps align staff, board members, and stakeholders around common goals and ensures that resources are deployed effectively. For example, if a nonprofit identifies technology as a key driver of future program delivery, the strategic plan might prioritize investment in digital infrastructure and staff training. Long-term planning also promotes accountability, as progress can be measured against established goals. For funders, donors, and the public, a clear long-term plan signals professionalism, foresight, and the capacity to use resources wisely.

Yet long-term planning alone is not sufficient. Even the best-designed plans can falter if leadership transitions are mishandled. Leadership succession is therefore a critical component of sustainability. In nonprofits, leadership transitions are inevitable. Executive directors retire, boards rotate, and program leaders move on to other opportunities. Without a succession plan, nonprofits risk disruption, instability, and loss of stakeholder confidence. Too often, organizations are caught off guard by sudden leadership departures, scrambling to find replacements while programs and fundraising efforts falter. A well-prepared succession plan reduces uncertainty, ensures continuity, and reinforces confidence among staff, donors, and beneficiaries.

Leadership succession planning begins with recognizing that no individual is indispensable. While charismatic leaders often play central roles in nonprofit growth, building systems that can function without reliance on one person is crucial. Succession planning therefore focuses on both people and processes. On the people side, nonprofits must identify and develop future leaders, whether from within the organization or outside. This involves investing in staff development, mentoring, and cross-training to build leadership capacity across teams. On the process side, succession planning requires documentation of critical knowledge, policies, and relationships so that institutional memory is preserved even when leaders depart.

Boards of directors play a central role in succession planning. They are responsible for hiring and evaluating the executive director, and they must be proactive in planning for leadership transitions. A strong board does not wait until a resignation or retirement is announced but engages in ongoing discussions about succession. This includes considering both emergency succession (who will step in temporarily if a leader departs suddenly) and long-term succession, identifying the skills and qualities needed in future leaders. By engaging in this planning, boards ensure that leadership changes are strategic rather than reactive.

Executive directors themselves must also take responsibility for succession planning. Effective leaders understand that preparing the organization for their eventual departure is part of their legacy. This may involve developing senior staff, sharing decision-making responsibilities, and cultivating transparency so that leadership is not overly centralized. By empowering others and fostering a culture of shared leadership, executive directors strengthen the organization's resilience. When the time comes for transition, the nonprofit is better positioned to adapt without losing direction.

An important aspect of succession planning is aligning leadership transitions with long-term strategy. For instance, if a nonprofit is planning to expand nationally, the next executive director may need experience with scaling organizations and managing multi-site operations. Conversely, if the organization is focusing on deepening community partnerships, a leader with strong grassroots organizing skills may be a better fit. By considering the future direction of the nonprofit, succession planning ensures that incoming leaders bring the right skills and vision to advance strategic goals.

Communication is critical during leadership transitions. Stakeholders must be informed and reassured. Transparent communication about the succession process builds trust and reduces uncertainty. For donors in particular, leadership changes can raise concerns about organizational stability and the continued alignment of values. By proactively communicating the succession plan and highlighting the strengths of new leadership, nonprofits can maintain donor confidence and prevent funding disruptions. Similarly, staff members need reassurance that their work will continue to be valued and supported under new leadership.

Leadership succession is not limited to executive directors. Board succession is equally important. Boards provide governance, oversight, and strategic direction, and turnover in board membership can affect stability. Succession planning at the board level involves cultivating a pipeline of committed, diverse, and skilled members who can step into leadership roles as terms expire. This may include developing a governance committee responsible for identifying and recruiting potential board members, mentoring newer members, and ensuring continuity in board leadership positions such as the chair or treasurer. A well-functioning board succession plan ensures that governance remains strong even as membership changes.

Long-term planning and leadership succession are interconnected. Effective long-term plans anticipate leadership needs, while succession planning aligns leadership transitions with organizational strategy. Together, they create a framework for resilience and sustainability. For example, a nonprofit focused on environmental advocacy might develop a strategic plan to expand into new policy areas over the next five years. Succession planning would then ensure that future leaders have the policy expertise and networks required to advance those goals. In this way, planning for the future is not only about programs and funding but also about the people who will lead the organization forward.

Despite the importance of long-term planning and succession, many nonprofits struggle in these areas. Limited resources, urgent program demands, and a culture of informality can push planning aside in favor of immediate needs. Some boards may hesitate to discuss succession for fear of signaling instability, while executive directors may be reluctant to confront their own eventual departure. Overcoming these barriers requires a cultural shift that views planning not as a sign of weakness but as an act of stewardship. Organizations that embrace long-term and succession planning demonstrate maturity, responsibility, and commitment to their missions.

Funders increasingly recognize the importance of these practices and may even require evidence of long-term planning and succession strategies as part of grant applications. For nonprofits, this creates both an incentive and an opportunity to strengthen planning processes. By investing in strategic planning sessions, leadership development programs, and governance training, nonprofits can build the capacity to plan effectively for the future. Collaborating with consultants, peer organizations, or associations can also provide valuable expertise and resources.

In conclusion, long-term planning and leadership succession are indispensable for nonprofit sustainability. Long-term planning provides the vision and strategy to navigate future challenges, while succession planning ensures that leadership transitions occur smoothly and strategically. Together, they create a foundation for resilience, enabling nonprofits to continue fulfilling their missions even in the face of change. These practices require foresight, commitment, and open communication, but the benefits far outweigh the challenges. By embedding long-term and succession planning into their organizational culture, nonprofits can build continuity, preserve stakeholder trust, and ensure that their missions endure across generations of leadership.

Avoiding Mission Drift

Mission drift is one of the most pressing risks faced by nonprofit organizations. It occurs when an organization begins to move away from its core purpose, often in subtle ways, until its activities, programs, or funding strategies no longer align with its stated mission. While nonprofits may not set out to deviate from their founding principles, the pressures of fundraising, competition for resources, and external expectations can slowly pull them off course. Avoiding mission drift is crucial because a nonprofit's credibility, effectiveness, and long-term sustainability depend on staying true to its mission. When stakeholders perceive that an organization has lost focus, they may lose confidence in its leadership and withdraw their support. To safeguard against this risk, nonprofits must adopt deliberate strategies that preserve mission alignment across programs, partnerships, and funding decisions.

One of the most effective ways to avoid mission drift is through clarity and discipline in defining the mission. A well-crafted mission statement provides the compass for all organizational activities. It should be specific enough to establish clear boundaries, yet broad enough to allow some flexibility as community needs evolve. A mission statement that is too vague or aspirational risks leaving room for interpretation, making it easier for the organization to justify activities that are outside its core purpose. By contrast, a clear and focused mission statement ensures that everyone (board members, staff, volunteers, and funders) understands what the organization stands for and how it intends to achieve its goals. This clarity enables the nonprofit to evaluate opportunities and challenges through the lens of mission alignment.

Governance plays a central role in preventing mission drift. Boards of directors are responsible for safeguarding the mission and ensuring that all organizational decisions reinforce it. Strong governance practices include reviewing new initiatives in light of the mission, asking whether a potential partnership or funding source aligns with core values, and holding leadership accountable for mission fidelity. Boards that are disengaged or overly focused on fundraising at all costs are more likely to allow mission drift to occur. By fostering a culture of thoughtful oversight, boards provide the necessary checks and balances to keep the organization on track.

Leadership is equally important in avoiding mission drift. Executive directors and senior staff set the tone for organizational priorities, and their decisions about programs, funding, and partnerships influence whether the mission is upheld or compromised. Leaders who are clear about the mission can inspire staff and stakeholders to remain focused, even when faced with attractive but misaligned opportunities. For example, an environmental nonprofit might be offered a large grant to expand into general health services. While the funding may be tempting, a disciplined leader would recognize that pursuing this path could dilute the organization's impact and confuse its stakeholders.

Financial pressures are often the most significant drivers of mission drift. Nonprofits may accept funding opportunities that come with requirements or restrictions inconsistent with their mission. A youth development nonprofit, for instance, might take on a grant focused primarily on job training for adults, stretching its programs beyond its intended audience. While this may bring in money, it risks diverting staff attention and resources from core programs. To mitigate this, nonprofits should adopt a diversified funding strategy that reduces dependence on any single source. With multiple streams of revenue, nonprofits have more flexibility to decline funding that does not align with their mission. Transparency with donors is also key, as communicating the mission clearly helps attract supporters whose values align with the organization's purpose.

Program design and evaluation also play a critical role in avoiding mission drift. Nonprofits must regularly assess whether their programs are aligned with their mission and delivering intended outcomes. Evaluation systems allow organizations to measure not only effectiveness but also mission fidelity. For example, a literacy nonprofit might track whether its programs are indeed improving reading levels, rather than expanding into unrelated services like general tutoring that may be less mission-focused. When programs are evaluated against mission-based outcomes, the organization can identify areas where it may be drifting and take corrective action. Program reviews also ensure that resources are invested in initiatives that genuinely advance the mission, rather than in peripheral activities that dilute impact.

Communication, both internal and external, reinforces mission alignment. Internally, staff and volunteers must be consistently reminded of the mission and how their work contributes to it. Training, staff meetings, and performance evaluations can all emphasize mission focus. Externally, nonprofits must clearly communicate their mission to donors, funders, and the public. Messaging that is consistent with the mission helps set expectations and attracts stakeholders who share the organization's values. When nonprofits communicate a clear sense of purpose, they reduce the likelihood of pressure to pursue off-mission activities simply to satisfy external demands.

Partnerships and collaborations can also test mission alignment. While working with other organizations can expand reach and impact, it can also lead to compromises if partners' goals are not fully aligned. A nonprofit must carefully evaluate potential partners to ensure that collaborations reinforce rather than dilute its mission. For example, a nonprofit focused on nutrition might consider partnering with schools to provide healthy meals but should avoid alliances with corporations whose products contribute to unhealthy lifestyles. Establishing clear partnership agreements that reflect mission values ensures that collaborations remain supportive of core objectives.

Another strategy to avoid mission drift is embedding mission into strategic planning. A strategic plan provides a framework for growth and decision-making, ensuring that all initiatives align with the mission. By setting clear priorities and measurable goals, nonprofits can resist the temptation to pursue opportunities that fall outside the strategic focus. Strategic plans should be reviewed regularly to account for changes in the external environment, but they should always remain anchored in the mission. Involving board members, staff, and stakeholders in the planning process reinforces collective commitment to mission alignment.

Succession planning is another safeguard. Leadership transitions are moments when nonprofits are particularly vulnerable to mission drift, as new leaders may bring different priorities or approaches. Succession planning ensures that future leaders are selected based on their alignment with the mission and that institutional knowledge is preserved. Documenting policies, procedures, and program rationales helps incoming leaders understand and respect the mission rather than unintentionally shifting focus.

Finally, nonprofits can avoid mission drift by cultivating a culture of accountability to the communities they serve. When beneficiaries are engaged in program design, evaluation, and decision-making, the nonprofit is less likely to veer away from its purpose. Community engagement ensures that programs remain relevant, responsive, and mission-centered. It also reinforces the idea that the nonprofit exists to serve its stakeholders, not external funders or institutional interests.

In conclusion, avoiding mission drift requires intentionality, discipline, and vigilance. Nonprofits must establish clear missions, reinforce them through governance and leadership, and make decisions about funding, programs, and partnerships with mission fidelity in mind. Diversified funding strategies, program evaluations, and strong communication all help maintain alignment. Strategic planning and succession planning further safeguard against drift by embedding the mission into long-term frameworks and leadership transitions. Above all, accountability to beneficiaries and stakeholders ensures that nonprofits remain rooted in their founding purpose. By staying true to their missions, nonprofits not only preserve credibility and stakeholder trust but also maximize their impact, fulfilling the promises that inspired their creation.

CASE STUDY

Background

City Harvest, founded in 1982 in New York City, began with a simple mission: to rescue excess food from restaurants, grocers, and manufacturers and deliver it to organizations feeding people in need. At its inception, the organization relied almost entirely on volunteers using their personal cars to collect and deliver food. Over time, the nonprofit confronted both growing demand and operational challenges, which pushed it to evolve strategically. By focusing on its mission, diversifying revenue sources, and strengthening infrastructure, City Harvest transformed from a small grassroots operation into one of the nation's most prominent food rescue organizations, while maintaining long-term sustainability.

Strategic Long-Term Planning

From the outset, City Harvest recognized that hunger in New York City was a systemic challenge, not a short-term crisis. By adopting multi-year strategic plans, the organization aligned growth with realistic goals. For example, in the mid-2000s, City Harvest's strategic plan shifted from simply rescuing food to also addressing the root causes of hunger. This expansion included nutrition education and community partnerships. Each plan was rooted in measurable objectives, such as pounds of food rescued, number of community partners engaged, and people reached with nutrition programs. By embedding evaluation into its strategy, the nonprofit avoided mission drift and demonstrated accountability to stakeholders.

Mission Discipline and Adaptation

The mission of alleviating hunger remained central, but the organization adapted its methods as conditions changed. After Hurricane Sandy in 2012, City Harvest scaled up dramatically to meet emergency needs. Instead of drifting into general disaster relief, it stayed true to its focus by ensuring food rescue and distribution were central to its disaster response. In recent years, as food insecurity surged during the COVID-19 pandemic, City Harvest again scaled operations, delivering tens of millions of pounds of food while maintaining its mission integrity. This ability to adapt while staying mission-centered strengthened trust with donors, partners, and the communities it serves.

Revenue Diversification

Sustainable growth was made possible through revenue diversification. City Harvest built a balanced mix of funding from foundations, corporate partnerships, government contracts, individual donors, and special events. Corporate sponsors not only contributed financially but also provided volunteers, in-kind support, and visibility. Individual giving campaigns, such as "Share Lunch, Fight Hunger," tapped into community engagement and grassroots support. Government contracts supported large-scale food distribution, while foundations provided resources for innovation and program expansion. By diversifying funding streams, City Harvest reduced vulnerability to shifts in any single source and secured the financial flexibility to scale sustainably.

Investment in Infrastructure

Sustainability also required investment in systems and infrastructure. City Harvest professionalized its operations by acquiring a fleet of trucks, establishing warehouses with cold storage, and building technology systems to track food flows. Rather than relying solely on volunteers, it created a professional staff structure while still maintaining a strong base of community volunteers. Investments in logistics capacity allowed the nonprofit to scale up operations during crises without losing efficiency. These infrastructure investments were supported by capital campaigns and long-term funding strategies, ensuring that growth was sustainable rather than reactive.

Leadership and Succession Planning

Another key to sustainable growth has been leadership development and succession. City Harvest maintained strong executive leadership that balanced vision with operational competence. The board of directors actively engaged in oversight, governance, and fundraising, ensuring continuity during leadership transitions. Clear succession planning and board recruitment strategies allowed the organization to weather changes in leadership without disruption.

Community Engagement and Partnerships

City Harvest sustained growth by building robust community partnerships. Rather than operating in isolation, it partnered with hundreds of food pantries, soup kitchens, and community-based organizations across New York City. These partnerships ensured that rescued food reached those most in need while strengthening community trust. The nonprofit also partnered with local schools to deliver nutrition education, creating long-term impact by addressing the root causes of food insecurity. These partnerships reinforced mission fidelity and provided opportunities for innovation.

Measuring and Reporting Impact

Transparency and accountability were essential for sustaining donor confidence and community trust. City Harvest reported on measurable outcomes, such as pounds of food rescued and distributed, numbers of families served, and improvements in nutritional access. It also shared stories of individuals impacted by its services, combining data with narrative to demonstrate both scale and human impact. This practice built long-term relationships with donors, partners, and volunteers, ensuring that funding and support continued even during economic downturns.

Sustainable Outcomes

Through these strategies, City Harvest achieved sustainable growth. What began as a small volunteer effort grew into an organization that now rescues and delivers over 100 million pounds of food annually. Its programs address both immediate needs and long-term solutions, balancing scale with mission focus. The organization's diversified revenue base, investment in infrastructure, community partnerships, and commitment to evaluation have allowed it not only to expand but also to sustain operations through crises such as 9/11, Hurricane Sandy, and COVID-19.

The case of City Harvest illustrates several principles of sustainable nonprofit growth. First, nonprofits must balance adaptability with mission discipline, ensuring that new opportunities or crises are met without losing focus. Second, diversification of revenue reduces vulnerability and provides stability for long-term planning. Third, investment in infrastructure and systems is critical to scaling effectively. Fourth, strong governance, leadership succession, and board engagement ensure continuity. Finally, measuring and reporting impact builds trust and sustains support across stakeholders.

Summary

Expanding nonprofit programs and services is both a challenge and an opportunity, requiring a balance of vision, planning, and discipline. Successful growth depends on aligning expansion with mission, building sustainable funding models, and leveraging partnerships and innovation. Strong governance, leadership succession, and investment in infrastructure ensure that growth is not only achievable but also sustainable over the long term. Continuous evaluation and communication strengthen trust with stakeholders and safeguard mission integrity during times of change. Ultimately, thoughtful expansion allows nonprofits to reach more people, address pressing community needs, and create lasting impact.

Glossary

A

Articles of incorporation. The legal document filed with the state to establish a nonprofit corporation and define its purpose.

B

Board of directors. The governing body responsible for overseeing a nonprofit's mission, finances, and compliance.

Bylaws. Internal rules that govern how a nonprofit operates, including board duties, elections, and meetings.

C

Charitable solicitation registration. A state-level filing required before a nonprofit can legally raise donations from the public.

Conflict of interest policy. Rules requiring nonprofit leaders to disclose personal interests that could compromise decision-making.

D

Donor restrictions. Conditions imposed by donors on how contributed funds may be used.

F

Functional expenses. Costs categorized by purpose (program, management, fundraising) as required in nonprofit reporting.

Fund accounting. An accounting method that tracks resources by funds to ensure compliance with donor restrictions.

G

Grant. Funds provided by governments, foundations, or institutions that support specific nonprofit programs or activities.

I

Internal controls. Safeguards such as segregation of duties and approval hierarchies that protect nonprofit assets.

M

Mission statement. A formal declaration of a nonprofit's purpose, guiding its programs and decision-making.

N

Nonprofit organization. An entity created to pursue a mission that benefits the public rather than generate profits for private individuals.

O

Organizational lifecycle. A The stages nonprofits typically pass through: startup, growth, development, maturity, and decline.

P

Program evaluation. The process of measuring outcomes and impact to demonstrate a nonprofit's effectiveness.

S

Stewardship. The ethical responsibility of nonprofits to manage donor contributions and resources with accountability and transparency.

T

Tax-exempt status. A legal recognition that exempts nonprofits from paying federal income taxes if they meet IRS criteria.

U

Unrelated business income tax. A tax applied to revenue from activities unrelated to a nonprofit's exempt purpose.

Index

www.ingramcontent.com/pod-product-compliance
Lightning Source LLC
Chambersburg PA
CBHW051209200326
41519CB00025B/7056